PERFECT GAME, IMPERFECT LIVES

A Memoir Celebrating the 50th Anniversary of Don Larsen's Perfect Game

Other Books By Albert A. Bell, Jr.

Mystery
Death Goes Dutch
All Roads Lead to Murder
Kill Her Again

Historical Fiction
Daughter of Lazarus

Young Adult Mystery
The Secret of the Lonely Grave

Non-Fiction
Exploring the New Testament World:
An Illustrated Guide to the World of Jesus
and the First Christians
Resources in Ancient Philosohy

PERFECT GAME, IMPERFECT LIVES

A Memoir Celebrating the 50th Anniversary
of Don Larsen's Perfect Game

Albert A. Bell, Jr.

Almont Books

2006

Almont Books
from
INGALLS PUBLISHING GROUP, INC.
197 New Market Center, #135
Boone, NC 28607
www.ingallspublishinggroup.com

Cover design by Steve Beckwith
Text design by Ann Thompson Nemcosky

Library of Congress Cataloging-in-Publication Data

Bell, Albert A., 1945-

    Perfect game, imperfect lives : a memoir celebrating the 50th anniversary of Don Larsen's perfect game / Albert A. Bell, Jr.
            p. cm.
        ISBN-13: 978-1-932158-41-0 (trade pbk. : alk. paper)
        ISBN-10: 1-932158-41-3 (trade pbk. : alk. paper)
1. Larsen, Don. 2. Pitchers (Baseball)--United States--Biography. 3. Perfect games (Baseball) 4. New York Yankees (Baseball team) I. Title.
        GV865.L32B45 2006
        796.357092--dc22
        [B]
                                        2006018199

Printed in the United States of America
First printing, October 2006

PERFECT GAME, IMPERFECT LIVES

Albert A. Bell, Jr.

For the rest of the 14.
Perfect? Of course not, but they have meant so much in my life

". . . in short measures life may perfect be."
Ben Jonson

"Dear Mr. Larsen,
It is a noteworthy event when anybody achieves perfection in anything."
Dwight D. Eisenhower

The preface of a book is the part many readers skip. Please don't skip this. It isn't a preface; it's the warm-up for everything that follows. If you're going to play baseball – or any sport – you can't just step onto the field and start playing. You have to warm up first or you could hurt yourself. If you don't read this, you'll miss some important clues about where this book is going.

"We reach perfection not by copying, much less by aiming at originality, but by constantly and steadily working out the life which is common to all."
Richard Baxter

Early in 2005 I was adding a few baseball cards to my collection when it dawned on me that the fiftieth anniversary of Don Larsen's perfect game in the 1956 World Series was on the horizon. Because it remains the only perfect game ever pitched in a World Series (or any other post-season play in the major leagues) and because it has exercised such a fascination for me for most of my life, I wanted to write something to commemorate the event (and I had to hope no one would pitch a "perfecto" in the '05 World Series).

Other projects had to be completed first, but I finally realized that, if I was going to do a book, there was a time limitation. And what could I write about the game that others had not already said? Larsen himself wrote a book, *The Perfect Yankee*, which offers background on his life and takes the reader through the game pitch by pitch. There are several books on baseball's perfect games and no-hitters. Each gives Larsen's game the appropriate chapter. Could I find a fresh approach?

My first idea was to contrast the rather imperfect lives of the Yankee players in the game with the notion of perfection. Hence, my title. As I thought about that time period, though, I came to see it as a significant chapter in my own imperfect life. I was hitting puberty and my family moved from a home in South Carolina that felt nearly perfect to Cincinnati, Ohio.

Reflecting and reading further, I saw how often people referred to the 1950s as an idyllic, almost perfect, time. But I lived through the 1950s, so I know the decade saw increasing tensions in the U. S. and abroad, as the Civil Rights movement gained impetus and the Cold War threatened to turn hot. And a social revolution was taking place, symbolized by Elvis Presley's appearance on Ed Sullivan's show. The fact that there was a television show for Presley to appear on was a key part of that revolution. What I decided to do was look at the perfect game and at a number of factors surrounding it through my eyes as an eleven-year-old Everykid who was very much aware of the imperfections of his own life and trying to find some bit of perfection to hang on to.

At one point I was writing about an incident that occurred while I lived in Cincinnati but which had no connection to baseball. How can I justify including this? I asked myself. I feel like it needs to be in here, but it's not about baseball or Don Larsen. It's about *my* life experience. Suddenly the heavens opened, a shaft of light shone down on me, and music surrounded me – a full-blown epiphany. As clearly as if someone else was speaking, I heard, "This book isn't about Don Larsen or baseball. It *is* about me. The perfect game is the metaphor, not the theme." When I mentioned this revelation to my writers' group, they said, We knew that weeks ago. What took you so long to figure it out?

The book then took on its present purpose and subtitle: A Memoir Inspired by etc. That means it's not primarily about Larsen's perfect game but about the game's impact on my life and about my life as pretty typical of that era. It contains 27 chapters because that is the number of consecutive outs required to complete a perfect game. The chapters are of unequal length because some batters make an out on the first or second pitch, while others foul off pitches and stay at the plate for a long time.

The autobiographical material is fact, even if it has been dramatized here and there to illustrate a point. Things like this happened to me and to kids all over America during that period. As Miller and Nowak observe, it's hard for people who grew up in the '50s to write about that era without drawing on "personal experience to illustrate some of the decade's major social and cultural trends" (*The Fifties*, p. 12). I just hope I don't start to sound like the character in an "Arlo 'n' Janis" comic strip who said, "I remember when Cokes were only a nickel . . . I remember when gas cost 25 cents a gallon . . . I remember when movies were half a dollar . . . I remember when I didn't remember so much!"

I realized how much I was touching on some universal themes – what Richard Baxter called "the life which is common to all" – when I read Roger Kahn's *The Boys of Summer*. I had known of the book's existence for years but hadn't read it because it was – I thought – about the Brooklyn Dodgers in the early 1950s, and I had no interest in the Dodgers of that era, or of any other era.

Then, late in the writing of this book, I ran across a quotation from Kahn's book which suggested there was more to it than just a history of the Dodgers. The book is, in fact, about Kahn, about how he grew up a Dodger fan and eventually covered them as a newspaper reporter in 1952 and 1953. Many of his early life experiences were similar to mine. He talks about playing catch with his father, as I do, and getting hit in the ribs by a baseball, as I do, experiences common to just about any boy growing up in the 1950s. (Although I went through my own pubescent sexual awakening, I cannot top Kahn's encounters with his family's maid [*Boys*, pp. 30-31]).

Every good baseball book I've ever read was about something more than just baseball. As Michael Coffey says, "True, libraries are groaning under the weight of paeans to baseball, its American character, its importance to fathers and sons. And for good reason. It is a wonderfully absorbing sport that has managed to appeal to an American's sense of fair play" (*27 Men Out*, pp. 268-269).

So many books and articles have been written about baseball because it is such a perfect metaphor for life. Just look at Thomas Boswell's *How Life Imitates the World Series* or his "99 Reasons Why Baseball is Better Than Football." Comedian George Carlin does a routine comparing baseball and football "and what they tell us about ourselves and our values." He points out that "football has hitting, clipping, spearing, piling on, personal fouls, late hitting and unnecessary roughness. Baseball has the sacrifice . . . . In baseball the object is to go home! And to be safe!"

In preparing to write this book I read several recent histories of America in the post-war period and went back through magazines and newspapers from 1956. In the process I was reminded of two old axioms:

1) "No one who can read can ever clean out an attic." I was looking for certain things but kept finding all sorts of other wonderful stuff. And some unsettling stuff, like a 1956 article warning about the increased risk of cancer among smokers. Why wasn't anybody listening?

2) "The more things change, the more they remain the same." How discouraging it was to read articles from 1956 about US efforts to "westernize" and "democratize" Iraq and about the fighting in the Sudan between Muslim Arabs in the north and non-Muslim Africans in the south. The word "Darfur" seemed to jump off the page.

Does the world need another book like this one – a coming-of-age story with a baseball motif? That question loomed before me while I was writing it. As a justification I cite the words of Lucian of Samosata, a Greco-Roman essayist and satirist of the late second century AD:

> Athletes . . . do not confine their attentions to physical exercise . . . . Similarly, literary people should, after extended reading of serious authors, relax mentally, to refresh themselves against subsequent exertions. They will find this interlude agreeable if they choose as company such works as not only afford wit, charm, and distraction pure and simple, but also provoke some degree of cultured reflection. I trust the present work will be found to inspire such reflection. My readers will be attracted not merely by the novelty of the subject, the appeal of the general design . . . but also by the humorous allusions in every part of my story to various poets, historians, and philosophers of former times.
>
> *A True Story*, 1.1-4.

If you're old enough to remember 1956, I hope you'll enjoy having those memories refreshed. Perhaps you'll find some points of similarity between your life and mine. If you're too young for that – and the majority of America's population is – I hope this book will give you some insight into a period of America's past that may look idyllic as our world becomes more and more complicated but was actually as nerve-wracking as any era in our history.

The historian in me requires that I say a brief word about citing sources. I have used the parenthetical form rather than footnotes or endnotes because I hate having to flip back to the end of a book to look at endnotes and because footnotes create a nightmare for the typesetter. If I may say so, I have been meticulous in citing material I've read. The problem comes in citing quotations from baseball players. It's very difficult to determine where their most famous lines appeared in print for the first time. Most of them appear in numerous anthologies, such as Dickson's and Leventhal's, and on more web sites than one can count. I've contented myself with getting the quotations right – which isn't always easy – and have not tried to attribute them to one particular source, unless it was something I read in a newspaper or magazine myself.

Thanks are due to a number of people. The library staff at Hope College, in Holland, Michigan, procured roll after roll of microfilm for me. Several of my cousins called up reminiscences of life in our grandparents' house in the 1950s, especially Connie Hood, John Willard, Juanita Compton, and Joan Crowder. As always, my writers' group contributed mightily. They didn't like the first installment I shared with them but soon after that began encouraging me. One member, Greg Dunn, suggested having a quotation about perfection at the head of each chapter. My colleagues, Professors Jeanne Petit and Fred Johnson, read the chapters on American history and made helpful suggestions. My editor, Judy Geary, and the owners of Ingalls' Publishing Group, Bob and Barb Ingalls, have not been afraid to take some risk with this book, as different as it is from anything else they've put out. My wife, Bettye Jo, has supported me unfailingly through this and many other projects. And my grandson, Cameron Carter, gives my spirits just the lift they need just when they need it. Thanks are also extended to the Topps Company for permission to reprint the baseball cards included in this book.

Well, I think I'm warmed up. Let's play ball!

	Runs	Hits	Errors
BRKLYN	0	0	0
YANKS	2	5	0

"Of the 1,200 pitchers to pitch in the World Series, only one, Don Larsen, hurled a perfect game. Like Sophia Loren's marriage to Carlo Ponti, the continuing popularity of Danny Thomas, and the political career of Spiro Agnew, there is no explanation for this. It just is."

Boyd and Harris, p. 102

That's the story the scoreboard in Yankee Stadium told shortly after 3:00 on the afternoon of October 8, 1956. If there had been a column for **Walks**, there would have been another **0** on the Brooklyn side. On the field umpire Babe Pinelli had just called a third strike on Dodger pinch-hitter Dale Mitchell, who had started to swing but held up. Yankee catcher Yogi Berra ran to meet pitcher Don Larsen between home plate and the mound and jumped into his arms as over 64,000 fans erupted in pandemonium.

The reason for the celebration? Larsen had just pitched the first perfect game in World Series history. Twenty-seven Dodger batters came to the plate and not one of them reached first base. Fifty years later it still stands as the only perfect game in a century of World Series (or any kind of major league post-season) play. As Richard Lally says, "Mention the 1956 World Series and most baseball fans recall little else but Don Larsen's perfect game, one of those events so momentous it cold-cocks memory, jamming the brain cells until they are incapable of storing any competing data or images" (*Bombers*, p. 101).

Even as I watched the game, at age 11, I didn't understand what I was seeing. The term "perfect game" wasn't common in those days. There hadn't been one since 1922. Shirley Povich rhapsodized about the game the next day without using that term: "The million-to-one shot came in. Hell froze over. A month of Sundays hit the calendar. Don Larsen today pitched a no-hit, no-run, no-man-reach-first game in a World Series" (*Washington Post*, Oct. 9, 1956). The Cincinnati *Enquirer* and *Sports Illustrated* referred to it as a "perfect, no-hit, no-run game," as though they had to clarify what the term meant.

The game was significant for several reasons. First, it gave the sport a badly needed publicity boost, much like the home-run race between Sammy Sosa and Mark McGwire in 1998. Baseball was the national sport in the 1950s, easily overshadowing football, basketball, or hockey, but since WWII the game had been dominated by the three New York teams: the Yankees, Giants, and Dodgers. Of the eleven World Series between 1946 and 1956, only two did not involve a New York team; seven were played between the Yankees from the American League and either the Giants or Dodgers from the National League. The Yankees won a record five straight Series from 1949 to 1953, beating the Dodgers three times, the Giants once, and the Phillies from far-away Philadelphia once.

The dominance of these three teams continued for another decade. The Yankees were in the Series in 1957 and 1958, the [Los Angeles] Dodgers in 1959, the Yankees from 1960-64, playing the [San Francisco] Giants in 1962 and the Dodgers in 1963. The Dodgers were back in the Series in 1965-66.

For New Yorkers, it was a Golden Age. As Whitey Ford said in 1987, "You have to be in your fifties, or close to it, to appreciate what it was like when there were three major league teams in the city of New York, all within minutes of one another . . . . Unless you lived through it, you can't imagine what a baseball-mad city New York was in the fifties. The rivalries were intense, the loyalties fierce" (*Slick*, pp. 106-107).

But as far as most Americans outside of New York were concerned, nothing really exciting had happened in baseball since Joe DiMaggio's 56-game hitting streak in 1941. The Cincinnati *Enquirer*'s sports editor, Lou Smith, observed that "the rest of the baseball world is tired of seeing the Dodgers and the Yankees in the World Series . . . . Outside of the closely knitted boroughs of this sector, it seems safe to assume that nation-wide interest in the World Series has been on the decline because there has been too much of the sameness" (Oct. 2, 1956).

Larsen's achievement also gave the country something upbeat to think about at a time when news headlines were full of conflict over desegregation in the South, President Eisenhower's health, escalating tensions in the Middle East, the Soviets' suppression of their satellite states in Eastern Europe, and Red China's threats against Taiwan.

For me the perfect game – and the Yankees' entire season leading up to it – had a profound impact. I turned eleven in September of 1956, and my life felt very imperfect. While I was hitting puberty, my family was uprooted by a move from Greenville, South Carolina, to Cincinnati. The Yankees were my pole star. I hadn't read *The Old Man and the Sea*, but I would have known exactly what Santiago meant when he said to the boy, "Have faith in the Yankees, my son."

Larsen's perfect game has exercised such a fascination for me that, over the years, I've acquired items autographed by all nine of the Yankee players in the game. One does have to be careful about such things, especially about Mickey Mantle's memorabilia. He didn't like to sign baseballs. Many of those bearing his signature were actually signed by the Yankees' clubhouse man (*Ball Four*, p. 30). The autographed ball I have came from *Sports Illustrated* with authentication, so I don't think I have to worry.

My most cherished item, though, is a copy of the famous picture of Berra jumping into Larsen's arms which is signed by both of them. I bought it with Larsen's authenticated autograph on it and, through Berra's web site, discovered I could send him the picture, a small check and a return envelope, and get his signature on it, too. What I have not acquired, and never will, is a ticket stub from the game. Those go for about $2,000 apiece.

As with any major sporting event, the number of people who claim to have been there far exceeds the seating capacity of Yankee Stadium. But the game was on television. In the 1950s Major League

Baseball told TV when the games would be played, not the other way around. And they didn't get in any hurry about it. An article in the Greenville *News* on Sept. 11 explained the scheduling for the Series, which had just been set the day before in a meeting in the Commissioner's office. The teams attending were Milwaukee, Cincinnati and Brooklyn, the contenders from the National League, and the Yankees and Cleveland Indians from the American League, even though "it was regarded as a practical certainty that the New York Yankees will represent the American League in the series."

The Series, it was decided, would begin on Oct. 3, unless a playoff was needed in the National League. And there was a strong possibility of even a three-way, round-robin playoff which would push the opening of the Series back a week. The games would start at 1:00 local time, except for a Sunday game in New York, which would start at 2:00. Finally, "if Brooklyn should oppose the Yankees, there will be no open dates."

The fact that World Series games were played in the afternoon prompted numerous cases of "World Series flu" among males of all ages. A cartoon in the Greenville *News* on Sept. 27, 1956, showed two men sitting in front of a TV. One says to the other, "I'm taking a week's 'sick leave' to see th' Series." Most schools and businesses were lenient about absences during the Series. That's one reason you often see men in coats, ties and hats in pictures of the crowds in the stands from that era. They left the office at lunch and never went back.

The only way I could have seen Game 5 was to have played hooky. Like a lot of kids, that's what a friend and I did, leaving school at lunchtime and holing up in his family's apartment to watch it. On my way home after the game, I felt guilty for skipping school and deceiving my mother, but I also wondered what it must have felt like to stand on that mound and get *every* batter out. Mickey Mantle, my idol, made a spectacular catch to preserve the perfect game, but that was just one play. For the first time I began to look at the game from a pitcher's perspective.

A perfect game! Batter after batter – Out! Out! Out! I pumped my arm like an umpire making the 'out' signal. Amazing!

"Trying to Reach Perfection"

Kids want their world to be perfect, and they believe it's possible for it to be that way. As we grow up we learn that perfection isn't achievable. Some of us adjust to that reality sooner and better than others. The ones who don't, gravitate toward careers or hobbies which challenge them to keep chasing perfection. As far back as I can remember, I've had a strong urge – I won't admit to a compulsion – to do things as well as possible. My wife still doesn't understand why I edge the sidewalk and dig up dandelions. But how else can I hope to have a perfect yard, even if I know it never will be perfect?

I think Billy Martin would have understood me. In describing the passion with which he played baseball, he said, "If you're in love with the game, you can't turn it on and off like a light. It's something that runs so deep it takes you over . . . . You're second-guessing yourself, but in a positive way, trying to reach perfection . . ." (*Number 1*, p. 11).

"Trying to reach perfection." Yeah, I can relate to that. But I also sympathize with the guy who described himself as "a perfectionist who can't do anything right." For a long time I felt other people had the ability to do things perfectly while nothing I did was ever good enough, let alone perfect. I was a young adult before it dawned on me that everybody else might be as clueless and imperfect as I was about most things.

I also realized that perfection, if it is attainable at all, can't be a permanent state. There are too many variables in our lives, beginning with the people around us. Something that Hall-of-Fame pitcher Sandy Koufax said struck home for me, even if he was a Dodger and did humiliate my beloved Yankees in the 1963 World Series. Koufax said he always took the mound intending to pitch a perfect game, and he did throw one. If he walked someone or a teammate made an error, his goal became a no-hitter, and he had three of those. Once somebody got a hit, Koufax was trying for a shut-out, and he had a passel of those. If the opponents scored a run, his objective was still to win the game, which he did with regularity.

After the '63 Series Yogi Berra said of Koufax, "I can understand how he could win 25 games. What I can't understand is how he lost 5."

So it becomes a matter of adjusting one's expectations, of accepting Ben Jonson's "short measures" of perfection.

Mickey Mantle knew the frustration of the disappointed perfectionist. Toward the end of his career the Yankees moved him to first base to spare his gimpy legs. "I wasn't great," he says, "just adequate. I should have been happy with that, but I had spent my whole career shooting for perfection" (*The Mick*, p. 238).

No one knows if he/she will ever realize a perfect moment, and there is no way to build up to such a moment or to prolong it beyond its natural half-life. It just happens. As William Hazlitt said, "No one ever approaches perfection except by stealth, and unknown to themselves."

And the very moment that feels perfect for one person may be a nightmare for someone else. I'm sure the Dodgers didn't feel as good as Larsen and the Yankees did when the perfect game ended. Pinch-hitter Mitchell has said that moment, with the bat twitching on his shoulder – his last major-league at-bat – defined his reputation as much as it did Larsen's. In spite of a solid eleven-year career, with a lifetime batting average of .312, what he is remembered for is that strike-out, while Larsen "is mainly remembered for being perfect where perfection is simply not possible" (www.baseball-almanac.com/ws/yr1956.shtml).

As I enter my 60s I would still like to find even an occasional one of Jonson's "short measures" of perfection in life. As a teacher I revise my courses and exams and read to keep up in my field, but I know I've never taught a perfect course, not even a perfect day of a course. As a writer I rewrite and listen to critiques from my writers' group and my editor, but I've never published a perfect article or book. I think I've been a good husband and father in spite of frequent reminders that I'm by no means perfect in those areas. I am "the World's Greatest Grandpa." I've got a card from my grandson to prove it, but does "Greatest" equal "perfect"?

So, what does it mean to be perfect or to do something perfectly? How did a man whose baseball career could be described as undistinguished at best (an overall record of 81 wins and 91 losses) step onto the mound one afternoon, with only a few hours warning, and pitch a perfect game under the gut-wrenching pressure of a World Series?

And why does it still matter fifty years later? In a broader sense, how did that game fit into the world of 1956? Can a look at the world of 1956 tell us anything about our world? Those are some of the questions I want to explore in this book.

But that doesn't mean the book is just about a baseball game. At the risk of sounding pretentious, it's about life – mine and, in some sense, everyone's. As William Saroyan said of the World Series, "This is a contest, a play, and all of the players together are yourself, and the play is about your life" (*Sports Illustrated,* Oct. 22, 1956).

CHAPTER 2

"I seem to be . . . ."
Looking back on her childhood, Annie Dillard concluded that at age ten children

> wake up and find themselves here, discover themselves to have been here all along; is this sad? They wake like sleepwalkers, in full stride; they wake like people brought back from cardiac arrest or from drowning: in medias res, surrounded by familiar people and objects, equipped with a hundred skills. They know the neighborhood, they can read and write English, they are old hands at the commonplace mysteries, and yet they feel themselves to have just stepped off the boat, just converged with their bodies, just flown down from a trance, to lodge in an eerily familiar life already well under way (*An American Childhood*, p. 11).

That is an accurate, if somewhat embroidered, description of how I felt in the summer of 1956, on the verge of turning 11. My life before that summer I remember as isolated incidents, not a continuous narrative, snapshots instead of a movie. Beginning in 1956, though, I have a sense of the wholeness of my life.

At ten – I would turn eleven on September 23 – I had no illusions about that life being perfect. I was a non-athletic kid who wanted to be an athlete, a short kid who wanted to be tall, a kid with a defective "snaggle-tooth" right in front who wanted to be able to smile, a shy kid who wanted to make friends like everybody else seemingly could – in short, to be something other than what I was.

The first time I heard the Platters sing "The Great Pretender," in the summer of 1956, I knew they were talking about me. Not that I had lost a love or that I was a gay clown, just that somehow the outward reality of my life didn't match how it felt inside of me. "Too real is this feeling of make-believe."

My primary avenue of escape from this imperfection was avid reading. I used to pick up a volume of our encyclopedia and just browse. I had to look up a lot of words, but the dictionary was handy. I still have my parents' dictionary (and a modern one, too). My parents didn't buy me many books, but they took me to the library. I still have my award from a summer reading program when I was nine. I began working crossword puzzles at age ten, and I read my daily newspaper with closer attention than most ten- or eleven-year olds. My father and I read it over breakfast, in part to avoid talking to one another, I think.

My family was as typical as families got in those days. My father served in the Marines in WWII, then spent five years working and going to school. After graduating from Georgia Tech in 1951 he got a low-level management job in the textile industry in Greenville, South Carolina, in the northwest corner of the state. My mother was a home-maker. My younger brother and I had everything we needed except a good fraternal relationship, a situation I've always regretted.

My life felt most nearly perfect when I was at my maternal grandparents' home on Irby Avenue in Laurens, thirty miles south of Greenville. I was born in Laurens while my father was still in the Marines. The house on Irby Avenue was – still is – huge, built in the 1880s, with 12-foot ceilings and rooms the size of two rooms in a modern house. Its thick plaster walls rendered it impervious to such updates as central heating or air-conditioning. Each room had its own gas heater (replacing the original fireplaces). Rooms were heated only when in use and the front hall was never heated. A monstrous attic fan brought us as close as we got to cool in July and August. As one of my cousins is fond of saying, "That fan would suck the sheets right off the beds."

The house sat well back from the street. Four steps led up from the public sidewalk to the yard. A long, broad sidewalk led to a flight of nine steps up to the front porch. We weren't an aristocratic family, but the people on the other side of the street did literally look up to us.

Upstairs the house had a hall, actually more of a mezzanine, with two large rooms and a bath off each side. One room on each side was outfitted with a sink and stove, to create essentially a set of two-room apartments. We ate a lot of our meals with my grandparents, though. At breakfast I would sit in my grandfather's lap and he would fix me a cup of 90% milk and 10% coffee. Yes, I was drinking lattes at age three.

My mother was one of five children (four girls, one boy) who, in their turn, produced fourteen grandchildren (eight girls, six boys), the youngest born in July, 1956. Due to death, divorce, or other family problems, ten of those children lived in my grandparents' house for some portion of their childhood, sometimes more than one family at a time. We spent so much time in the house that, when the stairs needed refinishing, my grandmother cried as the scuff marks we had left on the edge of the steps were sanded off.

Being together that much created a certain familiarity among the grandchildren. One of my cousins recently told me that her earliest memory is of following me into the bathroom when she was three and I was four. When her horrified mother found us, my cousin was watching with great interest as I peed.

We called my grandparents Ma-Ma and Pa-Pa, and their house was my home until I was four. After that I visited frequently and spent a week or more at a time there during the summer. Sharing holidays with grandparents on the other side of our family was never an option. Thanksgiving, Christmas, Mother's Day, Father's Day, Fourth of July – if it was a holiday, we were in Laurens.

The house itself meant so much to my cousins and me that, after my grandparents died and it was sold, we avoided driving by it for years.

It was too painful to know it was no longer ours. I did not see the house for twelve years and then was appalled to see how poorly it was being maintained. So holy a site deserves reverent owners.

I still own a piece of the house because my grandfather, like George Steinbrenner remodeling Yankee Stadium, made an unfortunate decision in the early 1960s. Typical of any Victorian-era house, this one had a lot of "gingerbread," fancy decorative work on the eaves. That made painting the house

difficult and more expensive, and some of it was in poor condition, so Pa-Pa had it all removed. My mother, the quintessential packrat, kept one piece, which I, every bit the son of the quintessential packrat, still have.

As an adult I've come to treasure old houses, and I'm sure that affection was imprinted on me by my childhood experiences in my grandparents' house. When I got my first job out of graduate school, I knew I was going to buy an old, two-story house, even if I couldn't afford one as big as theirs. Fortunately my wife shares my attraction to such places. As we get into our 60s, though, the word "condo" keeps cropping up in her conversation. But what would we do about our divorced daughter and grandson, who live with us? And he calls me Pa-Pa.

Damnedest thing, that circle of life.

"Perfect Days"

Just as Yankee Stadium, the largest park in the majors, seemed to me the perfect place to play baseball, so my grandparents' big house seemed the perfect place for a kid to spend time, outside as well as in. Their deep lot ran from Irby Avenue all the way through to the street behind. And they owned the vacant lot on one side of them, which also ran from one street to the other. Except for their house and garage and a dilapidated storage shed, the land was open, with trees only on the edges, so we had a huge L-shaped play area. As a child my mother had kept a pet goat there, until the animal butted somebody and had to be taken away. That urban "pasture" was where we spent summer days playing ball.

Since my cousins and I were not numerous enough to make two full teams, we often played Dollar-ball. It's nothing like the stickball played in big cities (Kahn, pp. 19-20), but variations of this game are found all over the country. For Dollar-ball you need a pitcher and a batter. Everybody else is a fielder. A catcher is optional because he/she doesn't have much chance to field the ball, and if you can't field the ball, you'll never bat.

Sometimes my grandfather would play with us. I remember him, at age 70, catching a pop-up barehanded and teasing us kids for needing our big gloves. My mother would also pick up a bat now and then.

The rules of Dollar-ball are simple. If you catch a ball on the fly, you get a dollar, which means you get to bat. First bounce equals fifty cents, second bounce is a quarter. If the ball is still rolling when you reach it – and kicking it and then picking it up doesn't count – you get a dime. If it has stopped rolling, you earn a nickel. When somebody reaches a dollar, everybody else's count resets to zero. When a new batter comes in, the pitcher moves to the field and the retiring batter becomes the pitcher.

The game does teach some skills applicable to regular baseball. Catching fly balls earns the highest reward. Every time I took off after one I envisioned myself as Mickey Mantle. Since there's no catcher, you have to learn to be a "bad-ball" hitter or you spend a lot of time running after the ball. Maybe that's where Yogi Berra developed his hitting style: "I swung at anything near my ears and golfed at balls near my ankles" (*Ten Rings*, p. 72). And, if you want to stay at bat for a while, you have to learn to hit the ball to the weak fielders or to places where nobody is playing. "Wee Willie" Keeler built a .341 lifetime average on this strategy of "hit 'em where they ain't." He did it 2,932 times.

On the porch that wrapped around the front and one side of the house, we played canasta or week-

long games of Monopoly, combining money from several sets and letting people go deeply into debt. The porch had a circular bulge at the corner of the house. When we were young we imagined that the conical roof over that part of the porch, with its black shingles, resembled a witch's hat.

One of my cousins summed up our feelings about the porch: "I loved lying in the big hammock on the witch's hat part of the porch, and vowed that someday when I got rich, I would own a hammock like that, and I do. I'm not rich, but I have a Pauli's Island hammock that reminds me of Ma-Ma's every time I curl up in it."

If you stayed at Ma-Ma's and Pa-Pa's for more than a day, you would find yourself doing chores. As loving as she was, my grandmother liked having things done for her. One of my older cousins spent a good bit of time in Laurens during the summer of 1956. She said Ma-Ma had her doing "amazing amounts of work. She was a slavedriver! . . . I remember cleaning the front and side porch and sweeping and scouring those infinite steps and that endless sidewalk."

Ma-Ma particularly disliked grass growing between the cracks in that sidewalk. Getting rid of it was a job assigned to visiting grandchildren. We sometimes joked about getting my mother's goat back to nibble the stuff away.

One side of the front yard was entirely taken over by a magnolia tree. When we reached about age nine or ten, the family rite of passage required us to see how far we could climb up that tree. Only the bravest of us got high enough to see where my mother had carved her initials when she was a girl. One of my cousins recalls climbing the tree "against Ma-Ma's express warnings" and finding her own "mother's initials with an old boyfriend's . . . . I carved my initials with my current boyfriend's above theirs."

The most perfect of those perfect days came when my grandfather piled us all into the back of his pickup truck, the "Little Red Truck" (the one in the background of this picture) and – oblivious to safety – we rode to the Dairy Twirl for ice cream. I thought Pa-Pa owned the Dairy Twirl and I sometimes mentioned that to win games of one-up-manship with friends. I never saw him pay for the ice cream and we were always treated like royalty. Some years later I learned he owned the building and leased it to the Dairy Twirl. They simply deducted the ice cream tab from their monthly rent. One of my cousins still has the Little Red Truck.

Three of my cousins came to live with my grandparents in 1955, after their father was killed in an auto accident and their mother had trouble caring for them. I knew it was an awful thing to lose one's father, but I also envied them for living there. A few years later, when one of my aunts got a divorce, she and three other cousins came to live there.

"Our splendid failure"

With adult eyes I can see that Ma-Ma and Pa-Pa weren't perfect people. And there were family secrets I didn't learn until I was in high school. That was also when I began to read Faulkner and Tennessee Williams. I immediately thought, "My God! They're writing about my family."

But my grandparents were caring souls. At 60 they took on the challenge of raising three very young children, one of them disabled. Pa-Pa lost his grocery store in the Depression because he couldn't refuse to sell food to people even when they had no money. One of my cousins remembered "long talks with Pa-Pa about faith and doubt and my many questions about the Bible and his patiently trying to answer them . . . . I would feel a sting of regret that I was too big to sit in his lap any more."

One cousin who grew up in my grandparents' house reflected on what that experience meant for him:

> Pa-Pa taught me more about being a man than my own father did, about honor and character . . . I remember vividly once that some girl was calling the house. She was apparently interested in me, though at the time I considered her a nuisance. I must have been around 12 or so. Pa-Pa answered, and I was sitting in the den. He told me the call was for me, a young lady. I asked him to tell her I wasn't there. He put his hand over the mouthpiece, then told me softly, "I will tell her you do not wish to speak to her, but I will not lie and tell her you are not here." I got up and answered the call. Obviously, I've never forgotten the lesson. I didn't appreciate it at the time, though.
>
> I would come down early in the morning to use the shower because I didn't like the tub upstairs. One morning I barged through the hallway door – with its translucent glass – only to find Pa-Pa on his knees at that old pinkish couch, praying. He gave me a look that told me I had interrupted something very important, and I backed out into the hallway. Many mornings after that I would peer through that glass to make sure he was finished. Sometimes I would have to wait in the unheated hallway, shivering if it was winter. I would hurry through the den as soon as he got up. On a couple of occasions, as he got up and I was making my rapid dash to the shower, I noticed a tear running down his cheek as he fumbled to dry his eyes. He was a gentle, humble, thankful man who started every day on his knees . . . . He never said a lot. It was more the example of his actions, but I was too young and stupid to appreciate the wealth of teaching I was receiving.

I thought Chaucer described Pa-Pa as well as anybody: "He was a verray parfit gentil knight." Of course, it was unrealistic, even ridiculous, of me to expect my family to be perfect. For a while, though, in the mid-1950s it felt like we were pretty close to it. But, as Faulkner observed, "All of us failed to match our dreams of perfection. So I rate us on the basis of our splendid failure to do the impossible."

CHAPTER 3

Never to Perfection?

I believe something about growing up white and middle-class in the South in the 1950s made us feel perfection was attainable. We enjoyed a perfect climate and an ideal pace of life. Before our eyes was held up the ideal image of the Southern Gentleman, a descendant of the Cavalier of ante-bellum days and the gallant knight of the Middle Ages. Our women were Damsels, Fair Maidens, for whom we opened doors and gave up our seats. It was no accident that *Ivanhoe* was still required reading for white seventh-graders in many Southern public schools.

> "Perfection
> does not exist;
> to understand it is the
> triumph of human intelligence;
> to expect to possess it is the
> most dangerous kind of
> madness."
>
> Alfred de Musset

All of that perfection contrasted starkly with our perception of the harshness of life in the north – home of snowy winters, smoke-belching factories, and dehumanizing jobs on production lines, where everything was run by money-grubbing robber-barons and their gold-digging wives and daughters.

Life in the South in that era hadn't changed much in several generations, for either whites or blacks. One of the characteristics of a state of perfection is that it doesn't change, nor would you want it to. But, of course, the South was a very imperfect society for those who did not enjoy the privileges, as small as they were, which my family and I enjoyed. Much of the turmoil the South went through in the 1950s arose from the change taking place because some people finally got tired of the imperfection while others were determined to resist that change and hold on to what they saw as perfect.

Perfect? Perfection? Can we craft a workable definition of those terms?

The dictionary I use defines "perfect" as "having all the properties naturally belonging to it . . . complete, sound, flawless, pure, utter, as in 'utter bliss'." If something is perfect, it cannot be improved upon or done any better.

We're taught to strive for perfection in whatever we do. "Practice makes perfect" people say, or, as Oscar Wilde phrased it, "practice must precede perfection." Martha Graham preferred to say, "Practice is a means of inviting the perfection desired."

But does it? I took piano lessons for years and spent hours each week practicing. I never played anything perfectly. I've never heard a virtuoso pianist pronounce his/her work perfect. Some of them nearly go crazy because they *can't* be perfect. As Eugene Delacroix said, "Artists who seek perfection in everything are those who cannot attain it in anything." To be honest, we ought to say, "Practice makes better, maybe pretty good or good enough, maybe even the best."

But can "the best" ever become perfection?

Some would argue that that doesn't matter. It is by the process of pursuing perfection, not in the achieving of it, that we improve ourselves. The makers of the Lexus automobile claim to be committed to the "passionate pursuit of perfection." Will they ever reach it? How will they know when they have?

Should they sell cars that aren't perfect?

It may be our expectation of the possibility of perfection that sets us up for disappointment. As one minister said, "Time after time after time – all evidence to the contrary – we expect other people and institutions and our relationships and communities to be perfect . . . . Our Great Expectations of perfection come up empty every time" (Bertschausen, "Trying"). Many others have made less than encouraging observations on the subject:

"It is reasonable to have perfection in our eye that we may always advance toward it, though we know it can never be reached."

Samuel Johnson

"The indefatigable pursuit of an unattainable Perfection, even though it consist in nothing more than in the pounding of an old piano, is what alone gives a meaning to our life on this unavailing star."

Logan Pearsall Smith

"Perfection is a trifle dull. It is not the least of life's ironies that this, which we all aim at, is better not quite achieved."

W. Somerset Maugham

"By degrees the comforting light of what you may actually do and be in an imperfect world will shine close to you and all around you, more and more. It is this that will lead you never to perfection, but always toward it."

James Lane Allen

"Have no fear of perfection; you'll never reach it."

Salvador Dali

Perhaps, as Dali suggests, there is something even a little scary about the search for perfection. Sports writer Roger Angell concluded that many fans rooted for the inept New York Mets instead of the Yankees because of "a new recognition that perfection is admirable but a trifle inhuman, and that a stumbling kind of semi-success can be much more warming" (*Summer Game*, p. 41).

How Shall We Know It?

The problem in the quest for perfection is that in most fields of endeavor there is no absolute standard against which to measure our performance. Perfection may mean different things to each of us. Like beauty, it's in the eye of the beholder. Or, like pornography, we may not be able to define it, but we know it when we see it, even if others don't see it in the same places we do. In a "Zits" comic strip fifteen-year-old Jeremy says, "All I did today was eat, sleep and lie around." His mother says, "Well, with a little effort you can make tomorrow a better day." Jeremy looks stunned. "How do you improve on perfection?"

In some lines of work a kind of perfection may be achievable, even necessary. Workers on an assembly line each have to do their jobs exactly right or there will be a problem at the next step. Inevitably, some don't. That's why we get imperfect cars that we have to keep taking back to the dealer.

Electricians and plumbers have to achieve perfection. If there is any flaw in an electrical circuit, you have no power. Or, worse yet, something catches on fire. But if the plumber doesn't do a perfect job, there'll be water all over the place to put out the fire.

Airline pilots don't have much margin for error, either. We talk about a "perfect landing." But that just means the plane didn't crash. Is every successful landing necessarily perfect? Is an electrician's work perfect just because the lights come on? Could either of those jobs have been done any better?

There may be a problem in terminology involved here. Is excellence anything like perfection? Can something be excellent but not perfect? Actor Michael J. Fox has said, "I am careful not to confuse excellence with perfection. Excellence, I can reach for; perfection is God's business."

"Old-timers weekends and airplane landings are alike. If you can walk away from them, they're successful."

Casey Stengel

In most areas of our lives, how the results are evaluated is subjective. No surgeon ever performs the perfect operation, unless, as in landing an airplane, "successful" = "perfect." No architect ever designs the perfect building. No chef ever cooks the perfect meal (although Orville Redenbacher claims "forty years of making the perfect popcorn"). No parent ever raises the perfect child. No couple ever enjoys the perfect marriage.

If we're lucky we may find some perfection in Jonson's "short measures" – a walk on the beach at dawn, an evening with a lover – but those moments always merge into something else and we have to return to the reality of our imperfect lives, just as Larsen and the Yankees did the next day, when they lost Game 6, by a score of 1-0 in ten innings, in what *Sports Illustrated* considered the best game of the Series. Larsen himself got precious little time to savor his perfect moment. Alongside the report of the game in many newspapers on Oct. 9 was an article about his estranged wife suing him for child support.

"There is something that falls short of perfection in every book, without exception."

Josef Skvorecky

There's always something we could have done better, differently, more effectively, but how do we know what that something is? Will doing it result in perfection, or merely in excellence? A little more salt in a stew might improve it to one person's taste, but ruin it for another.

Maybe that's why something like Larsen's game, something described as "perfect," intrigues us. We want to see how it is perfect, and we suspect all along that it can't be, because nothing is ever perfect. Life has taught us that.

Making the Grade

The best place to look for perfection might be in an environment where performance is graded or ranked not subjectively but numerically on some recognized scale. We often ask people to rate something on a scale of 1 to 10, with 10 being . . . best? Perfect? In the movie "10," which etched this process into our collective psyche, Dudley Moore is asked to rate Bo Derek on a scale of 1 to 10. What's his answer? (You can win a bar bet with this.) He says she's an 11. So even this commonly used gauge seems imperfect, if something can exist which exceeds the top number.

In school we're often graded on a numerical scale. We know a score of 90 on an exam is better than a 70. But does 100 necessarily imply perfection? In an old "Peanuts" strip Snoopy went to school with

Charlie Brown and aced a true-false test. The teacher and principal were amazed. "They don't believe you could get a perfect score on a 'true or false' test, Snoopy," Charlie Brown reported. "So you know what they want you to do? They want you to take an essay test."

If the only tests we took were those with numerical scores, we might have a way to judge objectively how close to perfection a student has come. That assumes, of course, that the tests are perfect instruments. As a teacher for thirty years, I know there is no such thing as a perfect test, objective or otherwise. A score of 100 on a particular test might qualify as one of Ben Jonson's "short measures" of perfection, but what does it mean in terms of a student's overall achievement?

Then there are writing assignments and essay tests, the evaluation of which is highly subjective. Does an 'A' imply the essay/paper is perfect, or just the best possible? Does an 'A' in a course mean the student has achieved perfect mastery of the subject, or the best mastery possible, or just better mastery than anyone else in the class?

So the search for perfection in school seems destined to come to imperfection.

One for the Record Books

But wait, all sports keep statistics, and all athletes strive to do their best. Can we find perfection in sports?

We can know who has scored the most points or had the most assists or the highest batting average. Statistics like that are what make sports interesting off the field. On the field, though, the objective is to win. And even winning doesn't imply that an athlete has performed perfectly. Mark Spitz's seven gold medals made him the best in Olympic swimming in 1972, but no one claims he swam perfectly. He was just better than all the other swimmers. And no matter how many times Mr. Armstrong wins the Tour de Lance, no one can say his performance was perfect. It was just always better than anyone else's.

Likewise, no basketball player can ever say, "I played a perfect game." No set number of points or percentage of shots made is regarded as a perfect performance in a basketball game. Not even Wilt Chamberlain's 100-point performance on March 2, 1962, rates as perfect. After all, Chamberlain hit "only" 36 of his 63 shots (57%) and 28 of 32 free throws. NPR commentator Frank Deford asked, "Is there any other individual performance in a team game more glorious?" Glorious, yes. Perfect, no.

But there was a "perfect" performance in Chamberlain's 100-point game. His teammate Al Attles hit 8 of 8 shots and 1 of 1 from the free-throw line. Attles groused, "No one ever accused me of being a great shooter. But the only time in my life when I was perfect, when I had the hot hand and literally couldn't miss, Wilt had to go out and get 100." But was Attles really perfect? Should his play on defense be factored in? Oh, wait. They don't play defense in the NBA.

The core of the dilemma is that in basketball there is no standard which says, X is the best a player can possibly do and if he does X, his performance will be deemed perfect. Should Al Attles have taken ten or twelve or thirty shots and hit them all if he wanted to be considered perfect on that

To illustrate the magnitude of this achievement, the second highest point total in an NBA game is 81 by Kobe Bryant, on Jan. 22, 2006. Chamberlain scored 78 on Dec. 8, 1961. He scored 73 twice, a total which David Thompson matched in 1978. It must be noted that Chamberlain and Thompson played without the 3-point shot, which the NBA instituted in 1979. Bryant hit seven 3-pointers in his game.

night? Would he have been perfect if he hit his first shot and didn't take another shot for the rest of the game? Bill Walton hit 21 of 22 shots in UCLA's championship game in 1973. His performance was awe-inspiring, dominating, almost legendary, but perfect?

Football also lacks a standard to differentiate between "very good" and "perfect," although, years ago, *Sports Illustrated* claimed that "for professional football men, perfection is the rule" (Sept. 3, 1956). A west Michigan newspaper once carried a headline on its sports page: "Joey Perfect in Pre-season Opener." Detroit Lions' quarterback Joey Harrington completed nine of nine passes. The opposing quarterback completed six of nine and had one intercepted, but his team won.

Does being perfect mean anything if one's team loses? If one quarterback completes twelve passes out of twelve while another completes twenty out of twenty, are both perfect? Can one be more perfect than the other? If the quarterback who completes twelve passes accounts for three hundred yards gained and two touchdowns, while the guy with twenty completions gains only one hundred and fifty yards but four touchdowns, which is better? Is either perfect? Does it matter which quarterback's team won the game?

The NFL now has a "passer rating" system that ranks quarterbacks by a formula under which 158.3 is the maximum "grade." But, as James Buckley points out, "even a quarterback who reaches that number in a game can lose, and oddly, can have statistics that aren't as good as another quarterback who reaches the same grade. Do they call that a 'perfect' game? No" (*Perfect*, p. xviii).

Is it possible for a team, as opposed to individuals, to be perfect? The Miami Dolphins won all sixteen of their games in 1972. UCLA's men's basketball team won 88 consecutive games between 1971-74 and were national champions for seven straight years. But we refer to their "undefeated" seasons, not their perfect seasons. Whitey Ford felt the 1961 Yankees were "as close to being perfect as I've ever seen, a wonderful balance of offense and defense" (*Slick*, p. 166). But they didn't win all their games.

All of these teams were obviously excellent, superb, but is there a mark called "perfect" against which we can measure them?

Other sports have the same deficiency. There is no perfect score in golf. Have Arnold Palmer or Tiger Woods ever shot a perfect round? Par isn't perfect; it's just a typical score for a round. Pro golfers don't win tournaments by shooting par. I suppose a hole-in-one on every hole would qualify as perfect, but perfection should be within the realm of possibility. In September of 1956 Cary Middlecoff shot a 59. *Sports Illustrated* called it "a really stunning round of golf." Nobody called it a perfect round.

Gymnasts and ice skaters can receive perfect scores, but they are dependent on the subjective judgment of the scorers. (At least we don't have the notorious East German judges to contend with any more.) Before 1976 no gymnast ever received a 10 for his/her performance. In the 1976 Olympics, though, Romanian Nadia Comaneci was awarded a 10. Since then other gymnasts have been given that "perfect" score. Must we conclude that no one before Nadia, in all the history of gymnastics, had ever given a performance that could be deemed perfect? Did gymnasts suddenly get better after 1976? Or did the judges begin to see things differently?

The problem in all these fields – plumbing, surgery, school, football, basketball, swimming, gymnastics, etc. – is that there is no defined standard of perfection which lets a participant know at the beginning of the activity what would be regarded as perfect. There are degrees of accomplishment – poor, fair, good, better, best – but there is never a final term in the sequence which can be dubbed "perfect."

Where does that leave us? In Samuel Crothers' words, "Try as hard as we may for perfection, the net result of our labors is an amazing variety of imperfectness."

4

You know you're perfect when . . . .

Experience and the wisdom of the ages seem to suggest the quest for perfection is doomed to frustration. Surely this can't be. Is there no human endeavor in which we can even dream of doing something we can call "perfect"?

In all of life I'm aware of only two fields in which a participant can actually achieve perfection in an objective sense, independent of the biases and subjective opinions of teachers or judges. In these two cases you know when you start the activity what the standard is and you know as you go along whether or not you're meeting it. Those two fields are – and feel free to laugh – bowling and baseball. A bowler can roll a 300-game, and a baseball pitcher can hurl a perfect game.

The two accomplishments aren't exactly equivalent. The bowler is throwing a ball at ten inanimate objects. The pins aren't trying to thwart him or dodge out of the way. But there is that objective: bowl twelve consecutive strikes, and you cannot have done any better. This is not an impossible standard to meet. So many bowlers – amateur and professional, men and women – have done it that no one knows how many perfect 300-games have been rolled in the history of the sport. In December of 2005 a Michigan man bowled a 300-game – his second – and then died of a heart attack. In January of 2006 a Michigan newspaper reported on two 300-games as a ho-hum affair: "Another week, another two 300-games." One issue of the on-line newsletter of the Bowland Centers of Southwest Florida reported 300-games by an 11-year-old boy and a 74-year-old man. The record for 300-games by a father-daughter combination is 49 (45 by the father, 4 by the daughter). Ironically, it would be possible to bowl a perfect game but not defeat your opponent if he/she duplicated the feat.

A baseball pitcher, though, is trying to get the ball past opponents who have a weapon in their hands. As Hank Aaron said in 1956, "The pitcher has got only a ball. I've got a bat. The percentage in weapons is in my favor." Unless a pitcher manages to strike out 27 opposing batters, he has to rely on eight teammates to play their positions flawlessly. With 27 strike-outs, he would still have to rely on the catcher not to miss a third strike and, if the batter didn't swing, on the umpire's judgment about whether a pitch was a ball or a strike.

In spring of 2005 a Little League pitcher– a girl – in New York struck out all 18 batters in a six-inning game. (How boring it must have been for her teammates!) In the Little League World Series in August of 2005 a pitcher recorded all 18 outs in a game by strike-outs, but he gave up several hits and a couple of runs along the way.

Don Larsen summed up the pitcher's situation perfectly:

> . . . the perfect game in baseball is unique among all sports achievements. Except in bowling which has the 300 game, baseball has a finite number of outs that must be achieved for a victory. In a regular nine-inning game, that number is 27, and if a pitcher can retire the required number of batters in order, he has pitched the perfect game.
>
> Because of the absolute standard by which the winning or losing of a game is measured, the baseball pitcher knows firsthand the goal for which to strive. Before a game, pitchers, whether it be in little league, pony league, Babe Ruth league, semi-pro, the minors, or in the major leagues, realize that they have a chance for perfection if they can retire in order 27 straight batters (*The Perfect Yankee*, pp. 125-126).

Defining the 'Perfecto'

The very concept of the perfect game is tied up with one of baseball's most glaring peculiarities. It is a team sport, but one player on the team is designated as the winner or loser of each game. And he gets that record, no matter whether the win or loss is his doing. The third baseman may make an error which lets the winning run score, but the guy standing on the mound when that happens is the "loser." And he might not even be on the mound.

Sounds a lot like life, doesn't it? Sometimes you get credit or blame, regardless of your contribution to a situation.

Baseball is also the only sport in which the defense controls the ball. If an offensive player touches the ball with anything but a bat, he is out. Furthermore, it is the only team sport in which a ball that touches the "foul" line is "fair." Touch the line in football or basketball and you're out of bounds.

Imagine a tie ball game, in the bottom of the ninth. The lead-off batter is safe when the third baseman makes an error. The next batter lays down a sacrifice bunt to move the runner to second. The runner then steals third. The pitcher is not doing a poor job. The other team has not gotten the ball out of the infield, but they have the winning run on third with only one out. The next batter is a power-hitting lefty, so the manager brings in a left-handed relief pitcher to face him, since baseball wisdom says left-handed pitchers have an advantage over left-handed hitters. The runner on third would "belong to" the original pitcher. If the relief pitcher gives up a hit or a sacrifice fly or if a teammate makes an error – if the runner scores by any means – the run is charged to the original pitcher and he would be the loser, even though he did not give up a hit and was sitting in the dugout when the run scored.

On the other hand, a pitcher may do a mediocre job, but if his teammates score enough runs to overcome it, the pitcher is the "winner." In the Yankees' first game of the 1956 season Don Larsen gave up three home runs, but the Bronx Bombers lived up to their name with a homer by Yogi Berra and two mammoth shots by Mickey Mantle, so Larsen "won" the game. On May 5 of that year the *New York Times* reported Bob Grim was the winning pitcher in a game, not because of his outstanding performance, but "by virtue of having been around when the decisive rally was launched."

In no other team sport is one player singled out as the winner or loser of a game. There is no winning point guard in basketball, no winning goalie in soccer or losing quarterback in football, but every baseball game has a winning and losing pitcher. Some sportscasters these days do mention that a football team has so many wins or losses when a particular quarterback starts the game, but we don't talk about his Won-Loss record the way we do with pitchers. In no other sport is there a standard comparable to a pitcher winning 20 games, nor does any other sport have anything like an E. R. A. (Earned Run

Average) for an individual player.

This odd concept of one player winning or losing in a team sport is magnified when talking about a "perfect" game. A perfect game is defined as

    *a complete game
    *of at least nine innings
    *by one pitcher
    *in which no opposing batter reaches base.

No matter how well he pitches, if a teammate makes an error and allows a runner to reach base, the pitcher gets credit for a no-hitter but not for a perfect game. A pitcher can also walk any number of batters and still get credit for a no-hitter. A perfect game, though, means that at least 27 opponents came to the plate and not one of them reached first base. It also means that the pitcher's team managed to score at least one run.

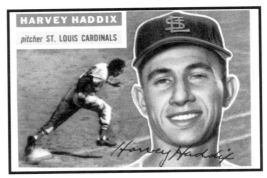

There have been two cases where a pitcher threw a perfect game for nine innings, only to lose it in extra innings. In 1959 Harvey Haddix retired 36 consecutive batters but lost his perfect game on an error in the thirteenth inning and went on to lose the game. Pedro Martinez gave up a hit in the tenth inning of a game in 1995. He pitched a complete game and won, but that hit in the tenth inning disqualified it as a perfect game. One commentator said at the time, "This [game] belongs in the annals of baseball. You can't pass this off as just another game, but that's how it will go down – as just another game."

Both of these games are reminders of how a pitcher's record is affected by the performance of his teammates. If Haddix's or Martinez's teams had scored just one run by the ninth inning, both men would have had their perfect games.

There have also been cases where pitchers were perfect until the last batter in the ninth inning got on base. And it wasn't always a hit that spoiled the perfect game. In 1908 Hooks Wiltse of the New York Giants had retired 26 batters and had two strikes on the 27th, pitcher George McQuillan of the Philadelphia Phillies. But Wiltse hit McQuillan with his next pitch. Wiltse got his no-hitter and won the game, but what a way to lose a perfect game. (Lew Burdette of the Milwaukee Braves also lost a perfect game in 1960 by hitting a batter, but his *faux pas* lacked the drama of Wiltse's because it occurred in the fifth inning.) In 1972 Milt Pappas of the Chicago Cubs got to a count of one ball and two strikes on the 27th batter. The umpire called the next three pitches balls. Controversy still surrounds those calls. Pappas retired the next batter and got credit for a no-hitter and a victory, but not a perfect game.

In the 180,000 or more games that have been played in the modern era of American major league baseball (since 1903, when most of today's rules were standardized) there have been only fifteen perfect games pitched. Two more were pitched in 1880, within five days of each other, but in those days the mound was 45 feet from home plate, the pitcher threw underhand, and the batter could call for a high or low pitch, so those two games are best left in a category of their own.

Don Larsen's perfect game in the 1956 World Series also stands in a category of its own. As the Cincinnati *Enquirer* put it, the other perfect games "hardly deserve to be mentioned in the same breath with Larsen's masterpiece" (Oct. 9, 1956). Sports writer Donald Benn said at the time, "That Larsen did it in a World Series game when the pressures are great and the stakes are high places his achievement on a pinnacle that will shine high above the greatest achievements in any competitive sport anywhere, any time."

Fourteen of the modern "perfectos" occurred during the regular season. For the record:

Date	Pitcher	Team	Opponent	Score
May 5, 1904	Cy Young	Boston (AL)	Philadelphia A's	3-0
Oct. 2, 1908	Addie Joss	Cleveland (AL)	Chicago White Sox	1-0
Apr. 30, 1922	Charlie Robertson	Chicago (AL)	Detroit Tigers	2-0
June 21, 1964	Jim Bunning	Philadelphia (NL)	New York Mets	6-0
Sept. 9, 1965	Sandy Koufax	Los Angeles (NL)	Chicago Cubs	1-0
May 8, 1968	Catfish Hunter	Oakland (AL)	Minnesota Twins	4-0
May 15, 1981	Len Barker	Cleveland (AL)	Toronto Blue Jays	3-0
Sept. 30, 1984	Mike Witt	California (AL)	Texas Rangers	1-0
Sept. 16, 1988	Tom Browning	Cincinnati (NL)	Los Angeles Dodgers	1-0
July 28, 1991	Dennis Martinez	Montreal (NL)	Los Angeles Dodgers	2-0
July 28, 1994	Kenny Rogers	Texas (AL)	California Angels	4-0
May 17, 1998	David Wells	New York (AL)	Minnesota Twins	4-0
July 18, 1999	David Cone	New York (AL)	Montreal Expos	6-0
May 18, 2004	Randy Johnson	Arizona (NL)	Atlanta Braves	2-0

A few observations about that chart before we move on. First, perfect games were extraordinarily rare before the 1960s. Jim Bunning's in 1964 was the first during the regular season in 42 years and the first ever in the National League. One hears a lot about how much stronger hitters have become in recent years, but the 1980s saw three perfect games and the 1990s had four.

Second, most perfect games are low-scoring. Four were 1-0 games, and in only five of them did the winning team score more than three runs.

Third, the names of some of these pitchers aren't exactly household words. Where are some of the dominant pitchers of the late twentieth century, such as Bob Feller, Robin Roberts, Whitey Ford, Bob Gibson, Don Drysdale, Nolan Ryan, Roger Clemens, or Greg Maddux? "Why not other mediocre pitchers, why not other great pitchers?" (Coffey, *27 Men Out*, p. 274)

Jim Bunning also pitched a no-hitter when he was with the Boston Red Sox, making him the only pitcher ever to throw no-hitters in both the National and American Leagues.

In addition to the perfect games, since 1900 there have been 108 no-hitters pitched in the American League and 97 in the National League. One of the American League "no-no's" was pitched by Clyde Wright of the California Angels against the Oakland A's on July 3, 1970. Three walks were all that separated Wright from a perfect game (Stewart, *Fathers, Sons*). I mention that particular game to show how close a pitcher can come without grabbing the brass ring. Oh, and because I attended Carson-Newman College with Wright in the mid-1960's. Six degrees of separation and all that.

Considering how many no-hitters there have been, a pitcher might not be overly optimistic to think he could throw one, or too arrogant if he was casual about having done it. After pitching a no-hitter, the Angels' Bo Belinsky said, "If I'd known I was gonna pitch a no-hitter today I would have gotten a haircut." When Paul Dean pitched a no-hitter in the second game of a double-header, his older brother Dizzy, who had pitched a one-hitter in the first game, said, "If I had known what Paul was gonna do, I would have pitched one, too."

No-hitters are common enough that two almost occurred on the same day. On May 12, 1956, the day Carl Erskine pitched his no-hitter in Brooklyn, Don Ferrarese of the Baltimore Orioles, pitching against the Yankees a few miles away in the Bronx, took a no-hitter into the ninth inning. It was broken up by Andy Carey, who attended the same college Ferrarese did.

But those are merely no-hitters. Pitchers themselves have a slightly different view of what constitutes a "perfect" game, as Jerome Holtzman discovered when he interviewed a number of them for an article in *Baseball Digest*. For Greg Maddux, "My definition of a perfect game would be throwing every pitch where you want to throw it. And, you know what? So what if you give up a run or two." Tom Glavine, John Smoltz, and others offered similar comments. Sour grapes from guys who've never done it? Woody Williams finally had to admit, "The baseball standard is 27 up, 27 outs."

A perfect game isn't a record built up over a season or a career. It's a one-time achievement, and all the more special for that. No one can look at a pitcher's career record and predict whether he'll throw a perfect game. As Michael Coffey observed, "There are no factors you can isolate that will even begin to suggest what might affect the probability of perfection" (*27 Men Out*, p. 275). The pitcher who does it can't prepare for it the way a mountain climber studies a peak and decides on the best approach. He won't be able to tell us how he did it, or what he did differently that day from every other time he's taken the mound. As Larsen himself said, "Why I had such incredible pinpoint control on October 8, 1956, is still a puzzle to me. It was the best it ever was" (*Perfect Yankee*, p. 150).

The pitcher who throws a perfect game knows he cannot expect to do it again, if history is any guide. Several pitchers have thrown more than one no-hitter. Johnny Vander Meer threw two in consecutive games in 1938. (The second was the first night game played in Brooklyn.) Dean Chance pitched two no-hitters within three weeks in August 1967, but he could still observe, "One day you can throw tomatoes through brick walls. The next day you can't dent a pane of glass with a rock." Nolan Ryan threw seven "no-no's." In his "best" no-hitter he walked only two batters; in the "worst" he walked eight.

But no pitcher has ever thrown two perfect games. Jim "Catfish" Hunter explained his failure to pitch a second in earthy terms: "The sun don't shine on the same dog's ass all the time." Mike Witt was more clinical: "I was always trying to figure out a way to find what I had that day again. I was always watching that tape, when I would get in a slump or something, to figure out what I had been doing right . . . . I'd get glimpses of it, but I never got that stuff back" (in Buckley, *Perfect*, p. 166).

What are a pitcher's chances of pitching even one perfect game? H. W. Lewis reasoned that a pitcher's chance of retiring any given batter is 0.7 (since a .300 batting average is considered good). To get the odds of a pitcher throwing a perfect game, we simply multiply 0.7 by itself 27 times. The result shows that a pitcher should accomplish a perfect game once in every 15,000 games he pitches. A hard-working major league pitcher might start forty games in a season. If he managed to pitch for 375 years, the odds are that he would throw one perfect game (*Why Flip*, pp. 161-162).

Even against those odds, pitching a perfect game does not make a man a star. Not every pitcher who accomplished the feat is in the Hall of Fame. Those who are enshrined made it because of their overall records, not because of their perfect games. As Blaise Pascal said, "The strength of a man's virtue must not be measured by his special efforts, but by his habitual acts."

That points up the basic difference between a perfect game and a season-long or career-long record. Babe Ruth's record of 60 home runs in a single season stood for thirty-four years. Roger Maris' mark of 61, with or without the asterisk, set the standard for thirty-seven years and was surpassed only by players who are under the shadow of accusations of using body-building substances. Hank Aaron never hit more than 47 homers in a season, but his 755 home runs are the best anyone has done over a career. Denny McLain recorded 31 victories in 1968, the only time since 1934 that a pitcher has won 30 games. But those are all records – "habitual acts" as Pascal would say – built up over a season, not "special efforts," one-time bursts of perfection.

Larsen's special effort, his perfect game in the World Series, has not been equaled in fifty years. And it can only be equaled; it can never be surpassed. No one can pitch a "more perfect" game. Someone could retire 27 batters on fewer pitches, but pitch count isn't what makes the game perfect. Outs are all that count. Get 27 of them in a row, no matter how, and you have a perfect game. As Arthur Daley said in the *New York Times* the day after the game, "Larsen faced twenty-seven men. He retired twenty-seven men. It's impossible to improve on such a performance. That's why they call it a perfect game."

Watching the game, at a time in my life when very little made sense, I felt like my faith in baseball and in the Yankees in particular was being justified.

CHAPTER 5

Damn Yankees

How does a ten-year-old boy living in upstate South Carolina become a New York Yankees fan in the 1950s? First he becomes a baseball fan. That I did at an early age. My father had played ball in high school and in the Marine Corps; he was a catcher. He was a loving but taciturn man who worked long hours. Throwing a ball – usually an old rubber ball or a dead tennis ball – was one of the most important ways we communicated, even though we talked very little while doing it. Mickey Mantle had the same experience with his father, using his "glove and a tennis ball" (*The Mick*, p. 3). Baseball and the bond it provides between generations of males is important enough that a whole book has been written on the subject (Stewart).

Not every kid was as lucky as I was. Yogi Berra's son, Dale, said, "Dad never did anything with us . . . . I remember asking Dad to have a catch with me when he came home from a game and he said, 'That's what you've got brothers for.' He didn't play with us" (in *Growing Up Baseball*, p. 40). In one source Don Larsen recalled that his father "did not play with me a lot" when he was a kid (in *Growing Up Baseball*, p. 140). However, in his book *The Perfect Yankee*, Larsen says, "Dad and I spent hours

"This is the very perfection of a man, to find out his own imperfection."

St. Augustine

together, especially on Sundays, with him throwing the ball as I tried to hit it . . . . as I got a little older, I told my dad that I wanted to be a pitcher. That's when he and I switched positions" (pp. 35-36).

Only in the last few years before his death did I come to understand some of what made my dad the way he was. His own father had not hesitated to hit his four sons (but never his three daughters). When he was 15, my dad told me, and big enough to stand up to the abuse, he doubled up his fists and told his father not to hit him again. According to my father, my grandfather said, "You'd better take me down with your first shot 'cause I'll kill you if you don't."

As my father told that story, it was hard for me to imagine the scene because, by the time I was born, my grandfather had been crippled by arthritis. I knew him only as bent-over, hobbling on a cane. No blows were exchanged, my dad said, but his father never hit him again.

My father never abused my brother and me, but he was incapable of opening up emotionally. That was something else I learned that I shared with my idol, Mickey Mantle. He said of his father,

"Any outward display of affection between us would have been considered a sign of weakness" (*The Mick*, p. 57).

In addition to throwing with my dad, I played baseball at recess during the school year, except in the winter, and winter in South Carolina was only November to early February. When spring training started for the major league teams, we were ready to play in Greenville. Until fifth grade I played ball in a vacant lot across the street from our semi-rural house during the summer and, as I've mentioned, at my grandparents' house. If there was noone around to play with, I would use a dinged-up old bat to hit rocks into the open field next to our house, something I later learned that Mickey Mantle also did.

"Not even sex . . . ."

In 1956 no other sport really mattered. Jacques Barzun said in 1954, "Whoever wants to know the heart and mind of America had better learn baseball, the rules and realities of the game – and do it by watching first some high school or small-town teams." Legendary Giants' manager John McGraw was more concise: "There is but one game, and that game is baseball."

Things have changed today, but in 1956 what Herbert Hoover said could still apply: "Next to religion, baseball has furnished a greater impact on American life than any other institution." As William Saroyan saw it, "More Americans put their spare (and purest?) caring into baseball than into anything else I can think of – and most of them put at least a *little* of it there . . . . Why not existentialism instead of baseball, for instance? Well, for one thing, you've got to be tired to care for old existentialism, and Americans just aren't ready to be that tired yet" (*Sports Illustrated*, Oct. 8, 1956). Robert Frost was more succinct: "Some baseball is the fate of us all" (*Sports Illustrated*, July 23, 1956).

In that day we didn't have ESPN trying to convince us poker is a sport. In the Greenville *News* local high school and college sports got good coverage, but no professional sport except baseball was worth the ink. And it got a lot. For the last week of the '56 season, as Milwaukee, Cincinnati, and Brooklyn remained neck-and-neck, the *News* updated the previous day's scores on the front page. When the Dodgers clinched the pennant on the last day of the season, they rated a front-page banner headline all the way down in South Carolina. On Sept. 30 the paper ran an editorial cartoon showing a baseball labeled "World Series" rising like the sun over "this troubled old planet."

What about pro basketball? The NBA was still playing in places like Syracuse and Fort Wayne. The NBA finals in 1956 were between the Fort Wayne Pistons and the Philadelphia Warriors. The *News* barely mentioned them, and then only in small, filler articles. The *New York Times* apparently didn't consider the NBA news that was fit to print either. On April 4 the *Times* summarized the results of the first three games in a filler article and gave the dates and places for the next two, then added, "Dates and sites of other games have not been scheduled." In October the Cincinnati *Enquirer* ran a small article announcing the opening of the NBA season. "Beginning December 15, there will be a 12-game series of Saturday afternoon telecasts . . . . In addition, three Saturday afternoon telecasts are planned during the league playoffs next March." *Sports Illustrated* featured Bob Cousy in a couple of issues in January, but their only other mention of the NBA was an article about the National Boxing Association.

Change was on the horizon, though. Bill Russell was about to turn pro, and Wilt Chamberlin was starring for the University of Kansas. A *Saturday Evening Post* article wondered, "Can Basketball Survive Chamberlain?" (Dec. 1, 1956).

Football? Pro football games were broadcast on TV and radio, but the season didn't start until the end of September and ended around Christmas. The *Saturday Evening Post*'s "Pigskin Preview" on Sept. 8 covered college football. The *Post* ran articles on Ole Miss (Oct. 13) and West Virginia's football teams (Nov. 10) but nothing, except for an article on Otto Graham's retirement (Sept. 29), on professional football until Dec. 15. The Colts-Giants title game that would establish the NFL wouldn't be played until 1958. *Sports Illustrated* covered college football beginning in September but hardly mentioned professional football, even after the World Series was over.

Hockey? Some weird game played by Canadians and a few Americans in those frozen states bordering Canada. All it meant to me and my friends was that we could say "H-E-Double-hockey-sticks" instead of "H-E-L-L." Today, ironically, I live in one of those frozen states and three of my children are avid hockey fans. My grandson got his first hockey stick when he was three. Long before that, though, I had given him a baseball glove and a bat and ball.

All of these other professional sports have gained in popularity in the last twenty years, in part because of television and in part because they suit the video-game pace of modern life better than baseball. But they have also evolved dramatically, while baseball has changed very little. Sportscaster Jon Miller summed up the situation:

> Baseball is the best arguing game. If you're passionate about baseball, you argue. It's not even optional. Everything is a potential argument in baseball. Were the seventies better than the nineties? Were the fifties as good as the seventies? Will there ever be a season as glorious as 1961?
>
> Do football fans ever argue about the old days? Or even discuss them? I mean, who'd bother comparing the NFL of 1995 with the NFL of 1955? Every player at every position in the NFL today is seven inches taller and outweighs those old-timers by 100 pounds. They're not even playing the same game.
>
> The difference in basketball is even more dramatic. Look at film of the NBA in the fifties – it's laughable. Two-handed set shots. Vertical leaps of a foot. It was slow, it was earthbound – it was basketball before the Wright brothers, before we learned to fly on Air Jordan.
>
> But baseball retains much more of its old character. Basically, baseball hasn't changed; you can defensibly compare Ken Griffey Jr. to Mickey Mantle . . . . Their careers were almost thirty years apart, yet it's the same game . . . .
>
> *Confessions of a Baseball Purist* (pp. 57-58)

Sports Illustrated admitted that other sports were growing in popularity but predicted "not even sex will ever take the place of baseball" (Feb. 27, 1956).

There were no major league teams in the South then; the Washington Senators and Baltimore Orioles didn't count as Southern, and hardly as major league teams. But Southerners played baseball, from elementary school through high school and into amateur leagues. Textile mills around Greenville sponsored leagues from which players sometimes made the jump to professional play. The connection between the South and baseball can be seen in the fact that about sixty percent of major league players in the 1950s were from the South. It's also important to remember that the "national game," like the nation, was segregated. Even though a few black players had made it to the major leagues, far more of them were playing in the Negro Leagues that proliferated across the South and into the Midwest (Dixon, *Negro Baseball Leagues*).

During the summer of '56 the National League teams grabbed more headlines in my hometown paper because they were actually involved in a pennant race. Milwaukee, Brooklyn, and Cincinnati stayed on one another's heels while the Yankees maintained a comfortable lead in the American League for most of the summer. In the last few weeks of the season, though, my paper did follow Mantle's chase for Babe Ruth's home run record. Mickey could garner a headline by *not* hitting a home run.

The Yankees played often on television. My family got our first set in the fall of 1954, just in time for me to see a couple of games of the World Series, over the vehement protests of my younger brother, who wanted to watch a western. The Yankees weren't in that Series, the only one they missed between 1949 and 1958, but I couldn't believe I was finally watching major league baseball. The experience far exceeded anything I had imagined while listening to games on the radio or reading about them in the paper.

Me and the Mick

Mickey Mantle said that, although he lived in St. Louis Cardinals territory, he became a Yankee fan because of Joe DiMaggio (Castro, p. 106). Mantle made me a Yankee fan. More than anything, I wanted to *be* Mickey Mantle. He seemed to embody everything I wasn't – strong, fast, sure of himself, popular. And he was doing what I wanted to do, playing the outfield for a winning team. A natural left-handed hitter, I worked hard to make myself a switch-hitter like Mantle. I would have given anything, starting with my younger brother, to have been in his cleats.

I remember being stunned to learn he got paid for playing. That was my greatest disillusionment from reading magazines and from the subscription to *Sports Illustrated* I got for Christmas of 1955. They ran articles on baseball as a business and talked about how much players got paid. The sums weren't exactly princely. In 1956 all 400 major league players together shared a total payroll of "around $5 million, which means average pay of about $12,500 for seven months work a year . . . . it would be hard to find any trade or profession that pays so well" (*SI* Mar. 5, 1956). I thought ballplayers played because they loved the game and loved their team. But Roger Kahn reported that Pee Wee Reese considered team spirit "ridiculous. What exists is money spirit. You help other players, bunt or hit-and-run and they help you, not for a team, but for themselves. You both want money" (*Boys*, p. 169).

In his article in *Look* about his performance in the 1955 World Series Johnny Podres mentioned that "I've already made $53,000 in five years of organized ball, plus about $20,000 for extra services. I have no kick coming." Mantle made $32,500 in 1956, the year he hit 52 homers and won the Triple Crown and the MVP award. *Sports Illustrated* estimated his endorsements would bring him another $40,000 or so (Sept. 10, 1956). For 1957 the Yankees doubled his salary.

If you want to know what's wrong with professional sports today, look at those figures and then consider the obscene amounts of money even mediocre athletes are now being paid.

That's all I'll say.

Mantle seemed to me to have the perfect life. This was before Jim Bouton's *Ball Four* and all the other revelatory books and articles that have since appeared, including several by Mantle himself. He was described by the *New York Times* that spring as "a shy young man of 24 who always seems embarrassed at the realization that he is a celebrity." I also thought he had a decent nickname, even if he shared it with a cartoon rodent. Not until I started collecting baseball cards did I learn Mickey was his given name. His father idolized catcher Mickey Cochrane and didn't know Cochrane's full name was Gordon Stanley Cochrane.

"The great trouble with baseball today is that most of the players are in the game for the money."

Ty Cobb, 1925

I shared a nickname with a cartoon character of that era, too. By the time I was ten I hated it. When your last name is Bell, you get enough kidding without having an obnoxious nickname to compound the problem. Only Mantle's mother and his first serious girlfriend called him Mickey Mouse (Castro, p. 101). I wasn't so lucky. Given an easy target, kids can be merciless. Roger Maris would know what I'm talking about. He was born Maras, a Croatian name, but he changed the spelling because kids called him Mar-ASS.

Mantle was known as "the Commerce Comet," after his hometown and his speed. Other players of that era had cool nicknames. Yankee pitcher Vic Raschi was "the Springfield Rifle," after his hometown and his strong arm. The best I could contrive for myself was "the Laurens Loser," after my hometown and my general view of myself.

Some people can deal with, even enjoy, odd nicknames. I admire them. As of this writing, the Boston Red Sox have a center-fielder named Coco Crisp. His full name is Covelli Loyce Crisp.

I especially envied Mantle his smile. There are few pictures of me smiling after age ten because I had a problem with my front upper teeth. Instead of a real permanent tooth, I had some sort of dental interloper, hardly more than a piece of bone, that came in when I lost my baby teeth. The permanent tooth was lodged high in my gum. My father had had the same problem. The dentist said it was genetic. In the summer before fifth grade I endured two bouts of oral surgery to remove the pseudo-tooth and expose the permanent one. It would come down of its own accord, the dentist assured

us, and the gum would grow over it.

But that wasn't happening. The tooth grew down all right, but the gum didn't grow over it. With nothing to hold it in place, the tooth was protruding. I would have to wear braces. My paternal grandfather told me one day he would put the tooth back in place without any braces. He jabbed his arthritic fist toward my mouth.

To cover up this deformity I tended to keep my head down and not smile. But kids did notice. One of my most vivid memories is standing in front of school one afternoon, waiting for my mother to pick me up. As the bus went by, a boy I barely knew leaned out the window and yelled, "Hey, snaggle-tooth!"

At least he didn't call me by my nickname.

I was supposed to get braces before I started sixth grade, but everything about my life changed that summer of 1956, as surely as a baseball player's life changes when he's traded to another team. My dad got a job in Cincinnati. That's Cincinnati, OHIO, the state that's round on the ends and high in the middle. The state that's on the wrong side of the Ohio River.

You Can – You Must – Go Home Again

For my mother's family there was profound truth in the old saying, "American by chance, Southern by the grace of God." No one in my family ever left the South except to do military service. And they came back as quickly as possible, preferably as close as possible to the holy city of Laurens. My mother and her four siblings spent their lives within thirty miles of Laurens. A few of the grandchildren have ventured farther afield, but eleven of the fourteen still live in South Carolina. Some have lived their entire lives in the same ZIP code. I am the only one north of the Ohio River. Most of the great-grandchildren have remained in South Carolina and North Carolina, although a few have escaped the gravitational pull of Laurens and wandered as far away as Tennessee, Kentucky, or Florida. My own children live in

Michigan and California.

My father's parents lived closer to us than my mother's, but we visited them infrequently and for only a few hours at a time. I never spent a night in their house. My paternal grandfather did not make it a welcoming place. He expressed his strong opinions with an acid tongue. My grandmother, on the other hand, might as well have been mute for all I can remember her saying. They lived on a small farm in a shabby three-room house heated by a wood-burning stove in the combination kitchen-living room. There was nothing to do there and never anybody to do it with. And you had to use an outhouse!

I can recall eating only one meal in my paternal grandparents' home. I remember it because it was the only time I ever ate squirrel (and it does *not* taste like chicken). They were decent folks, but I never got the chance to know them. I have cousins on that side – seven, I think. One I've never met. Some of the rest I would not recognize on sight. During my father's last years I did have the chance to connect with his youngest sister and have enjoyed getting to know her and coming to understand the family better. And I've gotten to know an uncle who is a lawyer and have benefitted from his advice.

In my mother's family, though, the urge to go home ran so deep that, when my father was at Georgia Tech, my mother would sometimes take my brother and me to Laurens for a weekend. I was five, my brother two. My mother would drive our station wagon – before interstates, seat belts, or car seats – and have me stand behind her and pull her hair to keep her awake.

The farther we moved from Laurens, the stronger her homing instinct grew. While we were in Cincinnati, a couple of times we left when she and my dad got off work on Friday and drove all night on two-lane roads through the mountains of Kentucky, Tennessee and North Carolina. We got into Laurens for breakfast on Saturday and left after breakfast on Sunday for the drive back to Cincinnati. Twenty hours of driving for barely twenty-four hours with the family. My brother, mother, and I slept on the trip. My dad slept most of the time we were in Laurens.

My mother's urge to go home nearly destroyed her marriage in 1970, when my dad's company transferred him to a plant in central Pennsylvania. After enduring it for a few months in the dead of winter, she told Dad if he wanted her, he would have to move back to South Carolina. She went to stay with her parents. Within two months my dad found a job in Greenville and a house on the south side of town, as close to Laurens as they could get and leave him a reasonable drive to work. Except for a few short trips, they never left the state again.

By saying all this, I don't mean to make my mother look ridiculous. She was an intelligent woman, the only one of her siblings to attend college, although she did not graduate. When I found her transcript among her papers, I was impressed that she had studied French, Spanish, and German and made good grades in all of them, as well as in her other courses. She was also a playful, vivacious, but volatile, woman, a tomboy whose life-long dream was to own a motorcycle. At 60 she settled for a Moped and rode my children around her neighborhood while I held my breath. If you were on her good side – where I usually was – she was a joy to be with. I used to get annoyed because, when my friends came over, they would often spend as much time talking to her as they did to me.

But if you were on her bad side – where my brother spent most of his childhood – she could be formidable. I will never forget her shaking her fist at my brother during one of their confrontations when he was twelve and yelling at him, "You're not worth shit!" Even as distant as I felt from him, I thought, *You shouldn't say that. You're his mother!*

I inherited my mother's attachment to home. I loved being at my grandparents' house with my cousins – some of whom were, and still are, closer to me than my brother. At age eleven, though, I was about to be uprooted. I wasn't losing a parent, as three of my cousins had. In some ways it felt worse. I was losing the whole framework of my life. It was one thing to cheer for a team called the Yankees.

It was quite another to leave South Carolina and go live among actual damn Yankees.

I was being thrust into a larger, and scarier, world than I had experienced – even imagined – to that point. In case you've forgotten what an imperfect place the world was in 1956, or never knew, let's take a few minutes to set the stage through the eyes of an Everykid.

CHAPTER 6

Through Rose-Colored Glasses

Phil Pepe, co-author of Mickey Mantle's book, *My Favorite Summer 1956*, described that era as "a wonderful time in this country when everyday life was much less complicated. It was a time of innocence, of peace and serenity, of simple pleasures and bigger-than-life heroes" (p. xii). Brendan C. Boyd and Fred C. Harris also characterized it as "a more innocent and less troubled era" (*Great American . . . Book*, p. iii). In its October 16, 1972, issue *Newsweek* celebrated the 1950s on the cover and lauded it as "a simple decade." On June 16 of the same year *Life* referred to the '50s as "that sunnier time."

> *"Man in the distant future will be a far more perfect creature than now he is."*
>
> Charles Darwin

Anyone who could say such things doesn't remember the 1950s or hasn't gone back and looked at even the newspaper headlines from those years. Stephan Pastis, in his comic strip "Pearls Before Swine," parodied this sentimental exaltation of the period. A character called Little Bear goes on a quest for someone who can reunite America. He settles on Willie Mays because Mays was "an icon of a past era that somehow seems better than today." He wants Mays to "go back to centerfield and everything will be okay." Mays reminds Little Bear that he's too old to play ball any more. Little Bear pleads with him: "I want to return to 1957 when this was one nation!" "When I couldn't eat in certain restaurants?" Mays retorts. "Please, Willie," Little Bear says, "I'm busy glorifying the past."

As Horace Greeley observed, "The illusion that times that were are better than those that are, has probably pervaded all ages." Historian Paul Boyer's summary of the period was much more realistic: "The United States in the 1950s was not as trouble-free as a quick visit to suburbia or a glance at television might have suggested" (*Promises*, p. 134). Let's be realistic, but I don't think we have to go as far as Norman Mailer, who described the '50s as "one of the worst decades in the history of man."

Listen to just a few voices from 1956. In his Easter address that year Pope Pius XII warned that "mankind is racing forward every day on the tragic road of suicide and extinction from atomic bombs and radio-guided missiles" (Greenville *News*, Apr. 2). On the same day Walter Winchell depicted that era as "a time when melancholia seems an almost slavish reflex to the tensions and anxieties" we faced. Assistant Secretary of the Army Hugh M. Milton II spoke of a "tense day" in a "complicated world" (Greenville *News*, Feb. 10, 1956). The winner of the South Carolina Collegiate Press Association's essay award, Dora Jean Johnson, wrote about "the source of present-day anxiety .. . . a fear of the scientific power being released that produces harassed expressions and tense minds" (Greenville *News*, Apr. 22, 1956).

How could the world have seemed serene, simple or sunny to people of the 1950s? Adults of that time had lived through World War I, the Depression, World War II, the Berlin Airlift, and the Korean

War. They went to bed each night under the cloud of the Cold War and the Soviet Union's nuclear capability. On March 30, 1956, the headline in the Greenville *News* carried a warning from Defense Secretary Charles Wilson: "Atomic Stockpiles Could Almost End World Soon." On April 30, this headline greeted me at breakfast: "Sea-Spanning H-Bomb Missile Warheads Certain." A week before that an article appeared under the headline "Speaker Says H-Bomb Alters Civil Defense." Another article on Feb. 1 promised "Few Would Survive Big Bomb Blast." As Yogi Berra said, "A lot of us were nervous about the atom bomb. Who really knew what was going to happen?" (*Ten Rings*, p. 74). On October 30, as Israeli tanks neared the Suez Canal, the headline of the Cincinnati *Enquirer* proclaimed "War Scare Spreads Around the World."

Racial tensions were mounting as well. It was a very unsettled, and unsettling, time. At ten or eleven, I didn't understand everything I was reading, but the adults around me seemed worried, and that scared me.

Shades of Gray

Our images of the world in 1956 are largely in black and white, literally and metaphorically. Color movies were common, but color television was still a dream for most Americans. We see the events of that year in grainy gray pictures. Newspapers were still the main source of information for most Americans. Pictorial magazines such as *Life, Look,* and the *Saturday Evening Post* had a readership and an importance they lost by the 1970s. Weekly newsreels shown before the feature films in theaters provided dramatic visual images as well.

Network news programs were in their infancy. In 1956 Douglas Edwards presented a fifteen-minute evening news broadcast on CBS. NBC had "The Camel News Caravan" until the fall of that year, when "The Huntley-Brinkley Report" began.

There was already evidence, though, of the power of the new medium of television. In 1954 Sen. Joseph McCarthy welcomed the cameras into his hearings on Communist influence in the Army. McCarthy had kept the country on edge for several years and ruined the careers of numerous artists, writers, and government employees with his witch-hunt for "Reds" in all areas of American life. In 1952 Charlie Chaplin went into self-imposed exile because of investigations of his left-leaning political activities. Singer Paul Robeson was denied a passport and hounded for years by McCarthyites because of his frank sympathy for the Soviet Union. Although titular head of the Republican party, Dwight Eisenhower, a decisive general and ineffectual president, was reluctant to rein McCarthy in and make himself appear "soft" on Communism.

What Eisenhower would not do, television accomplished. When people could see and hear McCarthy on the screen, they saw him for the sneering bully he was. His constantly repeated nasal yelp "Point of order!" became a national catchphrase. When the Army's special counsel, Joseph N. Welch, calmly asked McCarthy, "Have you no decency, sir?" the spectators in the hearing room burst into applause. McCarthy turned to his assistant, Roy Cohn, and asked, "What happened?" By the end of the hearings McCarthy had lost much of his influence. He was censured by the Senate and drank himself to death in 1957.

Communism frightened us because it seemed to be a conspiracy to undermine the foundations of American society. In its early days the civil rights movement looked to many white Americans like it had the same objective. These two issues – racial conflict within the U. S. and the Cold War between the U. S. and the USSR – dominated the news in 1956 and kept everyone on edge.

Some conspiracy theorists claimed the Communists were stirring up discontent among blacks to weaken America. Sen. Strom Thurmond drew the Senate's attention to a claim by Ohio's attorney general that the Communists were recruiting young people in a campaign for federal intervention in the desegregation process. "I hope this will serve as a red stop light to persons who have agitated for integration. They should be forewarned by this information from Ohio that such agitation serves the will of the Communists" (Greenville *News*, Mar. 27, 1956). During hearings by the Senate Internal Security Subcommittee in New Orleans documents seized in a raid were produced as evidence that "the Communists invited civil war in the South . . . proposing the creation of a Southern Negro empire" (Greenville *News*, April 7, 1956). As Mississippi's Senator James Eastland put it, the NAACP was supported by "organizations of all shades of red . . . the blood red of the Communist Party . . . the almost equally red of the National Council of Churches of Christ in the U. S. A." (*Time*, Feb. 6).

Putting such absurdity aside, we still must acknowledge that these two forces – the Communist threat and the civil rights movement – combined to make the mid-1950s one of the tensest periods in American history. The question seemed to be whether we would be torn apart from the inside before we were crushed from the outside.

From the Back of the Bus

The U. S. was prospering in the 1950s, but not everyone shared in the good life. Blacks were growing increasingly dissatisfied with the separate and inferior status imposed on them by laws passed by the white majority. The problem was most severe in the South, but not confined to that region. On June 26, 1956, *Look* published an article on "Jim Crow, Northern Style." A speaker before a meeting of Georgia Baptists expressed the opinion that "it will take the City of Chicago longer to complete the court's order [to desegregate] than almost any area in the entire South" (Greenville *News*, April 26, 1956).

Major league baseball was not exempt from the controversy. Jackie Robinson had broken the color barrier in the sport in 1947, but he and other black players often could not sleep or eat in the same places as their white teammates. The Yankees didn't exactly rush to bring up a black player from their minor league system but had done so by 1955. The Boston Red Sox were the last major league team to sign a black player, Elijah "Pumpsie" Green, in 1959 (Howard, *Shut Out*). Earlier in the decade the Bosox could have signed a young phenom named Willie Mays, but they declined to do so because of his skin color.

Skin color was the issue in a case that galvanized national attention in the summer and fall of 1955. A 14-year-old boy, Emmett Till, came from Chicago to Mississippi to visit family members. With a group of local black youths, Till went to a store owned by Roy Bryant, a white man. While there, he allegedly flirted with Bryant's wife. A few nights later Till was kidnapped from his family's house. He was pistol-whipped, had an eye gouged out, and was finally killed. His weighted body was dumped in a river.

When the body was recovered and brought back to Chicago for burial, Till's mother insisted on leaving the coffin open and not doing anything to disguise the brutal treatment he suffered. Photographs of the boy's mutilated face circulated around the country, especially in black newspapers and magazines.

Roy Bryant and his half-brother, J. W. Milam, were arrested and tried for the murder. Many historians contend that the very fact of a trial was a momentous step. The few blacks who dared to testify against them had to be escorted out of the state by the NAACP. After four days of testimony the all-white jury deliberated for 67 minutes before returning a not-guilty verdict. One juror said they took a "soda break" to make the deliberations last for an hour. In January of 1956 Bryant and Milam were paid $4,000 by *Look* magazine to tell their story. Since they could not be tried again, they freely admitted what they had done.

Racial tensions had been building across the country since May of 1954, when the Supreme Court handed down its decision in *Brown* v. *Board of Education of Topeka*, declaring "separate but equal" schools unconstitutional. But that did not bring overnight change, and it did not apply to public facilities other than schools. Many whites vowed resistance to integration at every step. Their attitude was summed up by a picture in *Life* (Feb. 6, 1956), showing a car in Nashville, Tennessee, carrying a Confederate flag and a sign that said, "Save Our Children from the Black Plague." Some black leaders were determined not only to integrate schools but to broaden the scope of the decision. All they needed was the right opportunity.

That opportunity presented itself in November of 1955, when Rosa Parks, a black seamstress in Montgomery, Alabama, refused to give up her seat on a bus to a white man. As was true in any Southern city, a Montgomery ordinance reserved certain sections of the buses for white passengers and gave whites preference for seats anywhere on the buses in case of crowding. Parks was arrested.

In addition to taking the case to court, black leaders in Montgomery, including Martin Luther King, Jr., called for a boycott of the city's bus system. This created tensions and hardship on all sides. Blacks had difficulty getting to work, and downtown businesses soon felt the loss of customers. Blacks organized car pools to help people who had no means of transportation and long distances to travel. Montgomery police retaliated by citing black drivers for the most insignificant violations and arresting those who were waiting for rides on loitering charges. Some whites gave rides or paid cab fare for their black employees, provoking an outburst from Montgomery's mayor: "When a white person gives a Negro a single penny for transportation or helps a Negro with his transportation . . . he is helping the Negro radicals who lead the boycott." State courts ruled the seating law constitutional, so the case was appealed to the U. S. Supreme Court. Similar laws in other states were also being challenged in court.

Early in 1956 the situation in Montgomery turned violent. Rev. King's house was bombed on January 30. Two days later the home of another minister prominent in the movement was also bombed. On April 24 the banner headline in my hometown paper read: "Segregation on City Buses Ruled Unlawful." The Supreme Court ruled unanimously in a case from Richmond, Virginia. On November 12, 1956, the Court heard the Montgomery case and again declared segregation on the buses unconstitutional. Even after the decision was announced and the boycott ended, trouble continued. Snipers shot at the buses. Several black churches, businesses, and homes were bombed.

The results were not so dramatic in all Southern cities. In Tallahassee, Florida, blacks began a bus boycott on May 28, 1956. In early July the city suspended bus service. When it was resumed on August 2, the city put two black drivers on routes used predominantly by blacks. No commitment was made to end segregated seating and "passengers took seats on the same segregated basis as before the boycott started" (Greenville *News*, August 3, 1956).

If it bleeds, it leads

Montgomery wasn't the only city whose racial conflicts made the evening news. And the fact that there were evening news broadcasts on television by 1956, even if they were only fifteen minutes long, made the entire country aware of things that could easily have been buried in the back pages of a newspaper or never depicted in weekly newsreels in movie theaters. In some cases, the presence of cameras recording events for those nightly broadcasts had an effect few could have anticipated.

In Anderson County, Tennessee, northwest of Knoxville, five black families, backed by the NAACP, had filed a suit against the county Board of Education to get their children into Clinton High School. On January 4, 1956, a federal district judge ruled that segregation had to end by the fall. Plans for integration proceeded quietly during the year, but when it came time for black students to register in late August, ardent segregationists from outside Clinton came to town to protest. The first day fewer than ten people showed up in front of the school with their signs. They left after only a few minutes.

But the news media were there, and those images were seen across the country on television that evening. The next day more protesters showed up. By the end of the week hundreds of people – almost all outsiders – had the streets of the small town in turmoil.

On September 1 violence erupted. A large crowd gathered at the courthouse. Gunfire forced the sheriff and his small band of part-time deputies to barricade themselves in the building. Tennessee State Highway patrolmen had to be sent in to force the crowd back. The next day the National Guard arrived.

The uproar made headlines in my hometown paper. Pictures of tanks rumbling into Clinton and people running from tear gas greeted me every morning for a week. On Sept. 4 I read that traffic was being detoured off of U. S. 25W, the main highway through that part of Tennessee. Suddenly I felt like the situation affected me. My dad was already at his new job in Cincinnati and U. S. 25W was the route he had taken to drive there. He had marked it on the map he left with us. It was the route we would take when we moved. Would we be able to get through? Would he be able to get back home to get us?

The National Guard remained in Clinton until the end of September. Black students endured harassment, but they did graduate in the spring of 1957 and thereafter. The principal of the high school resigned at the end of the school year and most of the teachers went with him. By the fall of 1957 it looked like the worst was over, though, and people were accepting the new reality. Then, on a Sunday morning in early October, 1958, the high school was blown up. No one was injured because of the timing of the blast, but the school was destroyed and took two years to rebuild. No one was ever charged in the crime.

Who is my brother?

School desegregation was a national issue by the fall of 1956. Southern schools were not the only ones where this practice had been entrenched for decades. Remember, it was the Topeka, *Kansas*, school board that was sued in the landmark Brown case. The elementary school I attended in Cincinnati was all-white. In some Northern cities it would be the mid-1970s before desegregation was in full force. Cincinnati was still trying to desegregate its schools in the early years of this millennium.

Southerners admonished Northerners to get their own house in order before presuming to shake their finger in someone else's face. An article such as one in the *New York Times* on May 10, 1956, would seem to Southerners to support their case. Four white teenagers were arrested after they stoned a black couple's home in a previously all-white neighborhood in the Bronx: "One of the stones thrown Monday was wrapped in a note containing obscenities, racial references and a warning that the two-story dwelling would be burned down unless the couple left the neighborhood." In early April a crowd of 500 people stoned a house in suburban Detroit because of a rumor that a black man and his white wife had moved in. The man, it turned out, was of Southern European origins and darker-complected than anyone else in the neighborhood (Greenville *News*, April 6).

Adlai Stevenson, campaigning for the Democratic nomination for the presidency, admitted blacks were denied rights "in my own state of Illinois" and that discrimination was a fact of life across the country (Greenville *News*, March 3, 1956). In a speech in Montgomery, Alabama, on March 11, Gloster B. Current, an official of the NAACP, reminded his audience that "in the North we struggle with the subtleties and hidden aspects of discrimination and segregation. In no community in this nation where there is a sizable Negro population can you say the problems of race relations have been com-

An article in the Detroit News on Feb. 15, 2006, under the headline "Schools Remain Segregated," reported that "close to 75% of black students in Michigan attend segregated schools." One official said, "You would think after 50 years we would see some progress. In Michigan, there hasn't been any progress."

pletely solved" (Greenville *News*). An editorial cartoon in the *News* on March 17 showed figures representing "All-white" churches, schools, businesses, and unions picking up rocks from a pile labeled "Northern condemnation of segregationists" while a heavenly voice says, "He that is without sin (such as race bias) let him first cast a stone."

In August and September of 1956 protests or violence severe enough to rate national news coverage flared up in Richmond, Virginia, Birmingham, Alabama, and Mansfield, Texas. In Sturgis, Kentucky, nine blacks entered school with the help of 160 National Guardsmen. The front page of my hometown paper ran a bold headline "Riot Guns, Fixed Bayonets Needed" to get the children into and out of the school. Some in the crowd yelled, "Let's hang them all tonight. There won't be a nigger come through town peacefully tonight." The 100 white students who came to school were derided as "nigger lovers" (Greenville *News*, Sept. 7, 1956). None of the blacks returned the next day. In Arista, West Virginia, only five of 39 whites came to their newly integrated school.

Things did go better in some places, such as Elmere and Frankfort, Kentucky, and Poolesville and Glen Burne in Maryland. In Princeton, West Virginia, about sixty percent of the white students attended after the school was integrated. *Life* described this as "The Halting and Fitful Battle for Integration" and expressed concern that "the continuing dispute could mean agonizing tension for the whole nation."

Out of sight, out of mind?

Race relations wasn't an everyday issue in my life. I didn't ride buses, and the elementary school I attended was segregated. Greenville was a large enough town that blacks and whites operated in their own spheres for long periods with no more direct contact than passing one another silently on the street.

Reading my hometown newspaper from fifty years ago to do research for this book made me notice something which I'm sure didn't register with me then: images of blacks did not appear in that paper except under unusual circumstances. In May, when group pictures of the graduating classes of all the local high schools were published, two black schools were included, but were not placed anywhere near the white schools.

Hardly any other black persons rated pictures in the *News* during that year. When the foreman of the boiler room at the hospital completed thirty years of service, he was pictured receiving an award from his (white) supervisor. A picture of white and black passengers on a Norfolk, Virginia, bus accompanied an article about the end of segregation on that city's buses (April 25). The whole thing had a "this could happen to us" tone. In June an article appeared about a black seminary student who was being financially assisted by a local white Baptist church as a mission project; the young man was pictured.

When I ran across these articles after hours of looking at microfilm, it actually startled me to see black faces. Analyzing my own reaction, I realized I was being conditioned by the absence of such images in the paper. I expected the Cincinnati *Enquirer,* as a "northern" newspaper, to be more egalitarian, but it followed the same practice. In October one black teenager was pictured on its Saturday "youth page." No blacks were ever interviewed for either paper's "Person in the Street" feature.

Pictures of black athletes were also rare. Willie Mays, Hank Aaron, and Frank Robinson were all having outstanding seasons, and they were mentioned in headlines and articles on the sports page, but pictures of them were few and usually included a white teammate or teammates.

Both Cincinnati and Greenville had black newspapers, the Cincinnati *Herald* and the Greenville *Black Star*. If the *News* (or the *Enquirer*) was your only source of information, you would not know blacks got engaged and married, had babies, or died. Both papers published announcements and pictures of whites only. The *News* even did an article, with a picture, about a party given by the Children of the Confederacy, the youth auxiliary of the Daughters of the Confederacy.

The only times blacks were mentioned in the "mainstream" papers were when the desegregation issue was discussed – often in the *News*, much less so in the *Enquirer* – or in small articles in the *News* that followed a template: "John Smith, Negro, was shot/arrested/etc." If there was any disturbance involving blacks anywhere in the country, it rated an article, and sometimes editorial comment, in the

"Bachelors' wives and old maids' children are always perfect."

Sebastian Chamfort

Greenville paper.

At the end of May an incident occurred in New York which disturbed the editors of the *News* greatly. Or perhaps it delighted them, since it appeared to them to make a strong argument for racial segregation. Violence broke out on a boat ride between Buffalo and an amusement park in Ontario. The *News* relied on the Associated Press report: "Of the approximately 1,000 persons who made the trip, about 80 per cent were Negroes. Most of the trouble was caused by gangs of Negro girls who walked the deck attacking and molesting young white girls." In case anyone missed the moral to be drawn, the *News* editorialized on June 5 that the incident demonstrated "the sound reasons why Southern states have chosen to keep the races apart by law in the interests of peace and good order."

Other non-whites hardly got better treatment in the papers. Considerable controversy about Japanese textile imports was brewing in 1956. The *News* almost always talked about the "Japs." When a local couple adopted a child from Japan, the picture that ran in the paper was captioned, "Couple adopt Jap infant." When someone wrote a letter questioning this practice, the editor explained it was just a way of saving space. The Cincinnati *Enquirer* frequently referred to Japanese in the same fashion.

In early June the *News* ran a piece about the sorry state of the "Once Mighty Catawba Indians," who lived on a 4,000-acre reservation in upstate South Carolina. The article was filled with phrases such as "bedraggled remnants," "meager existence," and "squalid houses." The Catawbas were Mormons because no other religious group bothered to send missionaries among them, even when the Catawbas requested them. The Indians had intermarried with whites to the extent that "there remain only two or three full-blooded Catawbas." But, not to worry, "there has been no intermarriage with the Negro race."

An unlevel playing field

Even though professional and college sports in other parts of the country were integrated, blacks and whites did not mix in athletic contests in the South. Several Southern states even broke away from the national Little League organization over the national organization's decision to allow black and integrated teams to participate. Many Southerners did not want the races to compete head-to-head. As Sam Smith, president of baseball's Southern League, said, "Let's face it, there are folks down here who just don't want their kids growing up to admire a Negro ballplayer, even if he's Willie Mays or Hank Aaron."

Louisiana legislators passed a law forbidding black or integrated teams to play against white teams. Then someone pointed out that they would probably lose the lucrative Sugar Bowl because college teams from other parts of the country were integrated. The Louisiana legislators tried to come up with some way of exempting the Sugar Bowl while not allowing intrastate teams to cross the integration boundary.

The closest contact I had with blacks occurred when I visited Laurens. It was a smaller town than Greenville, with a larger percentage of its population non-white. My grandfather's used furniture and antique store, "The Trading Post," was located on the edge of a black area of town, and many of his customers were black. The rear door of his store opened onto an alley where the police regularly arrested blacks for gambling, fighting, and occasionally stabbing one another. My cousins and I were sternly admonished never to set foot there, even in daylight.

One afternoon in July of 1956 several of my cousins and I were playing ball in our accustomed spot. We had been joined by some kids who lived on the street behind my grandparents. That gave us twelve players, enough to play something like a real game, but still a little short. We were arguing about how we might play when an unfamiliar car pulled into the parking area behind the house. A black man got out of the car, removed his hat, and knocked on the back door.

One of the kids from across the street asked, "Who's that?"

"That's Henry," one of my older cousins said. "He works for us. Sometimes he does stuff for Ma-Ma here at the house."

My grandmother came out of the house and explained, from the top of the steps, what she wanted Henry to do. He got a toolbox out of the trunk. As he started toward the front of the house, he said to

somebody in the car, "You boys stay there. Don't you be gettin' outta the car and don't be botherin' nobody."

As soon as Henry turned the corner of the house the heads of two boys appeared in the open window of the car's back door. One of them draped his arm over the door and rested his chin on it. They looked to be about my age.

"Let's play ball," one of my cousins said.

We decided to play with eight fielders and let four kids bat until they made three outs. Then we would send four more in to bat. It was an okay way to play, but to me it didn't feel like real baseball. In real baseball you have two teams and they take turns hitting and playing the field.

My cousin Buster and I were playing the outfield. Buster was closest to the back of our grandparents' house, when somebody hit a high fly in his direction. Even though the ball wasn't headed for me, I ran toward it, to back up the play like an outfielder is supposed to do. The ball, clearly foul, kept carrying toward the house and Henry's parked car. It was a long run for Buster and, even with his arm outstretched, the ball fell off the tip of his glove. He caught up with it as it stopped rolling next to Henry's car.

"Willie Mays woulda caught that," one of the boys in the car said.

"Willie Mays doesn't have to run uphill," Buster said, heaving the ball back to the infield. The backyard did have a slope to it at that point, gentle but noticeable if you were running up it.

"I coulda caught it," the boy said. One corner of his mouth turned up in a hint of a smile.

Buster turned to face him and pounded his fist into the pocket of his glove. Every boy knows when he's being challenged. "You think you could've caught it?"

"I *know* I could have."

"All right, let's see what you can do."

"What do you mean?" the boy asked. His half-smile vanished.

"I mean, get out here and show us how good you can catch."

"My . . . my daddy said for us to stay in the car."

"So you mean you could've caught that one in the car?"

"Well . . . no." The boy's face showed his regret that he had said anything to begin with. "I . . . I don't have no glove."

Buster opened the car door. "You can use mine."

That surprised me. Not that he was offering to let a black boy use his glove, but that he would let anybody use it. As Vince Staten said, ". . . gloves were personal . . . . Bats, we shared, but your glove, that belonged to you" (*Foul Pole*, p. 88).

"C'mon," Buster said, "show us how good you are. You and Willie Mays."

The boy looked at his brother like they were being called to the principal's office. "C'mon, Luke. Let's go."

Luke's doleful expression said 'You got yourself into this mess. You broke the main rule: never provoke a confrontation with whites, especially when you're outnumbered.' But he followed his brother out of the car.

I hadn't heard so many people get so quiet since my uncle's funeral. The two black boys followed Buster down to the infield. The younger boy, Luke, was barefoot and wearing a shirt and jeans his brother must have outgrown. Judging from the other boy's clothes, I suspected they had at least one older brother at home. He had on a pair of sneakers that didn't look like they would make it to the next boy down the line.

"We've got a couple of new outfielders," Buster said.

"Luke plays second base," the older black boy corrected.

We managed to play three "innings" and everybody was beginning to relax. The two new-

ELSTON HOWARD
catcher-o.f. NEW YORK YANKEES

comers were good ballplayers, but no better than most of us. Luke couldn't lay off a high inside pitch. I was thinking about how the Yankees had Elston Howard, and the Dodgers had Campanella, Robinson, Gilliam, and other black players, when a man's voice barked, "Mark! Luke! You git up here. Right now!"

By the time the boys rejoined their father beside the car, my grandmother and my mother had appeared on the back steps. Henry took off his hat and turned his face up to them. "I'm awful sorry, Miz Crisp. I told these boys to stay in the car."

"I'm sure they meant no harm," my grandmother said. Then she waved her hand at us. "The rest of you better come on in. It's almost lunch time"

From my mother's face I knew we weren't going in just to eat. And I was right. When they found out that having the boys play was our idea, she and my grandmother started throwing questions at us.

"What were you thinking? What are the neighbors going to say when they see you playing with Negroes? Do you want every Negro in Laurens to think they can come over here and play in our yard? Next thing you know, they'll be wanting to . . . come in the house to use the bathroom."

"No, they won't," I said.

"How do you know that?" my mother asked.

I knew because they had gone between the garage and the old storage shed to pee, like the rest of us did. It took too long to go all the way up to the house.

CHAPTER 8

White Fright

William Attwood, writing in *Look* (April 3, 1956), got to the core of the race problem when he said that, in spite of whites' fears of what political and economic power for blacks would mean, the real fear "is social, with profound sexual undertones . . . . The sexual neurosis makes many whites impervious to logic. They are obsessed by the notion that Negroes, given a chance, will take over their women as well as their golf clubs and legislatures."

One article that ran in the Greenville *News* (June 17, 1956) illustrates this point so well it's worth quoting in its entirety. The headline read "Pro-Integrationist 'Sickened' By Changes." A smaller headline above that said "Negroes 'Handle' White Girls":

> *"Don't blame us if we didn't turn out to be the perfection you expected."*
>
> Edna Ferber

> Julius Brenner, 35-year-old Arlington baker and one of three pro-integrationists seeking the Democratic nomination for Virginia's 10th District congressional seat, revealed today he posed as a student to study racial integration in Washington, D. C., schools and was 'sickened' by what he saw.
>
> Brenner said he favored voluntary integration. But he added, 'If integration is to be practiced in Arlington the way it is in the District of Columbia, then I'm not in favor of it.'
>
> He said he donned a T-shirt and slacks about three weeks ago and wandered around through five mixed schools in Washington to see for himself if integration was progressing 'satisfactorily' as had been reported.
>
> He said today he was 'disillusioned.'
>
> 'In one school,' said Brenner, 'I saw a White girl come up to a drinking fountain. Three Negro boys came up behind the girl and forced her to one side of the hall. They put their hands on her and patted her on the rear.'
>
> Brenner said the White girl cursed the Negro youths and pulled away.
>
> He said this type of incident was repeated, especially as students went up flights of stairs.
>
> Brenner said he still favors voluntary integration but he added, 'If the Negroes can't improve themselves and their race, there's nothing to be gained.
>
> 'I know mere forced mass integration is not the answer,' he said. 'I know as a result of my trip that the Negroes need culture, the kind that includes health education and social training, and they need self responsibility.'

Blacks had to be watched, many whites felt. When students at all-black South Carolina State College boycotted nearby white businesses, the governor of the state ordered the entire campus kept under surveillance to ferret out "subversive elements" (Greenville *News*, April 8, 1956). The NAACP and its alleged Communist allies were obviously meant. The students responded by boycotting classes. The school's all-white board of trustees threatened to close it.

The Southern strategy for opposing desegregation was to do everything possible to stall it. And there was nothing subtle about the plan. The headline of the Greenville News on April 9, 1956, proclaimed "Dixie To 'Harass Supreme Court' In Every Conceivable Legal Maneuver, Wofford Says." Thomas A. Wofford was South Carolina's junior senator, who hailed from Greenville. Speaking on a nationally televised show, he threw down the gauntlet: "I'll be an old man with a gray beard, or dead" before integration became a reality, he promised.

Mississippi Senator Eastland called the Brown decision "an unconstitutional and illegal act." Elected officials across the South urged the passage of state laws undoing it. Some Southerners argued states could nullify federal law, a process known as interposition or the "negative power," based on writings of Thomas Jefferson and other founding fathers. South Carolinian John C. Calhoun, whom my family claims as a not-too-distant relative, had worked out this nullification theory to its fullest extent in his "South Carolina Exposition and Protest" of 1828.

In March of 1956 a document officially titled a "Declaration of Constitutional Principles" but dubbed the "Southern Manifesto" was issued by nineteen senators and seventy-seven representatives from eleven Southern states. Texas Senator Lyndon Johnson was among the handful of Southerners in Congress who refused to sign it. The Manifesto accused the Supreme Court of exercising "naked judicial power" and substituting "their personal political and social ideas for the established law of the land." The signers argued that the education of children was a right reserved to the states but urged Southerners to "scrupulously refrain from disorder and lawless acts" in their opposition to the Brown decision (Greenville News, March 11).

No one in the South who had any pretensions to civility wanted to admit they were acting out of any motive so gauche as simple prejudice. G. T. Gillespie, president emeritus of Belhaven College, a Presbyterian school in Jackson, Mississippi, said, "Segregation is not a child of race prejudice . . . segregation can be defended because it is the only reasonable and practical means to prevent racial intermarriage." (Today the opening page of Belhaven's web site shows an African-American student.) North Carolina's Senator Sam Ervin took the same tack: ". . . racial segregation is not the offspring of racial bigotry or racial prejudice. It results from the exercise of a fundamental American freedom – the freedom to select one's associates. Whenever Americans are at liberty to choose their own associates, they virtually always select within their own race" (Look, Apr. 3, 1956).

"One drop of Negro blood"

In order to select within one's own race, one must be able to distinguish that race from others. For many Southerners – and evidence suggests perhaps for some outside the South – the great fear was that a black person might somehow be able to conceal his/her "true" identity.

An article in the Greenville News (Aug. 27, 1956) might have sounded like a promise, but could also be taken as a warning:

> The London Times said Sunday that scientists expect to have new pills available within the next 20 years that can change a person's color from black to white.
> It seems that pills are already perfected that will give a white person a protective tan. According to the article extensive research work is being done on skin pigmentation and there are good possibilities that within the next 20 years men can choose their color 'by swallowing the right pills.'

The editors did not offer any comment on this prospect, but it actually represented one of the white South's, perhaps white America's, greatest fears. There was more involved in the question of ethnicity than just skin color. The oft-stated rule was "one drop of Negro blood makes a person a Negro." Throughout the first half of the twentieth century books and movies were produced about blacks, usually women, who were light-skinned enough to "pass for white." They were always found out, however, and the consequences for the deception were severe. In Nella Larsen's 1930 novel *Passing*, Clare, who is living as a white woman married to a bigoted husband, returns to Harlem and falls from a sixth-floor window to her death. In the musical "Showboat," the character Julie discovers she has "Negro blood." Her white husband stays with her, but by the end of the story she is disgraced and an alcoholic.

In 1934 the movie "Imitation of Life" told the story of a young black woman who tried to dissociate herself from her family and pass herself off as white. It starred a light-skinned black actress, Fredi Washington. The movie was remade in 1959 with Susan Kohner, a white actress, in the starring role. The next year "I Passed for White" was released. In 1958 Natalie Wood starred as a "mulatto" girl in "Kings Go Forth." When two soldiers who are infatuated with her discover her father is black, they both desert her. At the end one, who has lost an arm in WWII, returns to her, in a sense now as "imperfect" as she is.

In these stories whiteness is obviously seen as the desired ("perfect"?) state, which anyone would want to reach. The tragedy of the light-skinned black was that he/she was so close to whiteness and yet could never achieve it. Many cosmetic products aimed at blacks were designed to de-emphasize racial characteristics. Lucky Brown's "Instant Brown Brighten Cream" and "Lemon Fragrance Bleaching Cream" would supposedly lighten a black person's skin, while Madam Jones' "Pressing Oil" would give their hair "that smooth silky" look. Some blacks ironed their hair to straighten it.

Roles for blacks in major movies or on TV were limited in number and type in the 1950s. Where white actors had played "Amos and Andy" and "Beulah" on radio, blacks were hired for those roles when the shows went to television. The programs were roundly criticized as degrading by organizations like the NAACP, which urged Hattie McDaniel not to accept the role of the maid Beulah. McDaniel's response was that she "could make $700 a week playing a maid or $7 a week being a maid."

There were no roles for light-skinned actresses like Dorothy Dandridge, in spite of the sensation she created in 1954's "Carmen Jones," an adaptation of Bizet's opera *Carmen*. She was the first black featured on the cover of *Life*, but Hollywood was not ready for a beautiful, even seductive, black leading lady. Dandridge finally moved to Europe where she died of a drug overdose at age 42.

Stories about the ethnicity of certain celebrities circulated widely. Dinah Shore was thought to be half black or to have had a black baby, which she gave up for adoption. For years Babe Ruth was rumored to be of black ancestry. Ty Cobb refused to share a hunting lodge with Ruth because "I never have slept under the same roof with a nigger, and I'm not going to start here in my own native state of Georgia."

Some Southerners did not object to sleeping with blacks. South Carolina Senator Strom Thurmond fathered a daughter by one of his family's black maids. Although he supported the child and his "secret" was known to family and a few friends, he did not publicly acknowledge her until very late in his long life. Her existence did not stop him from being an ardent segregationist until the 1970s.

Many Southern whites still thought of blacks as Uncle Toms or Step-'n'-Fetchits. One of the most remarkable pieces of evidence of that attitude was the daily presence in newspapers across the region of a one-panel cartoon called "Hambone's Meditations." It featured a broad-faced black man in baggy clothes and dilapidated hat, usually doing some menial task while he offered such observations on life as: "Dey tells me w'en a king 'ab-dicate', dat's runnin' off f'um home to save he neck – ef dat's de case, I ab-dicates 'bout oncet a week!!" What I didn't know as I read those panels was that the feature's creator, J. P. Alley, had died in 1934. Southern newspapers just kept reprinting it. The Greenville *News* in 1956 put it on the editorial page. It was still running in Memphis, Alley's home, as late as 1968. The mayor of the city at that time expressed his surprise that blacks found it offensive.

Although it was blatantly racist, the strip did strike one note of timeless truth. On August 27, 1956, Hambone said, "Baseball crank at de sto' keep sayin'de Yanks ain' raelly a good team – Hunh!! – ain' *nobody* kin have *dat* much *luck*!!" That must have been written about the great teams of the Ruth-Gehrig era (1925-1934), but it was just as true in 1956.

My mother's family practiced the sort of genteel, patronizing racism which this comic fostered. They employed and worked alongside blacks, and I never heard them make degrading remarks about blacks. But I never heard the last names of those employees either. For years two unrelated black men, Henry and Little Henry, worked in my grandfather's used furniture store and did odd jobs around his house. I was reminded of them years later when I became aware of Frederick Douglass' account of "Big Barney" and "Little Barney." Other than my encounter with Henry's sons, their names were all I knew about these men. My grandmother did express some concern that Little Henry drank too much, and I once heard somebody say he ought to be called Henrietta. For a long time I thought that was just a pun on "Little Henry." Only when I gained a little more knowledge of the ways of the world, did I realize it probably had greater significance.

Breaking the Color Line

By and large, the most desegregated institutions in America by the mid-'50s were professional sports teams. Roy Campanella's comment was widely quoted: "If life in general was a baseball game in the National or American League, this country wouldn't have these problems today." Some white athletes went out of their way to break down racial barriers. When the Dodgers played an exhibition game in Texas, after Jackie Robinson joined the team, the fans heckled him until Pee Wee Reese, a native of Kentucky and known as "the little Colonel," put his arm around Robinson's shoulder. When the Yankees' Elston Howard was denied service in Southern restaurants, "some of us would just stay in the bus with Ellie" (Berra, *Ten Rings*, p. 144; cf. Mantle, *The Mick*, p. 130).

Even in sports, though, institutional response to racism was slow. Sam Breadon, president of the St. Louis Cardinals when Robinson joined the Dodgers, thought he was "a good player. There may even be three or four other blacks in the country who can play well enough to get a chance in the big leagues." Even though the Yankees signed black players, it wasn't until 1962 that they changed the site

ROY CAMPANELLA
catcher BROOKLYN DODGERS

Roy Campanella

of their spring training camp because their hotel in St. Petersburg, Florida, had a "whites only" policy.

There was dissension about race within the ranks of professional sports, especially in baseball, with its large number of Southern players. Several Dodger players threatened to quit if Robinson was signed. The St. Louis Cardinals threatened to boycott games against the Dodgers to protest Robinson's signing. Enos Slaughter, a North Carolina native who would play in Larsen's perfect game, allegedly tried to instigate the boycott. National League president Ford Frick threatened to ban any players who participated, and the boycott never happened. Until the end of his life, Slaughter dismissed stories about the boycott as "baloney," but he did intentionally spike Robinson during a game. In another game the Cardinals' manager unleashed such a vicious stream of verbal abuse on Robinson that it galvanized the other Dodgers to come to their teammate's defense. Like the Red Sox, the Cardinals were slow to sign their first black player (Curt Flood in 1958).

Some of the old-time players never did change their attitudes. Long after his retirement Bob Feller said, "I don't think baseball owes colored people anything; I don't think colored people owe baseball anything, either" (*The Sporting News*, Aug. 9, 1969). The remark set off a feud with Jackie Robinson.

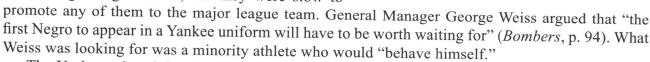

Robinson was also involved in a spat with Milwaukee pitcher Lew Burdette late in the 1956 season. While warming up, Robinson claimed he heard Burdette make racist remarks, including a reference to "watermelons." His next throw sailed past first base and into the Braves' dugout. "I aimed it right at Burdette's head," Robinson admitted. "Lucky for him it missed." Burdette denied he had said anything other than "needling him about his weight" (Greenville *News*, Aug. 27).

The Yankees had several black players in their minor league organization, but they were slow to promote any of them to the major league team. General Manager George Weiss argued that "the first Negro to appear in a Yankee uniform will have to be worth waiting for" (*Bombers*, p. 94). What Weiss was looking for was a minority athlete who would "behave himself."

The Yankees signed first baseman Vic Power, from Puerto Rico, but never brought him to the

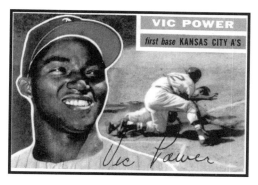

majors. Power felt it was because he was more flamboyant than someone like Elston Howard. He spoke out about the treatment he received at restaurants and hotels, and he dated white women (*Bombers*, pp. 95-99). He was traded to Kansas City and enjoyed a 12-year career in the major leagues. Roy Campanella faced the same questions when he came to the majors. Dodgers' General Manager Branch Rickey asked him "Did I drink? Did I run around with women? Would I embarrass the club with my conduct? That's what they had to be sure of before they signed any Negro player."

All deliberate speed

As opinions on school desegregation polarized in 1956 a few Southerners tried to find a middle ground. William Faulkner published a long letter in the March 5 issue of *Life* (I doubt he could write a short letter), urging those pushing for integration to slow down and let Southerners handle the process in their own way. Otherwise, Faulkner argued, there would be no middle ground left, only two extreme positions. In July, Robert Penn Warren chipped in with an article in *Life* on how the "Divided South Searches its Soul." Faulkner addressed a black audience in the September issue of *Ebony*, urging them to adopt Ghandi's tactic of non-violent protest, "inflexible and undeviable [*sic*] only in hope and will, but flexible always to adapt to time and place and circumstance." An editorial cartoon in the Greenville *News* showed a school bus labeled "School integration" barreling along while a black child in the rear seat asked, "Wouldn't it be better for *me* if the bus didn't try to go too fast?"

The extreme divisions which Faulkner feared showed clearly at the University of Alabama early in 1956. Two years before, Autherine Juanita Lucy had been admitted as a graduate student, apparently because the admissions committee didn't realize she was black. When they discovered their oversight, they reversed the decision. She sued and was finally admitted in January of '56, but was told she could not live in a dorm or eat in a university dining hall (most graduate students did not). Demonstrations broke out when Lucy came to classes. The demonstrators seem to have been townspeople as well as 'Bama students.

Lucy had to live with her family and drive a considerable distance to and from campus to attend classes. Her family armed themselves. Her brother-in-law said, "I'm not going to have her snatched from my care as they did the Till boy."

At the same time Lucy was litigating her way into the University of Alabama, over three hundred black students were being admitted to three state schools in Louisiana with hardly a ripple in the newspapers. A black coed at the State University of Iowa was chosen "Miss SUI." She was one of 150 blacks in a student body of 9,000 (*Saturday Evening Post*, Feb. 4). The NAACP reported that "orderly desegregation is taking place in such border states as Texas, West Virginia, Missouri, Oklahoma, Arkansas, Maryland and Delaware" (Greenville *News*, Mar. 4, 1956).

Why the difference in Alabama? Was it just geography? Lucy and her advisors, primarily attorney Thurgood Marshall, do seem to have created some ill will and controversy by driving her to campus in a Cadillac with an entourage. For many whites, who would never see the inside of a Cadillac, she became "the symbol of the determination of outsiders to force a change in 'the Southern way of life'" (Greenville *News*, Mar. 9, 1956). In a word, she was "uppity," the worst thing that could be said about a black person in this era. There seems to be a bit of criticism implicit in *Life*'s statement that "this was a new provocation by an organization which inflames the Negroes' most bitter enemies. And it alienated some who had deplored the earlier violence." Even after rereading that several times, I wonder if it is the provocation or the organization which inflames and alienates.

After several days of violence the trustees barred Lucy from campus "for her own safety." That led to more court action. This time the NAACP sued to have her readmitted and let into dorms and dining halls. Just before a court order to that effect could be enforced, the University expelled Lucy on the grounds that she and her attorneys had made "baseless" charges against the University of conspiring with the mobs who opposed her admission. The charges were in fact dropped because her lawyers were unable to find any corroboration. The whole business made front page headlines in my hometown newspaper on March 2.

The University's president promised: "Similar action would be taken against any student who is guilty of similar conduct regardless of race and color." He proved true to his word when a white student who had been highly visible in the riots and had spoken out against the University's administration, was expelled. Four others were suspended and unspecified "disciplinary action" was taken against 25 others (Greenville *News*, Mar. 13).

". . . a time of innocence, of peace and serenity"? Sorry, Mr. Pepe, not to those of us who were there.

CHAPTER 9

The Red Flag

The connections I'm making among racism, Communism, and baseball may appear tenuous. I'm commenting on these topics because racial tensions and fear of the Soviet Union (and Communists within the U. S.) underlay every waking moment of an Everykid in 1956. The same was true for adults. Yogi Berra recalled that "the Communist scare even hit us in the ballpark. Back then they'd fly a blue flag in Yankee Stadium if we won that day, and a red one if we lost," but in the early '50s "the Yankees stopped flying the red flag" (*Ten Rings*, p. 74).

"He that seeks perfection on earth leaves nothing new for the saints to find in heaven."

Francis Osborn

The regular season of baseball provided relief from those anxieties that I couldn't find anywhere else. The World Series, as long as the Yankees were in it, absorbed my attention completely for a few days because it booted everything else off the front page of the newspapers. And Don Larsen's perfect game restored my faith that this was, after all, a world in which anything was possible.

As Larsen himself said, the Series and the game came "at the end of a tumultuous year filled with friction and conflict on the national and international scene. The Fall Classic would in many ways allow people to take a deep breath and escape for a moment into the comfortable and exciting American tradition of crowning the world champion of baseball" (*Perfect Yankee*, p. xxi).

The Hunt for Red October, November . . . .

America's problems with race relations were a propaganda gold mine for the Communists. The North Vietnamese broadcast a letter which they claimed was written by Autherine Lucy, criticizing the U. S. and discussing her problems in gaining admission to the University of Alabama. In a rebuttal broadcast on the Voice of America, Lucy denied "that I have at any time written a letter to any Communist organization in either America or abroad . . . . I know very little about Communism and have not had any contact with any person or agent known to me to be a representative of the Communist party" (Greenville *News*, Mar. 8, 1956).

A small article buried on p. 22 of the *News* on Sept. 7 reported East German newspapers were playing up the disturbances over school integration in Clinton, Tennessee. Pictures showed blacks being threatened by Klansmen. Headlines in the *Berliner Zeitung* read: "Negroes must avoid the streets – atmosphere of terror – U. S. Southern states make own laws."

Frank Snowden, U. S. cultural attaché in Rome, found Europeans keenly interested in the issue, as he described in "They Always Ask Me About Negroes" (*Saturday Evening Post*, Mar 3, 1956). The Soviet Union and Red China were trying to gain toeholds in Africa, southeast Asia, and Latin America.

The U. S. did not look like a place where people with dark skins were welcome. When dignitaries from those parts of the world visited this country, the government had to pressure Southerners to set aside Jim Crow restrictions and allow the visitors to stay in decent hotels and eat in restaurants where non-whites ordinarily were not admitted. A speaker at the Georgia Baptist Sunday School convention declared the Supreme Court had to make the rulings it did against segregation "to offset Communist propaganda which . . . was winning the world through the promise of 'brotherhood and equality'" (Greenville *News*, April 26, 1956).

A letter to the editor of the *News* on July 8, 1956, described a small incident with international implications. Three college students stopped to have lunch at a restaurant in downtown Greenville. One of them, from India, "was assumed to be a Negro" and the students were asked to leave. The writer of the letter pointed out that India was "neutral in world politics" but Prime Minister Nehru was not kindly disposed to the West. How would this student feel about America when he went home "and Communism comes knocking at his doorstep"? An earlier article in the *News* (Feb. 7) had expressed the fear that "India Will Be Cloaked in Red In 5 Years."

Even though Sen. McCarthy was discredited, the fear of Communists and the urge to hunt them down still ran strong in 1956. In April the former president of the DAR urged the group's members to "help the government detect Communist collaborators who operate under the cloak of respectability." Such groups, she feared "exert greater influence and so are more dangerous than the actual members of the party itself" (Greenville *News*, April 16). An episode of "I Led Three Lives" in April of 1955 blamed juvenile delinquency on Communist instigators, while the venom-filled book *U. S. A. Confidential* claimed many disk jockeys were "Reds, left-wingers, or hecklers of social convention."

Early in the year Mississippi Senator James Eastland held hearings of his Internal Security Subcommittee specifically to investigate the presence of Communists in the media. The *New York Times* was singled out; 26 of 35 subpoenas went to its current or former employees. Several admitted to being members of small Communist cells back in the 1930s or 1940s.

Local authorities everywhere were active in the hunt for Reds. New York City passed a law "under which public employees were automatically fired for refusing to answer questions about Communism." That law was overturned by the Supreme Court (Greenville *News*, April 10, 1956). In May seven men accused of being Communists and conspiring to overthrow the government went on trial in Federal Court in New York City. On April 6 my hometown newspaper carried an article with the headline "Hellman, Reputed Commie Organizer, Is Arrested." John Cyril Hellman had been arrested in Butte, Montana, and charged with "violating the section of the Smith Act which defines as illegal membership in the Communist Party with the knowledge that it conspires to overthrow the U. S. Government by force and violence."

And we didn't even have the Patriot Act. The Smith Act, from the Virginia congressman who sponsored it, was the common name for the Alien and Registration Act of 1940, which is still on the books.

"Duck and cover"

Today, in the face of daily terrorist attacks, the world seems very hostile. But in 1956 it felt just as scary to an Everykid who was an avid reader of newspapers and magazines and whose parents watched the news every evening. The Soviet Union had nuclear weapons, and no one could guarantee they would not use them. They didn't have to cross our borders or get past airport security. All they had to do was push a button in Moscow. On Feb. 19 Russian Defense Minister Georgi Zhukov, under the headline "Zhukov Threatens Missiles If West Starts War," promised that the Soviet Union, while not desiring war, would "hurl atomic bombs on American cities" if it was attacked.

Fortunately, we school kids had been taught to "duck and cover" if the Ruskies did drop an atomic bomb on us. The town in South Carolina where I lived was home to an Air Force base, so we figured we were sure to be a target. On January 30 *Time* ran a story on "The Missile." The cover art showed a missile diving toward an unidentified city. One of ours or one of theirs? Could that be my town? It didn't help that Khrushchev was saying the Russians would soon have guided missiles with H-bomb warheads "which can hit every point in the world" (Greenville *News*, April 24, 1956).

Many newspaper and magazine articles of the time seem to assume "when," not "if," the Russians attacked. In an article on Feb. 1 Atomic Energy Commissioner Willard F. Libby warned a House subcommittee: "modern weapons would kill 85 per cent of those living within 12 miles of target zero if they were in ordinary two-story brick homes. The rest would be seriously injured." We lived in a one-story wood frame house. When I asked my dad how far we were from the Air Force base, he said, "About six miles." Obviously we were doomed.

Civil Defense Administrator Val Peterson didn't make me feel any better when he admitted, "Assuming a Russian attack with the element of surprise, they could do it, they could name the time, and there is no reason to believe that we could hit them with the same devastating result . . . . In the event of an attack, the day after will see a sad, stark, miserable situation in the United States" (Greenville *News*, Apr. 17, 1956).

Even if they didn't attack us directly, I learned on July 27, we would still be affected. Greenville was on a line between Atomic Energy Commission installations in Oak Ridge, Tennessee, and Aiken, South Carolina. An attack on either of those places would mean fall-out drifting over Greenville. We were advised "in case of an attack to go indoors and into a cellar." Fortunately my house had a cellar.

When I discussed the premise of this book with a friend who is my age, he said he moved from Iowa to California in 1956. Because of the controversy between Red China and Taiwan over some small islands which both claimed, he, an Everykid himself, went to bed each night expecting a Chinese invasion.

Fear of the Russians was even more deeply ingrained, I think, than fear of terrorism today. The "Red Scare" generated by McCarthy and Eastland may have passed its peak, but it had left a strong aftertaste of suspicion of anyone who acted differently. A family of Jehovah's Witnesses attended my elementary school in South Carolina. Every morning, when we stood for the pledge of allegiance (and we still stumbled over that phrase "under God" which had been added in 1954), they refused to do so. I know now they were acting on a religious principle, but at the time it looked like they were un-American. And being un-American meant you were a Communist.

The rule applied to baseball players, too. As Rogers Hornsby said, "Any ballplayer that don't sign autographs for little kids ain't an American. He's a communist."

"We Will Bury You"

What made it so hard to identify them was that Communists didn't look any different from the rest of us. They didn't wear turbans or other distinctive garb. They could even look like Methodists. A pamphlet called "A Handbook for Americans," published in 1956 by Senator Eastland's Internal

Security Subcommittee, listed the Methodist Federation for Social Action as a Communist-front organization. The Federation had to go to court to stop publication of the document.

According to historians of the period, this fear of the unidentifiable alien is one subtext of the movie "Invasion of the Body Snatchers," which came out in 1956. They look like us, they talk like us, but their minds have been taken over by this alien force (Marxist thought). And they want to overwhelm the rest of us. How can we stop them? In the words of film critic Tim Dirks:

> The theme of the cautionary, politicized film was open to varying interpretations, including paranoia toward the spread of a harmful ideology such as socialistic Communism, or the sweeping mass hysteria of McCarthyism in the 1950s and blacklisting of Hollywood, the spread of an unknown malignancy or virulent germ (read fear of annihilation by 'nuclear war') or the numbing of our individuality and emotional psyches through conformity and group-think. Yet its main theme was the alien (read 'Communist') dehumanization and take-over of an entire community . . . (www.filmsite.org/inva/html).

Communism itself was undergoing drastic change at this time. Stalin's death in 1953 opened the door to a power struggle inside the Kremlin that wasn't entirely over three years later. Nikita Khrushchev emerged as First Secretary of the Communist Party and eventually the USSR's Premier, but he faced challenges on internal and external fronts. If he wasn't seen in public for a few days, American newspapers speculated that he had fallen from power.

In February 1956 Khrushchev delivered a three-hour speech denouncing Stalin's brutality and his "cult of personality." Reports of this "Secret Speech" gradually leaked out, causing riots in Soviet Georgia, Stalin's birthplace. It wasn't until March 18 that the story became well known enough in the West for my hometown newspaper to run the headline "Denunciation of Stalin Triggers Protests in Russia." The dead dictator was characterized as "a murdering, blundering psychopath." Soviet officials were distressed that news of the speech was getting around.

At times Khrushchev talked like he wanted to relax tensions between East and West, but he was a mercurial man who took offense easily and held grudges deeply. He and Premier Nikolai Bulganin ruffled feathers and spread much ill-will, even among European Socialists, when they visited Britain in the spring of '56. In a speech there Khrushchev responded to hecklers by saying, "Never shake your fist at a Russian."

U. S. weather balloons drifting across Russian air space could look to Khrushchev like provocation for war (Greenville *News*, Feb. 10, 1956). As Joseph and Stewart Alsop warned in "The Reds' New Gimmick" (*Saturday Evening Post*, Feb. 5), "today most of those who know the ugly facts agree that the cold war has become more perilous than ever." When anti-Soviet protests erupted in Hungary in the fall, Khrushchev sent in 200,000 Russian troops to crush them. England, France, and the U. S. were too deeply involved in the Suez Canal crisis to offer more than verbal protests.

One Russian strategy for improving their status in the eyes of the world was to claim they invented or pioneered just about everything. A Russian magazine even explained to its readers that baseball (or 'beizbol') was an American perversion of 'lapta,' an old Russian village game. The American version, though, had been turned into a "beastly battle, a bloody fight with mayhem and murder . . . . in which both players and spectators frequently suffered terrible wounds or even death" (*New York Times*, Sept. 16, 1952).

"All the Angry Winds"

One of the places where Communist influence was most feared was the volatile Middle East. Egypt's president Nasser openly courted Russian aid. As he said in *Life*, (Apr. 16), "We asked the Soviet Union for help. For years we had asked everyone else. We turned to the Soviet bloc knowing that the Western powers had no intention of dealing with us as independent equals." General Sir John Bagot Glubb, recently ousted head of Jordan's Arab Legion, expressed his fears for the region in a long article in *Life,* (Apr. 16). Parts of it read as though it could have been written in the past year.

In 1956 tensions in the Middle East were strained to the breaking point. On January 23 *Time* spoke of "all the angry winds now loose" there. A front-page headline in the Greenville *News* on March 5 warned "War Danger in Middle East Mounts With New Clash." Two Israelis had been killed in a minor skirmish with a Syrian patrol, but the British Foreign Secretary was warning the world that "time is running out and trouble is getting worse" in the region. An editorial cartoon in the *News* on April 25 showed the world peering anxiously at a burning fuse labeled "Arabs/Israel" which led to a tank of "Middle-East Hi-Test Gas."

The establishment of the state of Israel in 1948 incensed the Arabs. As Nasser said, "Eight years ago you [America] unalterably changed my life and my children's lives" by thrusting "a foreign state among us Arabs." In January of 1956 the Committee of Senior Ulema at Cairo's Al-Azhar University, the highest Muslim authority in matters of faith, declared a *jihad* against Israel, regarded as land stolen from Muslims. They quoted the Koran, "Drive them from where they have driven you."

On the other hand, the establishment of Israel was seen by many Christian fundamentalists as a sure sign we were living in the last generation of human history. In the fall of '56 Egypt, backed by the Russians, seized the Suez Canal. Israel, with support from Britain and France, advanced to the east side of the Canal. Those who took Biblical prophecies too literally thought the sides were squaring off for the battle of Armageddon. The U. S. twisted diplomatic arms to get Britain and France to back down.

Denting the Iron Curtain?

The Eisenhower administration, with John Foster Dulles as Secretary of State, developed two doctrines that actually ramped up tensions around the globe. One was the threat of "massive retaliation." In an effort to cow the Soviet Union, Dulles warned that the United States had the will and the "capacity to retaliate, instantly, by means and at places of our own choosing." Those means included nuclear weapons.

The other thrust of the Eisenhower/Dulles foreign policy was containment. To check the growth of godless Communism, the U. S. entered into unholy alliances with any national leader who gave lip-service to anti-Communism. That sometimes meant we connived in the overthrow of governments which we considered socialist or proto-socialist in order to install leaders whose views sounded anti-Communist. If this meant they were fascists who systematically looted their national treasuries to enrich themselves and their families, we could overlook that as long as they were anti-Communist.

This containment policy led to U. S. involvement in such disparate places as Iran, Vietnam, and Guatemala. The U. S. did not belong to the Baghdad Pact, consisting of Turkey, Iraq, Iran, Pakistan, and Britain, but it did promise economic support to what it saw as a bulwark against Russian encroachment on that area (Greenville *News*, April 15, 1956). Some of the headlines sound ironic or eerily familiar. The *Saturday Evening Post* found South Vietnam a "Bright Spot in Asia" (Sept. 15), although the editors worried that "the departure of the French has saddled Americans with much heavier responsi-bilities in these exotic countries where the United States has no very sharply defined status." An article in *Life* explained why it was important that we confront the Soviets in Afghanistan, even though most Americans had never heard of the place. Soviet expansionism and America's resolve to contain it meant that the world's political climate remained extremely tense in the mid-1950s.

Eisenhower's and Dulles' determination to keep America strong militarily required us to maintain the strength of our armed forces. The draft loomed over the head of every young American male, even baseball players. Ted Williams did a second tour of duty during the Korean War. Every team lost play-ers, even stars, for a year or so, although most of the major leaguers drafted just played ball on service teams. Whitey Ford's commanding officer at Fort Monmouth, New Jersey, wanted him to pitch three times a week because it was "good for morale." Ford refused and was surprised he wasn't court-mar-tialed (*Slick*, pp. 80-81).

In addition to Ford, the Yankees lost Billy Martin, Jerry Coleman, and others to the draft in the first half of the decade. Before he came to the Yankees, Don Larsen spent 1951-52 in the Army, playing ball with service teams in Hawaii. He realized how fortunate he was: "The alternative certainly would have been combat" (*Perfect Yankee*, p. 82). Mickey Mantle was called up for a physical and deemed unfit for military service because of his knee injuries. Enough questions about his classification were raised in the press that he was called back for a second physical, which he also failed (*The Mick*, p. 58). It was hard for families whose young men were serving to understand how someone who could run as fast as Mantle did on a baseball field could be "unfit" to shoulder a rifle instead of a bat.

Magazines and newspapers of 1956, especially the *Saturday Evening Post*, kept everyone nervous with articles like "Timebomb in Germany" (May 3); a series of three articles: "I Saw Communist China: Nightmare for the West" (May 19, 26, June 2); "Red Surge in Southern Italy" (Aug. 25); "New Danger in Argentina" (Nov. 17). When the political angle wore thin, the weekly magazines would run articles on how far ahead of us the Soviet Union was getting in technology and weaponry, or maybe a general scare piece such as Lester Pearson's "Are We Losing the Cold War?" (*Look*, Jan 10).

". . . a time of innocence, of peace and serenity"? Sorry, Mr. Pepe, not to those of us who were there.

Is it any wonder Everykid – and grown-ups too – would seize on baseball as an escape? As Mickey Mantle said, "When you watch baseball at its best there's a tendency to forget the real world: wars, fam-ine, natural disasters, the day-to-day problems" (*The Mick*, p. 191). I knew how true that was. Whether I was reading the sports page or feeling the satisfying 'thump' of a ball landing in my glove, the world between the foul lines felt much safer than any other place I could find. I knew the rules there, and I knew who were the good guys, (the Yankees), and the bad guys, (everybody else).

Spring training offered hope. There was going to be baseball, and as long as there was baseball, the world's problems seemed manageable. As William Saroyan observed, without baseball "for all any of us know there might soon be no nation at all" (*Sports Illustrated*, Oct. 8, 1956).

CHAPTER 10

The Walking Wounded

Every baseball player aims at perfection during spring training. The youngster knows it's his chance to show the manager he has spent enough time in the minors and deserves a place on the big league team. The veteran wants to show that his skills have not diminished so he can fight off the rookies and reclaim his spot on the roster. Spring training is a beginning for some, an end for others.

"There is no place in all the world where things are so perfect as the spring training camp of the team that has just won the World Series."

Sports Illustrated,
March 19, 1956

That "we finished last" story appeared in Sports Illustrated *(July 16, 1956), but with Bill Veeck and pitcher Ned Garver exchanging the lines. This illustrates how difficult it sometimes is to establish a canonical version of a baseball story.*

Just as there is "no crying in baseball," there was no job security in the 1950s. Today a team may have to think twice about unloading a high-salaried player, depending on the complications of his contract. In 1956 all players were given one-year contracts, with terms typically dictated by the team's owner and general manager. The infamous "reserve clause" bound a player to his team until the team decided to get rid of him. An off-year for a player or a team could mean a salary cut. Ralph Kiner, after winning his seventh consecutive home run title in 1952, asked the woeful Pittsburgh Pirates for a raise. General Manager Branch Rickey replied, "We finished last with you; we could have finished last without you." Kiner was soon traded to the Cubs.

In short, spring training was a time when a player's prospects could be as variable as the weather.

That was truer of the Yankees in the mid-1950s than it had been for some time. As Yogi Berra put it, "There was an uncertainty about the Yankees in '56" (*Ten Rings*, p. 144). The Bronx Bombers had lost the 1955 World Series to the Brooklyn Dodgers – the first and only time "Dem Bums" would win a championship in Ebbets Field. To the extent that a 10-year-old Southern Baptist could curse, I was still reviling Johnny Podres for the magnificent way he pitched to win Game 7 and Sandy Amoros for a catch that simply shouldn't have been made. Both had had mediocre seasons, and yet they played beyond themselves to steal a title that clearly belonged to the Yankees.

The Yankees hadn't even gotten to the World Series in 1954, so this was starting to look like a serious drought for a team that had had a standing order for championship rings under Casey Stengel from 1949-53.

The road to the Series began in Florida. Fifty years ago spring training was really a time for players to start getting in shape. *Sports Illustrated* called it "Spring Straining" (Apr. 2, 1956). Because they made so little money playing ball, most players worked at "real" jobs, not at conditioning, during the off-season. Cincinnati's Gus Bell worked in the team's office, selling season tickets (*Sports Illustrated*, July 16, 1956). Don Larsen did construction work in the off-season because "my Yankee salary didn't stretch very far" (*Perfect Yankee*, p. 92). Yogi Berra, who worked in a men's clothing store and as a greeter at a restaurant, said, "hardly anyone lifted weights or ran in the off-season – that's what spring training was for. My main thing was not getting fat at those winter banquets" (*Ten Rings*, p. 84). Enos Slaughter, 39 years old, worked on his farm in North Carolina and credited chopping wood with keeping his wrists strong. Even so, he admitted to a reporter, "My legs really hurt the first few days, but they feel fine today. Yesterday every part of me was sore and I had to force myself. Today I feel loose and my legs don't hurt" (Greenville *News*, Mar. 7, 1956).

Mickey Mantle rarely did any off-season conditioning. After his horrendous injury in the 1951 World Series he was supposed to wear a brace with weights on it and exercise to strengthen the knee. But "I lazed around, feeling sorry for myself instead of doing the exercises . . . . I thought the muscles would automatically come back, good as ever. I was twenty years old and I thought I was a superman" (*The Mick*, pp. 82-83). In its July 16 issue *Sports Illustrated* ran an article showing eleven different spots where Mantle's right knee had been damaged. It left me wondering how he could even walk, let alone play baseball.

During spring training in 1956 some of the Yankees' regulars suffered injuries. *Sports Illustrated* referred to their "horrid list of cripples" (April 23). Gil McDougald, who was supposed to start at shortstop, pulled a tendon below his knee. Whitey Ford had problems with a sore foot and sprained an ankle. Elston Howard broke a finger. Mantle, not yet fully recovered from a leg injury at the end of the '55 season which many say cost the Yankees the Series, pulled a hamstring on March 28 and was still not in top form on opening day, although that wouldn't stop him from hitting two gargantuan home runs in that first game.

Once spring training started I devoured the sports page of the Greenville *News*. That was also when I finally got to enjoy my subscription to *Sports Illustrated*. The year had started badly, from my perspective, with Johnny Podres on the cover of the first issue, and there had been precious little baseball in the magazine until March. I didn't even mind when my dad took it to dream over the photo-essay on antique cars in one of the January issues. Our cars weren't classics, but he spent a lot of time maintaining them, especially his '49 Cadillac.

My father adored cars from the 1920s and 1930s. I always gave him something for birthdays, Christmas, and Father's Day, but I once took pictures of some old cars at a show being held on the street in front of my house and sent them to him. It was the only time he ever wrote to thank me for something.

Every time I read about one of the Yankees' injuries my spirits sank, even though I sometimes didn't know exactly what the problem was. Broken fingers and sprained ankles I understood, but what was a hamstring?

I raised that question with my three best friends, Ted, Dan, and Johnny. (Hey, it was the '50s. Nobody named their kids Jason or Phoenix or Fiona or Lourdes or Apple.)

"Hamstring? Isn't that what they tie around a ham you buy in the store?" Ted suggested.

"Ha, ha," I said. "It's got to be part of a person's body. Something you can injure bad enough so you can't play ball."

"Look it up," Ted said. "You're always looking stuff up."

So I did. The dictionary told me a hamstring was "either of two groups of tendons at the back of the knee."

I spent a lot of time that afternoon feeling behind my own knees. I could feel some kind of hard, stringy things. Those must be hamstrings, I concluded. During the night I woke up with an awful cramp in my right calf. When I limped into school the next morning, Ted, Dan, and Johnny asked what had happened.

"I think I messed up my hamstring," I said. They regarded me with awe for the rest of the day. My charley-horse cleared up by the end of the day, of course, and I couldn't understand why Mantle didn't get back into the line-up as quickly as I did.

My local paper featured a number of articles about the Yankees during spring training. In one Don Larsen promised he would reform his "bad boy" image. "I was getting such a reputation for horsing around that even my mother spoke to me about it," Larsen lamented (Greenville *News*, Mar. 8).

Mantle got his share of coverage in my paper. An article on March 9 reported he still hadn't lived up to expectations people had been forming since he came to the Yankees to take Joe DiMaggio's place: "Frankly, he never has come up to the Yankee Clipper's level. Perhaps he will in time." To me, DiMaggio was just a name. He retired at the end of the '51 season, when I was six years old. I resented people comparing my hero to someone I had never seen play.

In a *News* article on March 16 Mantle declared he was "tired of being a pushover for sucker pitches." He intended to concentrate on the strike zone and reduce his number of strike-outs. I was shocked to see him quoted in the article as saying, "Hell, it took Duke Snider a little while to learn the strike zone but he's got it down pretty good now. I know I can do it, too."

My hero cussing? Right there in the newspaper? If he could do it, maybe I could, too. Just not out loud. And not in front of my parents. The first time I said "Oh, hell" out loud, I felt myself getting warm. It felt like a foretaste of the fire and brimstone awaiting me if I continued down that path. Mantle cussed. Did that mean he was going to hell? Because of more than just his profanity, the question began to torment him toward the end of his life (Castro, p. 270).

Mantle later figured that, between his strike-outs and his walks, he played the equivalent of seven full seasons "without ever touching the ball"

(Favorite Summer, p. 56).

The headline of one little article on March 4 caught my eye: "Potential Mantles?" Who could be as good as Mickey? I wondered. The article said the Cleveland Indians had two young players who they hoped would "develop into a pair of Mickey Mantles one of these seasons, maybe this one. The two – Roger Maris, 21, and Carroll Hardy, 22 – are look-alikes and do-alikes . . . . Right now, [manager Al] Lopez rates Maris a shade ahead of Hardy."

A shade, indeed. Hardy played in the majors with four teams from 1958-67. He averaged .225 over his career and hit a total of 17 home runs. Maris hit 15 in the month of June, 1961.

When the Yankees headed north the second week in April, five players – McDougald, Irv Noren (surgery on both knees), Billy Hunter (broken ankle), Bob Cerv (pulled stomach muscle) and rookie sensation Norm Siebern (bruised knee) – were left behind in Florida to recuperate and join the team later. Manager Casey Stengel still didn't know whether Billy Martin would play second and Andy Carey third, or whether

Martin would take third and Bobby Richardson second. Bill Skowron would play first, backed up by Eddie Robinson and Joe Collins, both nearing the end of their careers. Robinson would be traded to Kansas City in mid-season.

The phrase "traded to Kansas City" appears in the biographies of many Yankees from the late '50s and early '60s. When the Philadelphia Athletics moved to Kansas City in 1955 the Yankees had a well-established AAA team there. The Yankees "relinquished the territorial rights of their American Association franchise," but the general manager of the Yankees' farm team, who had been hired by Yankees' General Manager George Weiss, became the G. M. of the new American League team. Throughout the late 1950s Kansas City "emerged alternately as a Yankee staging area and a rest-and-recuperation area" for Yankee players (*The Yankees*, p. 127), a kind of high minor league team. Enos Slaughter provides a perfect example. The Yankees got him from the St. Louis Cardinals in 1954, traded him to Kansas City in 1955, then got him back from the A's for the final weeks of the '56 season.

"Baseball Was Meant for Trains"

Younger readers will need to be reminded that in 1956 major league teams still traveled by train from their spring training sites to their opening day games. Along the way they stopped and played exhibition games against one another or against minor league teams. Mickey Mantle didn't like those trips: "All of these cities were the same to me. There was no time to go sight-seeing or to find out anything about the cities. Just get off the train, go to the ballpark, play the game, get back on the train and head for the next city" (*Favorite Summer*, p. 31).

Yogi Berra, though, "enjoyed the trains, as slow-moving as they could be. Our team had our own Pullman sleeper and private dining car. We played cards, ate together, talked baseball, read the papers . . . . Those train rides . . . were great for team togetherness. To me, baseball was meant for trains. It added to the intimacy of the game. We talked more about it . . . . When we finally started taking airplanes a few years later, you'd take a nap and you were there. It wasn't the same" (*Ten Rings*, p. 142).

Yogi wasn't the only player who enjoyed the trains. Hank Bauer said, "We were close-knit. It helped a lot that we traveled by train. We played cards together and we talked baseball together" (in *Men of Autumn*, p. 69). First baseman Joe Collins recalled a time when Casey Stengel sent him and several other players to St. Louis by plane ahead of the rest of the team. "I ended up sorry I missed the train ride. I heard they had a hell of a time" (in *Men of Autumn*, p. 169). Billy Martin regretted the demise of the trains: "Now you get on a plane and land in a city, and everyone rents his own car, and everyone goes off in a different direction" (*Number 1*, p. 120).

Baseball teams weren't the only ones who traveled by train in 1956. Without jets, airlines were not yet the accepted mode of transportation for long trips. As late as August 23, 1956, the Greenville *News* could report that "more high-speed railway trains are operated in the United States than in any other country in the world."

Railroads and airlines had roughly equal numbers of passengers in 1955, but the balance would shift to the airlines after that. The interstate highway system was barely off the drawing boards in 1956, so cars and buses took forever to reach their destinations. Few had air conditioning. An article in the *Saturday Evening Post* (Oct. 20) described plans for the new interstate highways and held out hope that one

Sports Illustrated *likened the Yankees in their train accommodations to "a caravan of rich gypsies" (Oct. 1, 1956).*

day we could travel "Coast to Coast Without a Stoplight."

The sad state of American railroading was the theme of an article entitled "So You Don't Ride the Trains Any More?" in the *Saturday Evening Post* on Dec. 22, 1956. The gist of it was this statement: ". . . the railroads today are the stepchildren of the transportation business, forced to struggle along under an antiquated set of regulations that give all the breaks to their competitors." The New York Central Railroad ran an ad which appeared in the Cincinnati *Enquirer* on Oct. 2. It showed Soviet leader Georgi Malenkov smiling over the caption, "Thank you, America, for what you're doing to your railroads!" Another article in the *Saturday Evening Post* (Jan. 21, 1956) lauded St. Louis' Union Station as the "American traveler's version of the Taj Mahal," where thirteen rail lines converged. The station's architectural splendor can still be appreciated today, but it's been restored as a shopping mall, as has the beautiful station in Indianapolis.

Train travel would still be comfortable and affordable for a few more years. It was an occasion for which one dressed. Manners maven Emily Post was asked, "Would it be proper when taking a long train trip for a woman to wear slacks while traveling, instead of a dress? I think they are much more comfortable and certainly do not muss as easily as a dress, but are they in good taste?" Mrs. Post replied, "I am sorry but even in these modern times I cannot approve of slacks on the train" (Greenville *News*, Aug. 12, 1956).

My mother, brother, and I made one trip from Cincinnati to South Carolina by train. My only memory is that it was long and boring. We rode overnight and sleeping upright did not come easy to me. We took the train so we could have most of Christmas break in Laurens. My father drove down for the last couple of days and we rode back with him, on roads so icy I vividly remember being scared all the way.

Train travel was still feasible for major league baseball teams because the sport was played primarily in New England and the upper Midwest. A popular definition of the World Series from that time was "Competition to determine what team of baseball players in the upper right-hand corner of the U. S. A., North America, Western Hemisphere, the world, wins the most games." On April 23 the *New York Times* described the Detroit Tigers' arrival as an "invasion" from "the West." In the American League the Philadelphia Athletics had moved to Kansas City in 1954, but the St. Louis Browns had balanced that by migrating to Baltimore in the same year. Look at a map and you'll see almost a straight line from Boston to New York, and on to Cleveland, Detroit, and Chicago. Washington and Baltimore are only a short train ride south from New York and Boston.

The Yankee brass weren't alone in their fear of planes. An article in the Greenville News *on May 24, 1956, reported the Hillsborough County (FL) Aviation Authority had trouble finding someone to send to a meeting in Miami since "three of its members won't ride in airplanes."*

In the National League the Boston Braves had moved to Milwaukee in 1953, but the teams in the senior circuit were already traveling to Chicago and St. Louis anyway. With two teams in New York, one in Philadelphia, another in Pittsburgh, and one in Cincinnati, the National League's travel route was more circuitous but did not cross the Ohio River and did not get far enough across the Mississippi to lose sight of that river.

Going by plane was not unheard of. The *New York Times* reported that, on April 24, the Giants flew home from Pittsburgh after a game with the Pirates was postponed because of cold weather. Mickey Mantle and Yogi Berra say the Yankees traveled by train because the people who made their travel arrangements were afraid to fly (*Favorite*

Summer, p. 39; *Ten Rings*, p. 142). Sportscaster Mel Allen doubted the feasibility of major league ball on the west coast because "at the present time, lots of players don't like to fly" (*Sports Illustrated*, Mar. 12, 1956). With the move of the Dodgers and Giants to California in 1958 and the addition of expansion teams on the west coast in 1961, all major league teams had to take to the air.

Train travel fit in with the slower pace of baseball in the 1950s. The season did not have to begin on April 1 because it was only 154 games long and did not have two weeks of playoffs crammed in between the end of the schedule and the World Series. They also played doubleheaders, as many as ten per year (including Memorial Day, July 4th, Labor Day), reducing the length of the season by at least another week. The season could start in mid-April and the World Series could still be played in early October, the way God intended.

> *"What could be better than a Fourth of July doublehaeder in Kansas City? Anything up to and including a kick in the ass."*
>
> Jim Bouton,
> Ball Four, *p. 242*

The Ol' Perfesser

One cannot write about the Yankees in the 1950s without saying something about Charles Dillon Stengel, whose life was as imperfect as that of any of his players. His hiring in 1949 was a surprise to New York fans. He had been a better than average player with the Giants, Dodgers, Braves, and other teams, appearing in three World Series in the 1920s. As a manager, though, he enjoyed little success until he came to the Yankees. When he managed the Boston Braves he was so unpopular that a cab-driver who accidentally hit him was castigated for not finishing the job. Stengel was regarded as something of a clown, but he took the Yankees to five straight World Series titles, a record that still stands. There was, as *Sports Illustrated* said, "nobody remotely like him in the game" (Oct. 1, 1956).

His critics said anyone could win with the talent Stengel had on his teams, but the 1953 team was quite different from the '49 team, and they still won. The Dodgers of that era had as much talent as the Yankees, but managed to win only one World Series.

> *Twelve players were part of all five of Stengel's championship teams from 1949-1953: Allie Reynolds, Vic Raschi, Eddie Lopat, Yogi Berra, Charlie Silvera, Bobby Brown, Jerry Coleman, Johnny Mize, Joe Collins, Gene Woodling, Hank Bauer, and Phil Rizzuto. Only Bauer, Berra, and Collins were still with the Yankees for the perfect game.*

Stengel seemed to have a knack for knowing which player to put where, but he had his faults as a manager. He exerted no influence on his players' off-the-field behavior, even when it affected their performance on the field. (By his own admission Mickey Mantle sometimes played when he was so hung-over he could barely see the ball.) Stengel favored some players over others, and he cultivated the sports writers so they would back him in disputes with management or players.

Some of Stengel's critics said he actually had little skill in developing young ballplayers or establishing rapport with his teams. He inherited a strong veteran team in 1949 and benefitted from the Yankees' excellent farm system. Each year they brought up strong players to replace aging veterans, and George Weiss made a number of strategic trades. As Jackie Robinson said, "They voted Casey the greatest living manager. That's a lot of bull – a joke. The only thing a manager has to do is relate to the players. Who did Casey ever relate to? Nobody but himself."

Stengel's biggest weaknesses might have been his handling of Mickey Mantle and the way he used his pitchers, especially Whitey Ford. He simply loaded Mantle's brawny young shoulders with such great expectations it would have taken a superman to live up to them. Although Mantle joined the Yankees in 1951, it was 1956 before he felt confident in himself and began to realize his potential. Some writers have suggested the childless Stengel wanted Mantle to be his baseball legacy. Mantle spent his childhood trying to live up to his father's expectations, then much of his baseball career trying to be what Stengel wanted him to be.

As for his pitchers, Stengel liked to use them in a five-day, rather than a four-day, rotation or start them in strategic spots. He saved Ford to pitch against the league's top teams or in ballparks which put right-handed batters at a disadvantage. For instance, Ford rarely pitched in Fenway Park, with its Green Monster in left field just waiting for right-handed hitters to unload. As a result, he never won 20 games under Stengel. Under Stengel's successor, Ralph Houk, he had two 20-game seasons, when he was already developing arm problems.

What cost Stengel his job was his age and his handling of the 1960 World Series against Pittsburgh. For reasons he never explained, he did not start Ford in Game 1. Standard procedure in the Series is for a manager to start his strongest pitcher in the first game so he can come back in Game 4 and Game 7, if necessary. That's what Stengel did in the '56 Series, even though it meant the lefty Ford had to pitch in Ebbets Field, a small park that favored right-handed batters. In 1960 Ford got to pitch only two games of the Series. He shut Pittsburgh out in both, but the Pirates won the Series in seven games. Any Yankee who has written about that Series has come to the same conclusion Mantle did: "I believe the whole Series revolved around [Stengel's] decision" (*The Mick*, p. 198). Ford himself felt "the way I was pitching, I know I would have beaten them three times and we would have been world champs again" (*Slick*, p. 150).

A few days after the Series Stengel was fired, after winning ten pennants and seven World Series in twelve years. He said he would "never make the mistake of turning seventy again." Two years later he became manager of the expansion New York Mets. He retired after three years and died in 1975. During his last years he had to deal with his wife's Alzheimer's.

Who's on First?

Casey Stengel was an early proponent of the platoon system. He tried to get as many left-handed hitters as possible in the line-up against a right-handed pitcher and as many right-handers as possible against a southpaw. Early in the '56 season a *Sports Illustrated* photo essay showed Mantle batting left-handed and right-handed on facing pages, a one-man platoon. If Stengel could have had a whole team of switch-hitters like Mantle, he would have been set, but he needed two strong starting players for each position, not just a starter and a sub. Amazingly, he had that throughout his tenure with the Yankees. Most of the Yankees in the dugout would have been starting players on any other team. In the immortal words of Yogi Berra, "we always had deep depth" (*Ten Rings*, p. 99).

But injuries and uncertainty about whom to start left Stengel facing some hard choices in the spring of 1956. On April 12 the *New York Times* summed up his dilemma: "Seldom has a manager been more in the dark, with the opening of a pennant race a few days away, than Casey Stengel, the New Yorkers' skipper. Certain it is that since he took charge of the Bombers in 1949 Stengel has not had his plans so unsettled as today's at so late a date."

Youngsters Jerry Lumpe and Tony Kubek might figure in his plans, Stengel said. Because of an overabundance of infielders and injuries to outfielders, Kubek, a shortstop, had played left field during spring training and had made some outstanding plays.

Moving players to different positions was something the Yankees did often, sometimes to take advantage of a strength, sometimes to squeeze an extra year or two out of an aging player. Mickey Mantle came to the major leagues as a shortstop with an erratic cannon for an arm. Yogi Berra was supposed to be an outfielder. The experiment didn't always work, though. Stengel put Joe DiMaggio at first base for one game late in his career. DiMaggio told Stengel never to do that to him again.

Stengel had not reached a decision about his opening day pitcher for 1956, either. Bob Turley, Whitey Ford, Don Larsen, Johnny Kucks, and Tom Sturdivant were listed as starters, with Mickey McDermott, Tommy Byrne, Rip Coleman, Bob Grim, and Tom Morgan in the bullpen. But starters and relievers were not the distinct species they've evolved into today. Over the course of the season all of the pitchers would start games and appear in relief.

Whitey Ford was "the crafty lefthander" or "the stylish portsider." The veteran Byrne, often described as "well seasoned," had a habit of talking to opposing batters or to catcher Yogi Berra about what pitch he was going to throw. Turley had an up-and-down spring, pitching brilliantly at times, then turning into a batting practice pitcher. Known as "Bullet Bob" for his speed, he admitted in an article in *Look* (May 29, 1956) that his control had plagued him throughout his big-league career. He would overcome the problem enough to win the Cy Young Award in 1958.

Larsen had "done some fine pitching" in Stengel's view, but early on the morning of April 3 the tall right-hander smashed his car into a telephone pole. The press, more discreet in those days, did not even hint at inebriation. But everyone knew Larsen's reputation. Pitcher Ryne Duren, who played with Larsen in Baltimore and New York, recalled that in 1954 he broke his hand. Instead of giving up on the season and going home, Duren says, "I just hung around for three weeks and drank with Don Larsen" (in *Sweet Seasons*, p. 51). In this case Stengel suggested Larsen might have gone out early to mail a letter. His punishment was to make Larsen run "for about an hour and a half."

Despite their mediocre spring – they finished with an 18-14 record – and the uncertainties about their opening day line-up, the Yankees were picked to finish first in the American League, as were the Dodgers in the National League. Brooklyn had won their title in 1955 by 13 games and, with their line-up pretty much intact, had added a promising rookie pitcher named Don Drysdale. Most sportswriters figured the season would be merely a long prelude to another Subway Series, just as the political season seemed headed toward a rematch between incumbent president Dwight Eisenhower, the nation's comfortable grandfather figure, and challenger Adlai Stevenson.

CHAPTER 11

Making the Team

"People ask me what I do in winter when there's no baseball," Rogers Hornsby said. "I'll tell you what I do. I stare out the window and wait for spring."

Baseball preoccupied me year-round, too. When the weather prevented me from playing it, I looked at my baseball cards and thought about playing it. During school, when my mind wandered, I drew pictures of ballplayers, and there was always one in pinstripes, wearing Mantle's number 7 on his back. My fifth-grade teacher, Mrs. Smith, confiscated one of my drawings done during social studies but hung it up as an example of good art work.

One day in May of '56, at lunch, my friend Dan said, "Did y'all see in the paper this morning? They're holding try-outs for youth league teams on Saturday. My folks said I can go."

Dan would turn 11 in early June. He had always been hefty and was growing into a big kid. Because he was so slow he played catcher. I had run into him on a play at the plate and bounced off of him.

"Let's all go," Ted said. "I'll bet we could all make it."

"Yeah," Johnny chimed in. "We're all pretty good players."

I liked the idea, too. It would be fun to play with uniforms on a real field, with real bases and foul lines we could actually see.

"Maybe I'll get to wear number 7," I said.

But first I had to get to the try-outs. My dad had the engine of his '49 Cadillac torn apart. My mother said she had to go to Laurens on Saturday in our other car. That posed a dilemma for me: baseball try-outs or a trip to Ma-Ma's and Pa-Pa's.

"I'll see if I can ride with one of the other guys," I was surprised to hear myself say.

That wouldn't be as easy as it sounded. Before we moved into our current house, we lived within three blocks of Dan, Ted, and Johnny, on the southeastern edge of the school district. Now we were on the northwestern edge, several miles away. Two more blocks north and I would have been going to a different school. Those guys could still walk home from school, like I used to do with them, and they could play together after school. They came to my house for my tenth birthday – soon after we moved – but I rarely saw them any more outside of school. When they talked about things back in the old neighborhood, all I could do was listen.

Looking back, it was as though I was being eased into the move to Ohio and the separation from family and friends that would be sprung on me later that summer. At the time all I knew was that I missed being part of my old "gang."

> *"Don't view*
> *me with a critic's eye,*
> *But pass my imperfections by."*
>
> David Everett

We arranged for my mother to drop me off at Ted's house on her way to Laurens. Ted's mom would bring me home after the try-outs.

Saturday morning I woke up nervous. As much as I loved playing ball, I had never played in a situation where an adult was watching and judging me. We just chose sides and played. We argued strikes and balls, fair or foul, but I was my own judge of how well I played.

I hoped the try-outs weren't going to turn out like playing the piano, which I was learning to do. I practiced and enjoyed playing at home, but at my teacher's house, with her sitting in her chair beside the piano, I messed up pieces I could rattle off easily in my living room. When we got in the car that morning I wished I was just going to Laurens with my mom and brother.

"The logic of worldly success rests on a fallacy: the strange error that our perfection depends on the thoughts and opinions and applause of other men."

Thomas Merton

The try-outs were held at our school, with two dads coaching. As each boy arrived, the coaches pinned a number to his back and wrote his name and number and the position he wanted to play on a roster sheet.

"Okay, y'all listen up," one of the coaches finally said. "Each team in the league is allowed to have twenty players. We've got twenty-eight here today, so we'll have to make some cuts when we finish. Everybody play hard and show us what you can do."

We all looked around, wondering who would be the unlucky eight who didn't make the team. In the 1950s, of course, adults had not discovered the importance of avoiding damage to kids' self-esteem. Disappointments and set-backs were regarded as growing experiences. They would toughen you up, prepare you for the hard knocks everyone had to face in life. Vince Staten remembered his baseball coach "putting his hand on my shoulder and walking me off the field. 'Maybe you ought to concentrate on basketball'" (*Foul Pole*, p. 89).

"We're gonna divide y'all into two groups," the other coach said. "Numbers one through fourteen in group one, over here in left field, and fifteen through twenty-eight over in right field. And anybody don't know left field from right field, please go on home now."

Most of us laughed.

The coach clapped his hands. "Okay, pair off, get a ball, and warm up for a few minutes."

Ted and I paired off. I was closest to the big canvas bag holding the balls, so I reached in and pulled one out.

Until that moment, I had never touched a real baseball. Whenever I played at school or at my grandparents' house, we used a rubber ball that looked like a baseball or a "dead" tennis ball, for the

sake of any nearby windows and of any girls who might be playing. Where all those old tennis balls came from, I can't imagine. Nobody I knew played tennis.

How to describe my first caress of a baseball? Even though it was scuffed up, it felt hard and sleek, so different from the flattened nap of those dead tennis balls with the bald spots that I was used to. Instead of a tennis ball's indented seam, it had a raised red seam running infinitely around it.

Writers more eloquent than I have described the sensation of holding a baseball. Roger Angell, in his *New Yorker* essay, "On the Ball," put it this way:

Any baseball is beautiful. No other small package comes as close to the ideal in design and utility. It is a perfect object for a man's hand. Pick it up and it instantly suggests its purpose: it is meant to be thrown a considerable distance – thrown hard and with precision. Its feel and heft are the beginning of the sport's critical dimensions; if it were a fraction of an inch larger or smaller, a few centigrams heavier or lighter, the game of baseball would be utterly different. Hold a baseball in your hand . . . . hold it across the seam or the other way, with the seam just to the side of your middle finger. Speculation stirs. You want to get outdoors and throw this spare and sensual object to somebody or, at the very least, watch somebody else throw it. The game has begun.

Pitcher Dave Dravecky had a similar reaction in his book *Comeback* (p. 12):

All you have to do is pick up a baseball. It begs to you: Throw me. If you took a year to design an object to hurl, you'd end up with that little spheroid: small enough to nestle in your fingers but big enough to have some heft, lighter than a rock but heavier than a hunk of wood. Its even, neat stitching, laced into the leather's slippery white surface, gives your fingers a purchase. A baseball was made to throw. It's almost irresistible.

Men aren't the only ones fascinated by the baseball. Annie Dillard, in *An American Childhood* (p. 100), found a baseball so much more satisfying than the softballs girls were expected to play with:

A baseball weighted your hand just so, and fit it. Its red stitches, its good leather and hardness, like skin over bone, seemed to call forth a skill both easy and precise. On the catch – the grounder, the fly, the line drive – you could snag a baseball in your mitt, where it stayed, snap, like a mouse locked in its trap, not like some pumpkin of a softball you merely halted, with a terrible sound like a splat. You could curl your fingers around a baseball, and throw it in a straight line. When you hit it with a bat it cracked – and your heart cracked, too, at the sound.

Poet Robert Frost also "despise[d]" softballs (*Sports Illustrated*, July 23, 1956).

As we warmed up, the coach on our side of the field walked along behind us. I could see he was making notes on his roster sheet. When he passed me I glanced to see if he was writing anything down. What was he thinking about me?

At that moment I committed baseball's unpardonable sin: I took my eye off the ball. Ted made a perfectly good throw, but I missed it because I wasn't concentrating. The ball nicked the top of my glove and I had to go chasing after it. When I picked it up I could see the coach writing something. I needed to redeem myself, so I threw the ball back to Ted as hard as I could. It sailed over his head and he had to chase it. The coach wrote something else down.

Next we played a scrimmage game. Each boy got to play the position he was trying out for. Once I took my place in the outfield, it didn't feel so different from a game of Dollar-ball at my grandparents'. I made a running catch of a fly ball and fielded a base hit cleanly.

Finally my turn came to bat. The pitcher was a kid who had already started his growth spurt. He looked huge and he threw hard. Dan was catching, doing the chatter he always kept up behind the plate. "Come on, bud. Put it in here, bud."

I took the first pitch because I had no idea it would be coming in so fast. (According to *Sports*

Illustrated, Little League pitchers could throw as fast as 65 miles an hour [Sept. 3, 1956].) The next one I swung at but missed, badly. I could see the third pitch was coming inside. It just kept tailing in toward me. Instinct told me this ball was going to hurt a lot more than getting hit by a tennis ball or rubber ball. As Roger Kahn says, "If the tennis ball struck you, it stung briefly, but no one was afraid of a tennis ball. That was all the difference. Soft dream and hard reality. Once hit by a real baseball, a boy (or man) crumpled" (*Boys*, p. 21).

Rereading the sports pages of the News, *I was fascinated to see how many perfect games and no-hitters were pitched at various levels of youth baseball in Greenville during the summer of '56. There must have been lots of big kids pitching and other kids like me who just wanted to get out of the way.*

Everything happened so fast that, by the time I knew I needed to get out of the way, I couldn't. The ball caught me in the ribs, on the right side. Dropping the bat, I spun around and went down on one knee.

"Shake it off!" the coach yelled. "Take your base."

"Are you okay?" Dan asked me through his catcher's mask.

"Let's go, Bell!" the coach yelled. "Next batter."

As I stood up, the other coach came out and told me to lift my shirt. A small dark spot was already forming on my side. When he touched it, pain shot through my rib. "It didn't break the skin," he said. "I think you'll be okay. Hustle on down to first."

I trotted down to first base. When I tried to take a deep breath, I felt a sharp pain where the ball had hit me.

Toward the end of the morning some of us who hadn't done well in our first at-bat got another chance. As the first pitch came toward me, I experienced what Leonard Koppett put into words:

> Fear is the fundamental factor in hitting, and hitting the ball with the bat is the fundamental act of baseball.
>
> The fear is simple and instinctive. If a baseball, thrown hard, hits any part of your body, it hurts. If it hits certain vulnerable areas, like elbows, wrist or face, it can cause broken bones and other serious injuries. If it hits a particular area of an unprotected head, it can kill.
>
> A thrown baseball, in short, is a missile, and an approaching missile generates a reflexive action: Get out of the way.
>
> This fact – and it is an unyielding fact that the reflex always exists in all humans – is the starting point for the game of baseball, and yet it is the fact least often mentioned by those who write about baseball.

> *(The Thinking Fan's Guide to Baseball, p. 3)*

Dodger pitcher Don Drysdale was more succinct: "The pitcher has to find out if the hitter is timid. And if the hitter is timid, he has to remind the hitter he's timid." Lots of hitters became timid when Drysdale took the mound, with his sneer and his blazing sidearm fastball.

I wasn't facing Drysdale, but I was timid and this time I was backing out of the batter's box as I swung, so I hit a soft grounder to third. Since every breath caused me pain, I couldn't run fast enough to beat the throw to first. I was out by three steps.

Roger Kahn experienced the same fear standing in the batter's box while Dodger pitcher Clem Labine warmed up: "Through a resolute act of will I held my ground. The impulse was not simply to duck, but to throw away the bat and throw my body to the thick-bladed Florida grass. 'Bailing out,' ball players call this. Resisting was the totality of my strength. I could no more have swung, let alone hit, one of Labine's pitches than run a three-minute mile" (*Boys*, p. 55).

The coaches told us to get a drink of water and sit down in the outfield while they decided who would make the team. They huddled in a little shed behind home plate where the scorekeeper sat during games. We could see them shaking their heads and crossing out names. Then they taped the roster sheets to the posts holding up the screen behind home plate.

"Okay, kids," the bossier coach said, "numbers one through fourteen over here, fifteen through twenty-eight over there. If your name is crossed out, I'm afraid you didn't make it. Like I said, we can only have twenty players on the team."

"Thank you all for coming out," the other coach said. "Those of you who made it, be here at four o'clock on Tuesday for our first practice."

Ted, Dan, Johnny and I headed for the list posted on the first base side of the screen. I didn't hurry because my side hurt when I ran and because I already had a bad feeling about what I would see when I got there.

And I was right. The three of them had made the team. My name was scratched out. Under the ink marks I could read a couple of the coaches' comments: "Wild throw. Slow runner. Afraid of the ball."

The ride home was so quiet we might as well have been in a hearse. I sat in the back by the door with Dan and Johnny. My glove, which I usually treated with the respect reserved for a family heirloom, lay on the floor under my feet.

My friends were true enough friends not to talk about the fun they were going to have playing on a real team that summer, and there was nothing else to talk about. I knew I would see very little of them from now on. And I didn't want to. While they were playing ball, I, the Great Pretender, would be throwing rocks at clumps of dirt in my yard, imagining I was Mickey Mantle throwing out runners at second base.

Or maybe I would just forget about all this stupid baseball stuff.

When I got out of the car my dad was up to his elbows in grease in the driveway. He had tried to interest me in fixing cars – he even bought me a toolbox, which I still use – but I couldn't stand being that dirty. "How did it go?" he asked.

"I'm not going to play. I didn't like the coach."

"Well, it's up to you." He took a rag to a piston or a carburetor.

I went in the house and got myself a Coke – one of the 6-ounce bottles that cost a nickel – and a couple of Oreos. Only when I put my glove down on the kitchen table did I realize I still had a baseball tucked in it.

Beanballs and batting helmets: an important digression

Since baseball began, pitchers have had that "missile" in their hands. If they can't control its trajectory, they can hit, and possibly injure, a batter. If they can control the trajectory, they can throw it close enough to the batter to make him uncomfortable about getting a firm toehold in the batter's box. As Leonard Koppett said, and as I learned in that try-out, the ball hurts when it hits you and the batter's fear of being hurt is what gives the pitcher his edge. (It took almost two weeks for my cracked rib to stop hurting.) Pitchers always argue that they have to throw inside, close to the batter, to keep him from "digging in."

Until the mid-1950s batters had no protection against a hard-thrown ball. Some pitchers, like Sal "the Barber" Maglie, developed reputations as "head-hunters," a reputation which Maglie denied. "I never threw intentionally at any batter to hit him," he claimed. "It's easy to hit a batter if you want to. I could say I never knocked anybody down but why say that? Let's say that I never tried to hit a batter intentionally" (Greenville *News*, May 20, 1956). In his no-hitter in September of 1956 Maglie did hit one batter, but on the foot.

Beanings – both intentional and accidental – were common well into the 1950s. If a player on one team was hit, his manager usually ordered his pitcher to hit someone on the opposing team in retaliation. In the early years of the twentieth century umpires did not remove dirty or scuffed balls from games. Nor was any effort made to provide a solid dark background for hitters. They often found it difficult to see a discolored brownish ball, coming out of a blur of the crowds' shirts and waving arms – or advertising signs – in time to get out of the way. That problem may have been a contributing factor in an incident that led to the only fatal injury of a major league ballplayer during a game.

The most successful pitchers won't hesitate to use a "brushback" pitch, sometimes in retaliation against a batter who has gotten an extra-base hit. In a spring training game in 2006 Roger Clemens' son hit a home run off his father in his first at-bat. When young Clemens came up the next time, his father, known for good reason as "the Rocket," threw a fastball right under his son's chin.

On August 16, 1920, pitcher Carl Mays of the Yankees beaned Cleveland's popular shortstop, Ray Chapman. Chapman got up and took a few steps before collapsing. He was carried to a hospital where he died the next day (Sowell, *The Pitch*). From that time umpires have been conscientious about keeping a bright white ball in play.

On May 25, 1937, catcher Mickey Cochrane's career ended when a pitch hit him above the right eye and broke his skull in three places. On June 23, 1956, Don Zimmer was seriously injured when a pitch hit him under the eye. Zimmer had barely survived a beaning three years earlier in the minor leagues (*Zim*, pp. 9-10). That first beaning prompted the Dodgers to order all players in their organization to wear protective liners in their caps.

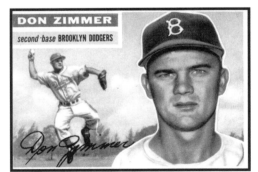

As early as 1941 a type of plastic helmet had been used by the New York Giants, but it did not catch on. Credit for giving players some real protection from the beanball goes to Branch Rickey, the man who brought Jackie Robinson to the Dodgers. Rickey was an innovator in many ways. His teams were the first to use batting cages and pitching machines. When he moved to the Pittsburgh Pirates, Rickey introduced the team to protective batting helmets.

Although he had his players' interests at heart, Rickey was not a pure altruist. He owned stock in a company called American Baseball Cap Inc. He asked an employee, Charlie Muse, to develop a helmet that would be light and comfortable and yet provide protection for a hitter's head above the ears.

In an interview in 1989 Muse recalled, "The players laughed at the first helmets, called them miner's helmets. They said the only players who would wear them were sissies." Frankie Frisch, of the St. Louis Cardinals' "Gashouse Gang" from the 1930s, sneered, "If we must have helmets, how about the one with a spike on the top – such as Kaiser Wilhelm's tough soldiers wore in World War I?"

Beginning in 1953 Rickey required Pirates' players to wear the helmets at bat and in the field. Other teams resisted the innovation, citing the discomfort. Some players feared that, if pitchers didn't have to worry as much about seriously injuring a batter, they would feel freer to throw at his head. Managers might also change their strategy. Casey Stengel said, "If we had them when I was playing, [manager] John McGraw would have insisted that we go up to the plate and get hit on the head."

The helmets didn't help the Pirates, perennial cellar-dwellers throughout the early '50s. Someone asked catcher Clyde McCullough – the last major leaguer to catch without a chest protector – if the helmets would be better with foam rubber in them. McCullough replied, "They would be better if there were ballplayers in them."

An incident that occurred in 1954 turned the tide in favor of the helmets. On July 31 Joe Adcock of the Milwaukee Braves hit four homers and a double in a game against the Dodgers in Brooklyn. The next day Dodger pitcher Clem Labine threw at Adcock's head every time he came to bat, finally beaning him. Adcock had started wearing a batting helmet that year. Labine's pitch shattered the helmet and left Adcock with a concussion. After the game Labine told Adcock he was under orders from his manager, Walter Alston, to throw at him.

Walter Alston's major league playing career consisted of a couple of innings in the field late in a game in 1936. He batted once and struck out.

When other players realized how much more seriously Adcock would have been hurt without the helmet, they became more receptive to the idea of wearing one. In 1956 the National League required all batters to wear a helmet. The American League left it optional that year but then instituted the requirement, with a liner that fit inside a standard cap as an option. Mickey Mantle "chose not to wear the helmet. I felt uncomfortable with it on. It bothered me, made me feel like a sissy" (*Favorite Summer*, p. 34).

In June of 1956 Giants' third baseman Henry Thompson was beaned and had a concussion. As a National Leaguer he was wearing a helmet. Yankees' General Manager George Weiss hoped Mantle and others would take a lesson from Thompson's beaning. Orioles' manager Paul Richards said "any player who doesn't wear a helmet is crazy" (*Sports Illustrated*, June 18).

In 1983 all major league rookies were required to use a helmet with an ear flap over the side of the face nearest the pitcher, a feature that is now standard for all players.

CHAPTER
12

"Ninety feet between home plate and first base may be the closest man has ever come to perfection."

Red Smith

Play Ball!

When the Yankees opened their season in Washington, President Eisenhower threw out the first ball. In those days players scrambled like bridesmaids after a bouquet for balls thrown out by celebrities. Guys making in the low five figures would be more likely to do that, I suppose, than guys making in the high seven figures. Gil McDougald got this ball and asked Eisenhower to sign it. The president autographed it to "Joe McDougald." McDougald's teammates never let him hear the end of it, but he kept the ball and passed it on to his children.

No one who knew baseball thought the Senators would be competitive, in 1956 or in any other year. For the Yankees the three-game series was merely an extension of spring training. Casey Stengel saved Whitey Ford for the opener that really counted, the first game of the series with the Red Sox which the Yanks would play when they reached New York.

The Senators played down to expectations on opening day. Mantle crushed two mammoth home runs, Yogi Berra added one, and Don Larsen pitched effectively enough – in spite of giving up three home runs – to win 10-4. The Yanks won the second game, 9-5, but lost the third 7-3.

If I may digress for a moment – and of course I may; it's my book – looking back at reports of games in the early days of the '56 season has made me aware of some evidence for global warning. The *New York Times* reported fewer than 3,000 fans "braved the chilly weather" in Washington on April 20 for that third game between the Yanks and Senators. In Philadelphia on that day fans lit bonfires in the stands to keep warm during a game. In New York itself it felt like "somebody had failed to shut the refrigerator door." Rain made the situation there worse. Reports of games into early May made frequent reference to the cold, even to snow flurries. Europe had the same experience. The Rhine and Danube Rivers froze for the first time in a century, and the French Riviera had snow for the first time in 75 years. *Look* ran an article on "Our Crazy Weather," forecasting short-term uncertainty and long-term changes.

Returning to Yankee Stadium, the Bronx Bombers took the first game against Boston, 7-1, as Whitey Ford pitched a five-hitter and Mantle hit a three-run homer and drove in another run with a drag bunt single before leaving the game with another hamstring injury. The headline in my paper read "Mantle Drives in 4 Runs, Injured." The article said he "aggravated a leg injury" on the bunt, but stayed in the game for one more at bat, when he hit the homer. I cringed when I saw he was expected to be out for five days.

But Mantle was back the next day with another home run as the Yanks took an 8-0 lead, lost it, and came back to win 14-10. In the third game of the series Don Larsen hit a grand slam but couldn't hold the lead and ended up with no decision as the Yanks won 13-6. Over his career Larsen hit 14 homers, was sometimes used as a pinch-hitter, and had a pattern of not being able to hold big leads. In Game 2 of the '56 World Series his teammates would give him a 6-0 lead, but he would not last through the second inning.

On April 24 the Yanks beat Washington in front of "a chilled gathering of 4,377 baseball fans" in Yankee Stadium. Games in Pittsburgh, Philadelphia, and Chicago were postponed that day because of cold weather. Next the Yanks and Orioles split a pair of games in Baltimore as Whitey Ford won his second game. The Bombers lost the second game largely due to errors by their infielders and – horror of horrors! – fell into second place behind the White Sox. Yankee-haters would not waste any tears on them, though. As Bob Feller said, "Sympathy is something that shouldn't be bestowed on the Yankees. Apparently it angers them."

On April 27 the Yanks opened a series in Boston, beating the Red Sox 5-2 behind Larsen, who had a double and a single to go with his strong pitching performance. In the second game Mantle hit what appeared to be a home run. Newspaper accounts say the ball landed several rows deep in the centerfield seats but bounced back onto the field. The closest umpire, however, ruled it was not a home run and Mantle, who had kept running, ended up on third with a triple.

This might be a good place to point out that, although baseball prides itself on its statistics, some of those numbers aren't as firmly established as one might think. For players in the pre-WWII period, records have been compiled by poring over box scores in newspapers. But that assumes the absolute accuracy of those reports. We may not know *exactly* how many hits Ty Cobb had. And when Babe Ruth was clouting more home runs than some teams hit in a season, the rules stated that a ball which hit the ground and bounced into the stands was a home run. Today that's a ground rule double. The question of how many such bouncing homers Ruth might have hit, especially in 1927, occasionally comes up. The confident answer for his record-setting year is, None.

It would be tedious to recap each game of the Yankees' season. Suffice it to say that by May 10 they had a 14-7 record and were in first place, where they would stay for the rest of the season. Mantle already had 10 homers and people were starting to compare him to the pace Babe Ruth set when he hit 60 home runs. That was the record everyone – not just an Everykid in Greenville, South Carolina – would be watching over the course of the summer.

The Yankees cruised for the rest of the season, with their lead growing to eight or ten games at times. Mantle, Bauer, and McDougald had the best seasons of their careers. Whitey Ford emerged as the ace of the pitching staff with 19 wins. Don Larsen started strong, then slumped. At mid-season *Sports Illustrated* listed him as one of the Yankees who had disappointed Casey Stengel. But Larsen rebounded with several victories at the end of the season and finished 11-5, the best record of his career. Toward the end of the season he began using a no-windup delivery, regardless of whether anyone was on base.

The origin of the no-windup delivery is obscure. Some sources say he started it because he thought opposing base coaches were able to tell what pitch he was going to throw. In the Cincinnati *Enquirer* (Oct. 5, 1956) he was quoted as saying it just occurred to him one day to do it because "all batting is in rhythm. So is pitching. So it's up to a pitcher to upset a batter's rhythm. When you don't windup, the hitters have to be ready faster." Even as great a hitter as Ted Williams admitted Larsen's unorthodox delivery threw his timing off.

An occasional slump allowed the rest of the league to draw closer to the Yankees now and then. By July 23, though, *Sports Illustrated* conceded the American League pennant to them.

Some critics groused that the Yankees played in a weak league. If they were in the National League, the argument ran, they would be just one more team, and possibly not even the best (*Sports Illustrated*, June 11, 1956). Milwaukee and Cincinnati were hitting more homers than the Yankees, and the Braves seemed to have better pitching. That was one reason some pundits were predicting by mid-summer that whoever won the National League pennant would win the World Series.

Where the action was

The National League race generated more excitement throughout the summer. The St. Louis Cardinals were picked by some as the team to beat. Most prognosticators, though, agreed with the *New York Times* and *Sports Illustrated* that Brooklyn would repeat as league champs. But the Dodgers were slow getting out of the gate.

The Dodgers' biggest problem in 1956 was age. As one newspaper article put it, "The Brooks lead the league in gray hairs" (Greenville *News*, Feb. 16, 1956). The Cincinnati *Enquirer* got in its digs toward the end of the season in an article headlined "Man With The Scythe Chasing Dodgers" (Sept. 7). To that writer the Dodgers looked like "seasoned athletes who are too many seasoned." Robinson's official age was 37, although *Sports Illustrated* thought he was at least two years older (July 2, 1956). Reese was 36, Campanella 34, Hodges 32. Whereas the Dodgers had run away from the rest of the league in 1955, winning by 13 games, they did not claw their way into first place in 1956 until the last week of the season.

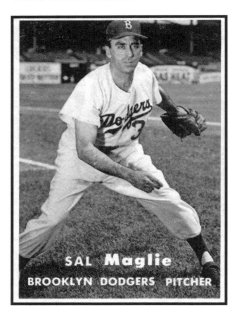

Pitcher Sal Maglie, who would win Game 1 of the World Series and pitch Game 5 against Don Larsen, was the oldest Dodger by age (although he had a 15-month-old child that summer). The Cincinnati *Enquirer* called him "the pasty-faced Barber" and suspected that his "official age of 39 falls short of the true mark by several years" (Oct. 11, 1956).

For ten years Maglie had been with the New York Giants, the Dodgers' bitter rivals. In 1955 the Giants traded him to the Cleveland Indians. In May of 1956 the Dodgers surprised everyone by getting Maglie from the Indians. Maglie had a reputation for being particularly aggressive when pitching against the Dodgers. That's a nice way of saying he was suspected of throwing at them. When he joined the team he was asked if he really "hated" them. "I hated anybody that was the best in any league I ever was in," he said. "In Cleveland, I hated the Yankees. Now who'll I hate? It kind of looks like St. Louis" (Greenville *News*, May 20, 1956).

One reason the Dodgers had been able to run away from the rest of the league in 1955 was their phenomenal start, winning 22 of their first 26 games. Another was that the Chicago Cubs rose up off the doormat that year and knocked off several clubs which might have challenged the Dodgers. In 1956 normalcy returned. The Dodgers got off to a mediocre start and other teams fattened their records in Wrigley Field. The Pittsburgh Pirates flirted briefly with respectability but went from fifth to first and back to fifth in less than two weeks. Dale Long of the Pirates electrified the country by hitting home runs in eight consecutive games in May, the first time that had ever been done.

Two teams in particular seemed ready to shift the balance of power in the league "out west." Milwaukee and Cincinnati both had hitters capable of turning a ball game around with one swing. Eddie Mathews, Hank Aaron, and Joe Adcock provided the muscle for the Braves, while Wally Post,

Gus Bell, rookie Frank Robinson, and Ted Kluszewski rattled the fences of little Crosley Field in Cincinnati. Kluszewski had such large shoulders and biceps that he cut the sleeves off his uniforms for comfort. Post, Bell, and Kluszewski made the cover of *Sports Illustrated* on July 16. When I found out I was moving to Cincinnati, I had to go back and reread that issue. I was surprised to be reminded that, from 1954-56, "Klu" hit more home runs than anyone else in the major leagues.

The Braves also got superb pitching from Warren Spahn and Lew Burdette. Burdette was accused of throwing a spitball, a charge he steadfastly denied, even though Whitey Ford said he learned to throw the pitch from Burdette in the last years of his career (*Slick*, p. 192).

The Braves led the league for much of the summer. As late as mid-September they were still three games ahead of Brooklyn and Cincinnati. The Reds could never quite make the final charge. Then the Braves collapsed in a four-game series against St. Louis in the last week of the season and had to watch the Dodgers snatch the pennant on the last day.

"All that money"

The objective of the season, of course, was to get into the World Series. That was where players made extra money, and the Yankees earned it so regularly it wasn't even extra to them. General Manager George Weiss used to tell players who were disappointed in their salaries that they would get World Series money. As Whitey Ford said, "You kind of took it for granted around the Yankees that there was always going to be baseball in October" (*Slick*, p 42). Mickey Mantle recalled a time when he stood in the on-deck circle, watching Phil Rizzuto drive in Joe DiMaggio and "already counting my World Series money" (*The Mick*, p. 77). That World Series money came from ticket sales, not television, so a seven-game Series in a big stadium would mean considerably more money than a four-game sweep in a small park.

It was disillusioning for me that summer to learn how big a role money played in baseball. Toward the end of the season Ed Bailey, Cincinnati's catcher, said, "You're tired but you can't afford to be with all that money at stake" (*Sports Illustrated*, Sept. 17, 1956). "All that money" would turn out to be about $8,700 for each man on the winning team in the 1956 Series. Some of the World Series money went to other teams in each league, as far down as the fourth-place finisher. In late September the St. Louis Cardinals knocked the Milwaukee Braves out of the Series, even though the Cardinals, in fourth place, would have gotten a larger payoff if the Braves, with their larger stadium, had been the National League winners.

Most of the Yankees rooted for National League teams with the biggest ballparks to win their pennant, so more tickets could be sold (*The Mick*, p. 78). Ebbets Field held only 32,000 people, while the Polo Grounds seated 55,000, but the Giants weren't in the race in 1956. Milwaukee's County Stadium would hold over 43,000. Cincinnati's Crosley Field had a capacity of 30,000, but it had character. As Vince Staten recalled, "Yankee Stadium was grand; Wrigley and Fenway historic. But Crosley Field, that was a ballpark" (*Foul Pole*, p. 34). Character didn't mean ticket sales, though. A cartoon in the Cincinnati *Enquirer* during the last hectic week of the '56 season showed a figure labeled "Yanks," with thoughts of "$erie$ Cut" in his head, urging on a running Brave: "Keep sprinting, Injun – I like that extra large cut we'll get outta County Stadium."

CHAPTER 13

Goodbye, Edgewood Avenue

Moving to Cincinnati meant leaving a house my parents had bought the year before, at 101 Edgewood Avenue in Greenville, South Carolina. It was the first house they'd ever owned, their piece of the American dream. My dad also bought his first Cadillac while we lived there. It was a '49, but it was a Cadillac. He took the engine apart and painted each piece a different color as he put it back together so he could spot leaks more easily. Service station attendants – remember them? – would do a double-take when they raised the hood to check the oil – remember "check your oil and water?" Dad had to sell the car when we moved to Cincinnati. As a child of the Depression, Cadillacs and steak – any type of beef, actually – were important symbols to him. A few years before he died, he bought himself an '83 Cadillac. We joked about burying him in it, like a Viking in his longboat.

The house on Edgewood is the first place I can remember, by feel and smell, rather than from photos of myself being there. It had only two bedrooms, so I had to share one with my brother. I drew a line down the middle of the floor because he wouldn't pick up anything and I liked to be able to walk and sit down without all the clutter. (I know, if he were writing this book, I would come off as an anal-retentive prick. Maybe I do anyway.) The house had what seemed at the time like a good-sized back yard, with a brick barbecue pit and a concrete patio.

What the place didn't have was other kids to play ball with or an open field across the street where I could play baseball.

Although we lived in that house only a year and a half, I have more memories of it than of other places we lived for longer times, maybe because, as Annie Dillard said, I was ten and I was "waking up." I remember my mother getting her hand caught in the old ringer-washer she still used. I had to help her turn the rollers backward to release her. And I'll never forget when she got word her beloved brother had been killed in an automobile accident. It's a frightening thing for a 10-year-old to watch his mother collapse on the floor in hysterics.

With no children our ages nearby, my brother and I played together on Edgewood more than we had in the house we'd lived in before. I wish I could say the experience brought us closer together, but the event I remember most vividly is when he shot me with his BB gun. It was no accident. We were shooting at targets and I was giving him some hints to improve his aim. He turned toward me and fired, hitting me in the leg. If he had followed my advice, he would have hit me in the crotch. That wasn't the first time he had inflicted physical injury on me. When I was six and he was three, he threw a metal pail at me, cutting me on the forehead so badly I needed stitches.

My parents took pride in the place on Edgewood and put sweat equity and money into it. While cleaning things out after my father's death, I found a receipt for the furnace they had installed in 1956. It was made in the town in Michigan where I now live (cue the "Twilight Zone" theme). In the spring of 2005 I drove past the house for the first time in over twenty years. Sadly, the neighborhood had deteriorated to the point that our house and most around it were abandoned. The yards were overgrown, the windows and doors of our house broken in. Someone had ripped off much of the vinyl siding which was applied to our house after we lived there.

My parents weren't able to sell the house before we moved to Cincinnati, so they had to rent it. Their inability to sell the house meant they could not buy one in Cincinnati. I, of course, understood nothing

about getting equity out of one house to buy another. All I knew was that we would be moving into an apartment "for a while." We had never lived in an apartment. I didn't know anyone who lived in an apartment. It all felt very unsettling, very imperfect.

The Visiting Scholar

Moving to Cincinnati meant I would have to change schools. And more than once. My dad went to Cincinnati in August to start his job. We wouldn't be moving until he found us a place to live, but we had to be out of our house to make room for the people who were renting it. In mid-September my dad found an apartment. I still have a letter he wrote to me, dated September 13. He says he hopes we will "like the new place to live." He also mentions "the Redlegs aren't doing so hot," so we probably "won't get to see the World Series this year."

"The Redlegs"?

That's what Cincinnati's baseball team called themselves officially in the mid-'50s because "Reds" smacked of Communism (*Sports Illustrated*, July 16, 1956). As noted earlier, even though Senator Joe McCarthy's witch-hunt had run out of steam by 1956, Senator Eastland and others still looked at anything "red" with a jaundiced eye. Sportswriters still referred to the team as the Reds, though.

I knew there was a major league team in Cincinnati, but they weren't in the American League and never made it to the World Series, so I knew little about them. During the summer of '56 my hometown paper carried stories about them because they were in the thick of the National League pennant race all summer. I even cut out one headline and kept it for a while: "Bell Hits Two-Run Homer."

That Bell was outfielder Gus Bell. No relation, of course, and a nickname I liked as little as my own. By looking through my baseball cards I learned his real name was David Russell Bell, Jr. I liked that. It had the same number of syllables as my full name, right down to the Jr. I wondered why he let somebody stick him with "Gus." He threw right-handed and batted left, like me. I appreciated the fact that he was traded to the Redlegs by the Pirates because he spent too much time

"GUS" BELL
outfield CINCINNATI REDLEGS

with his family of five children (*Sports Illustrated*, July 16, 1956). I did get his autograph while I lived in Cincinnati.

I began to root for the Redlegs for two reasons: I hated the Dodgers because they had beaten my beloved Yankees in the 1955 World Series. But, more importantly, I realized that, if Cincinnati won the pennant, the Yankees would come there to play in the World Series. Having not the vaguest notion of how one got tickets to a major league game, let alone a Series game, I imagined walking up to the ball park, buying a ticket – even if it cost more than the 25 cents it cost me to see a movie in South Carolina – and getting to watch Mantle play. Maybe I could even get his autograph.

Go, Redlegs!

Since we would be homeless for a while, we stashed our furniture in the back of Pa-Pa's store and moved in with my grandparents. It felt like going home. I would attend school in Laurens. Everybody there knew my extended family, but I didn't know anybody except my cousins and a few of their friends. After four and a half years in the same school – which would prove to be the longest time I spent in one place during my entire educational experience – I was the "new kid." I would be the new kid in Laurens for a few weeks, and then I would be off to become the new kid in some school in Cincinnati.

When you're shy, have a last name and a nickname that kids make fun of, and are snaggle-toothed as well, being the "new kid" is the equivalent of being sentenced to one of the lower levels of Dante's Inferno with a "Torture Me – Harder!" sign stuck on your back. This wasn't my first experience with "new-kidism," or my last. I started first grade in Greer, South Carolina. In March my family moved and I had to change schools. We always seemed to move during the school year. I was the new kid again in seventh grade, in tenth, and one last time in the eleventh.

How did all these moves affect me? When I was in graduate school, I ran into a girl I had gone to school with. I knew her name and we had a nice chat. As she turned to leave, though, I had to ask, "Where did I go to school with you?"

My parents never explained why we were moving. As a college student I began to suspect – almost hope – my father was having affairs with women at work. Only after I knew him as an adult did I get what I feel was an insight into the moves. My father could never talk about what was bothering him. I believe his work situation would become difficult; he would be unable to talk with his supervisor or co-workers, so all he could do was move. Added to this was the inexorable pressure from my mother to get back closer to Laurens.

Whatever my parents' reasons for all the moves, the main thing I learned from them was how much I hated moving. By 1956 whenever we moved I didn't say to myself, 'Here's my new home.' I said, 'I wonder how long we'll be here.' Yogi Berra expressed my sentiments quite well: "Stability I cherished. I saw too many families uprooted by trades, packing up to find new lives in strange places, kids going to new schools. It's hard on everybody" (*Ten Rings*, p. 182). His son Dale seemed to appreciate the stability Yogi provided his family: "I think one of the reasons we — meaning my brothers and I — handled it

The best example I can give of my father's inability to deal with emotions happened when my mother died after a long bout with cancer. When my family and I arrived in Greenville, I went with my dad to the funeral home. I had held up pretty well until we entered the room where her casket was. Then I broke down. Instead of trying to comfort me or share the grief, my father turned and walked out of the room.

[having a famous father] so well is that we stayed in one town when we were kids. We weren't moving around and having to make new friends" (in *Growing Up Baseball*, p. 40).

Even when my family stayed in one town, we moved from one house to another. Between first and fifth grades, I lived in four different houses. In high school I promised myself that, if I had children, they would not be put through moving. And they weren't. Once they started school we moved only once, a grand distance of six blocks, and all four of my children stayed in the same school system from kindergarten through graduation.

I don't remember much about my brief academic sojourn in Laurens. I do recall being aware my mother had gone to school in the same building in the1930s. My three aunts and my deceased uncle had also gone there. That gave me a sense of connection when all the other connections in my life were coming loose.

One thing I cannot forget is that Laurens was where I hit my first (and only) honest-to-god home run, not one where kids kept dropping the ball or throwing wildly so you just kept running, but one where the ball, even if it was a rubber ball, went over a fence on the fly, a perfect home run.

The field we played on at lunch had a diamond with a fence. I was always just a singles hitter, but one day some cosmic conjunction of bat speed and the ball finding the bat's sweet spot occurred and I actually hit that sucker over the fence. At its shortest point, true, but even Yankee Stadium had its 296-foot corner in right field. When I reached first base I stopped for an instant, out of habit. Rounding second I almost tripped because I was looking over my shoulder, still unsure of what had happened, expecting somebody to throw the ball back to the infield. Rounding third I thought, So *this* is how Mantle feels!

Sadaharu Oh, the "Japanese Babe Ruth," described what it feels like to hit a home run as well as anybody has: "No one can stop a home run. No one can understand what it really is, unless you have felt it in your own hands and body. As the ball makes its high, long arc beyond the playing field, the diamond and the stands suddenly belong to one man. In that brief, brief time, you are free of all demands and complications."

The other thing I recall about school in Laurens is that one of my teachers had a big wall chart with all her students' names on it. As various assignments were completed, stars would be awarded. She told me she wasn't going to put my name on the chart, since I would be leaving so soon. Having all those empty spaces beside my name for the rest of the year would make her chart look funny, she said. So, for three weeks, I was the snaggle-toothed kid with the awful nickname who didn't exist in her class.

But her chart looked really nice.

Just Don't . . . Because

While we were staying with my grandparents and awaiting – or dreading – the move to Cincinnati, I had what I would describe as the first experience when I was aware of a member of the opposite sex *qua* member of the opposite sex.

I was sitting on my grandparents' porch, reading a comic book. It was late afternoon on a warm Saturday. A group of my cousins had been there and we had played ball and Monopoly. Now most of them were gone. For a change I got to stay. One of my cousins came out of the house and plopped down on the glider beside me. She had turned nine in July, a pretty girl with long brown legs accentuating her white shorts.

"Whatcha reading?" she asked.

"My new 'Superman' comic."

She slid over until her leg touched mine. Then she put her head on my shoulder. "Read it to me."

She could read, and I could have given her the comic, but suddenly all I could think of was how *good* it felt to have her touching me. So I read her the comic book, slowly and with lots of unnecessary explanations. When I finished, I asked, "Do you want me to read it again?" What I meant was, *Whatever you do, don't move.*

"No, thanks," she said and got up. "I'm going to get a drink. You want one?"

I shook my head. "I'm just going to . . . sit here for a while."

With the comic book strategically across my lap, I sat there recovering from my first experience of sexual frustration. I must hasten to add that this incident did not leave me hankering after little girls. Nor did it lead me to marry one of my cousins. But it's the first experience I can identify as sexual. I didn't know what I wanted. I just knew having a girl touch me made me want something.

Where could I find an explanation for what I was feeling?

One place I looked for information was the movie ads. In my hometown paper they often appeared on the last page in the sports section. One theater in Greenville, the Roxy, usually warned: "ONLY ADULTS WILL ENJOY." Their ads featured scantily clad women with teasers like "Two Explosive Girls in Two Terrific Hits." That was an ad for a double feature: "Girls Marked Danger," starring Sophia Loren, and "The Barefoot Savage," which introduced "the sensational" Eleonora Rossi Drago. An ad for "Invasion of the Body Snatchers" at another theater carried this admonition: "PLEASE DON'T TELL WHAT THE BODY SNATCHERS DO TO WOMEN!"

Forget the Body Snatchers. I just wanted to know what *anybody* did with women.

When we moved to Ohio my curiosity was only heightened. Cincinnati had several adult theaters and the morning paper reviewed the films that played there along with mainstream films. In addition the city boasted two live burlesque theaters. The Gayety featured acts like "Sunny Dare, the girl with the acrobatic flair." The Glen Rendezvous offered dinner, dancing, and "Lyn Hayward and her all-girl Burlesk."

My baseball idols seemed to spend a lot of time thinking with their gonads, too. During spring training in 1956 the Greenville *News* ran a wire service photo of three members of the New York Giants pulling on a rope tied around the waist of some beauty queen in her shorts and halter top. The caption said they were "getting a line" on her.

Innocent enough, but there was a lot hidden behind that picture. I would have been disillusioned if I had known how puerile many of the players could be. Mickey Mantle said having his wife around "cramped my style" (*Favorite Summer*, p. 187). As he did in most other categories, he led the Yankees in womanizing, even carrying on two long-term affairs with his wife's knowledge. Vic Power said Billy Martin "offered to 'trade' me, to introduce me to the white girl he was dating if I introduced him to two black girls I knew" (*Bombers*, p. 98).

Women's bodies continued to mystify me for several more years. When I was in the seventh grade I called a girl to invite her to a swimming party my church was sponsoring. She said no and I, socially inept as I was, asked why not. She just couldn't, was all she would say. When I got off the phone – we had only one and it was in the living room – my mother told me, "If a girl tells you she can't go swimming, don't ask anything else."

"Why not?" I wanted to know.

"Just don't" was the only answer I got or would get.

One measure of how much the world changed in the next few years was that in 1963 I explained menopause to my mother when she was going through that process and I was taking an advanced biology course my senior year in high school. I can still see us talking in the kitchen and can hear the relief in her voice as she said, "So I'm not going crazy?"

For a family to move as far as mine did wasn't unusual in 1956. America was on the move. Suburbs were blossoming, new factories were being built. Much of the growth was connected with the auto industry and its suppliers in the Midwest, but a prophetic ad in *Time* proclaimed "the last half of the twentieth century belongs to the South." Homes, hospitals, and factories were being built in that region at a record pace.

Let's start with some bald statistics. In 1956:

> *"The great aim of culture [is] the aim of setting ourselves to ascertain what perfection is and to make it prevail."*
>
> Matthew Arnold

* the federal minimum wage was raised to $1.00 per hour
* the average income was just below $4,500 (a cartoon in the Saturday Evening Post showed two men standing at the water cooler under a January '56 calendar. One says to the other, "Well, another year – another $4,376.82.")
* the typical house cost $22,000
* you could buy a new car for $1,750-$3,150
* gas for that car cost 23 cents a gallon
* eggs cost 45 cents a dozen
* first-class postage was 3 cents
* the Dow-Jones Industrial Average hit a new high: 500.24
* a pack of 10 baseball cards cost 10 cents (and you got a piece of gum)

If you build it . . . .

The key element in the American dream of the 1950s was ownership of a house. The building boom that began after WWII, when Abraham Levitt and his sons began converting large tracts of land into housing developments in New York, Pennsylvania and New Jersey, was in full swing in the mid-'50s. Suburbs were springing up on the outskirts of all of America's cities. The homogeneity of the suburbs – in terms of the houses and their occupants – became a point of criticism. They did "cut off millions of whites from the poor and minorities of the inner cities" (Boyer, p. 123), but they also injected a new vitality into the American economy, as businesses followed their customers.

These houses symbolized independence and prosperity to a generation of young adults who had grown up in the Depression and known the rationing and hardship of WWII. Many young families of that day, like mine, had lived with their parents and in rental housing. Ownership of a house meant freedom to do what they liked with the property, room for their children to play, and some distance between themselves and their parents. When Whitey Ford got his World Series check in 1953, he used it for a down payment on a house so he and his family "could finally move out of our apartment" (*Slick*, p. 94). Other players, like Phil Rizzuto and Yogi Berra, also bought houses in the New Jersey suburbs (*Ten Rings*, p. 84).

The Berras could afford "a nice ranch house," but most suburban homes weren't elegant. The one nice touch our house on Edgewood offered was a fireplace in the living room. I don't recall us ever using it, and the lack of andirons or any fireplace equipment in the picture suggests we didn't, though the previous owners must have.

The average new house in 1950 offered 983 square feet of living space; by 1955 the figure was up to 1,170 square feet. By 1985 it had risen to 1,721 square feet. Twenty years later the average new MacMansion had over 2,900 square feet, and 4,000 square feet wasn't unusual.

In the 1950s many homes used coal furnaces. Fewer than 30% of U. S. homes were heated by electricity or gas in 1950. By 1960 12% of homes used coal, while 53% used gas (usually converted coal furnaces which were large and inefficient). In 1950 35% of U. S. homes did not have a complete bathroom (piped hot and cold water, flush toilet, and bathtub or shower). My wife and her family, in Evansville, Indiana, shared a duplex with another family in the early '50s. The bathroom, while it was complete, was used by both families. By 1960 16% of American homes were still without a complete bathroom. Today the figure is 1%. In 1956 more than 20% of U. S. homes did not have a refrigerator.

In March of '56 U. S. Housing Administrator Albert M. Cole invited 103 women to Washington to talk about housing. The women were given transportation costs and a daily stipend of $12 for the conference. A Pennsylvania congressman objected: "Why housing authorities . . . would be interested in learning what the women of this country want in a house is beyond my comprehension . . . . The government does not build houses. Its role, under the Federal Housing Administration, is the insurance of mortgages." Cole said he hoped to get information about what the minimum requirements should be for homes eligible for FHA mortgages (Greenville *News*, Mar. 26).

The women had little positive to say. They objected to the scalping of the landscape, poorly divided interior spaces, and the inclusion of impractical architectural details. Their conclusion was that the houses being built then were "a disgrace to the American standard of living: ugly outside and inefficient inside." What they wanted was a minimum of three bedrooms, a bath and a half, and larger kitchens, even if the other rooms of the house had to be made smaller to stay under $20,000 (Greenville *News*, May 5, 1956). The builders of my wife's family home must have taken those suggestions to heart; that's an exact description of the new house her parents bought in 1957 and which her mother still owns as of this writing.

A Car in Every Garage; A Garage for Every Car

Integrally linked to the growth of the suburbs was the growth of the automobile industry. As mentioned earlier, President Eisenhower signed the act authorizing the building of the interstate highway system in 1956. Car ads from that year emphasized bigness. Cars were on their way to the extremes of size they would reach in the last years of the decade. Magazine ads typically showed them in artists' idealized drawings, rather than photographs, and they looked like yachts with wheels. Cadillacs, Buicks, Lincolns, and Chryslers weren't the only ones sporting chrome and tail fins. You could still buy a DeSoto, a division of Chrysler.

The end was near, though, for some of the smaller companies. In an effort to remain viable, Hudson and Nash had merged, as had Packard and Studebaker. But in May of '56 Studebaker-Packard was "a critically ill company." The last Packard was produced in 1958. All of these cars were made in America. Only 108,000 foreign cars were imported in 1956, about 60,000 of them Volkswagens.

The increased use of automobiles spelled the demise of mass transit in the U. S. Coming out of WWII, Los Angeles had one of the best trolley and bus systems in the country. By the mid-1950s it was falling into disuse as cars clogged the city's inadequate streets. When *Sports Illustrated* asked if Los Angeles could support a major league baseball team, one of the negative respondents cited the way the city was spreading out (Mar. 12, 1956).

All in the Ideal[ized] Family

If we have any image of the mid-1950s, it is the conviction that the families who commuted in their cars to and from those new suburbs were more stable than families are now. Think of all those old sitcoms: Donna Reed cleaning the house in her heels and pearls, June Cleaver in her heels and pearls and all those petticoats telling Ward to take it easy on the Beaver, Margaret Anderson waiting for gentle Jim to come home. "Leave It to Beaver" premiered in 1957 and "The Donna Reed Show" in 1958, but "Ozzie and Harriet" and "Father Knows Best" were established shows in 1956. They were all cut from the same mold and designed to appeal to, and provide a model for, the rising white middle class of America. As Candace Rich said,

> We all wanted our families to be just like these. Perfect. Nobody ever raised their voice and all problems were resolved equitably – in less than half an hour! Women gladly cooked and cleaned, dressed in pearls and high heels, no less, while awaiting the arrival home of the all-knowing husband. While it all seems rather silly and innocent now, I am part of a generation who thought these women were what we were supposed to grow up to be (www.fiftiesweb.com/families.htm).

This 1950s family paradigm was not a continuation of an earlier pattern, but a creation of postwar prosperity (Coontz, pp. 26-28). We may idealize those families now, but figures show the real ones were outwardly more stable than families are today. In 1950 there were 385,000 divorces recorded in the U. S. By 1959 that number had risen to only 395,000. In 1998 the total was 1,135,000. (The U. S. government stopped compiling statistics on divorce rates in 1999.)

But more stable didn't necessarily mean happier. I got only inklings of it at the time, but several Yankee players of the mid-'50s had less than ideal home lives. In January of 1956 *Sports Illustrated* showed a picture of Enos Slaughter marrying his fifth wife. Billy Martin went through a bitter divorce. Don Larsen's first marriage ended in divorce. (His mother said she didn't even know he was married.) Mickey Mantle and his wife had a difficult marriage. He was often abusive to her and deliberately humiliated her in front of others (Castro, pp. 146-147).

After I grew up I learned perfection didn't exactly permeate my mother's family the way I thought it did in 1956. At least no one in my family ever got as desperate as a 13-year-old boy in a small town near Greenville. Unable to stop his father from beating his mother, he shot his father twice with a .22 caliber rifle. The father was only wounded and the boy was not charged (Greenville *News*, Aug. 2, 1956). In October an alcoholic father in Cincinnati wasn't so lucky. His 14-year-old son tired of the heavy physical abuse he received and shot and killed his father.

For every situation like these that erupted into the newspaper, there were scores – probably hundreds – that never saw the light of day. In 1956, if people did confront the unhappiness in their marriages, they weren't likely to get the help they needed. Consider the plight of a woman who wrote Billy Graham and got his answer on April 4:

> *How can any one expect a woman to be tied down like I am? I slave all day while my husband is away at work. He does not get home until 7 p. m. and goes to bed at 8. All I am doing is keeping a house clean and feeding a man (practically a stranger to me). I am very discouraged and my life is meaningless. C. W.*

> Life is meaningless for you because you are thinking of yourself more than of other people. There are many things you can do and the first thing of all is to invite Jesus Christ to come into your home and into your heart. Pray to Him daily; talk with Him while you are working; read about Him in the Bible. Then, be sure that you are the very best house keeper and wife possible. If you are cheerful and bright (and Christ can give you that kind of a disposition), you will make yourself attractive to your husband and he will enjoy your companionship more . . . . be sure that you show your husband that you love him. If he is working twelve hours a day and is so tired he goes right to bed after supper, let him know you are appreciative of him and of his work. With Christ in your heart, and others first in your thoughts, life will become wonderfully different.

Children and Child Brides

Donna and June looked pretty young to have teenaged children, but in that regard the sitcoms were reflecting reality. People married younger in the 1940s and 1950s. The median age at marriage for a woman in 1950 was 20.3 years; for men, 22.8. In 2000 the figures were 25.1 years for women and 26.8 for men. My parents were an anomaly in this regard. When they got married my mother was 24, my dad 20. My mother used to joke that she married a younger man because she didn't want to outlive him or have to take care of him in his old age.

Sometimes the women married a bit too young. On March 8 a large article on the front page of the Greenville *News* told about a 12-year-old girl who had married a 31-year-old man. She told the judge she was 14, the legal age for marriage in South Carolina at that time. Her husband said she acted like she was 16 or 17. They were living with her mother, who was divorced. A few days later a small article quoted her father as saying he would never have approved of the marriage.

Soon after I read about that girl my family was having Sunday dinner in Laurens. I remember looking at one of my cousins who was 12 and wondering how anybody that age could be married. My cousin certainly didn't act like she was 16 or 17. Of course, the oldest girl I knew was my 14-year-old cousin, so I wasn't sure how 16- or 17-year-olds acted, but my cousins just seemed like kids.

Such young brides and such age disparities were not strictly a Southern phenomenon. In Mosinee, Wisconsin, a 64-year-old retired teacher wed a 15-year-old girl, a former student of his. It was the first marriage for both. The teacher had also taught his bride's father (Greenville *News*, Sept. 2, 1956). In Lawrence, Massachusetts, an 80-year-old man and his 32-year-old wife had a baby (*News*, May 30, 1956). And roles could be reversed. On June 7 the *News* ran a front-page article about an 89-year-old woman and a 28-year-old man in Kentucky who were celebrating their tenth wedding anniversary.

Marrying at a younger age meant women had children when they were younger. Really young, sometimes. In March of '56 an article on the front page of the *News* told about another 12-year-old girl, also married, who had had a baby. On February 15 the *News* reported on a 20-year-old woman (with a

37-year-old husband) who had given birth to her sixth child. She had also been married at 12. In 1957 the birth rate among teenaged girls was 96.3 per 1000. In 2000 it was 48.7 per 1000. In 1957 most of those teenaged girls were married; by 2000 more than half of them were not.

My hometown paper did not publish announcements of children born "out of wedlock." What were then known as illegitimate births were on the rise during this period. In 1954 South Carolina recorded 7,150 such births; of those 699 were white. The previous year the total was 6,200; of those 580 were white (Greenville *News*, Sept. 9, 1956). In the 1950s abortion was illegal and contraception such a taboo subject it might as well have been against the law. One sociologist thought abortions were "performed most frequently for unwedded girls or sinning wives" (Sorokin, p. 13).

The subject of abortion came up a few times in my hometown newspaper in 1956. At the end of January a front-page story (also featured in *Time*) described an emotional scene in a Philadelphia courtroom when Gertrude Silver was given a suspended sentence as an accessory in the abortion death of her daughter. Mrs. Silver had driven her married daughter to the apartment of Milton and Rosalie Schwartz, where she was given an abortion and died as a result. Mrs. Silver "suffered a complete mental breakdown following her daughter's death," the article said. The Schwartzes were sentenced to several years in prison. The judge said he "had no doubt [Mrs. Schwartz] was an abortionist and that her husband undoubtedly took a greater part in the crime than he admitted."

On March 2 the *News* ran a small article about a doctor in Ohio who was sentenced to four months in jail for performing 300 abortions over a period of 22 years. He made over a million dollars for doing it, whatever it was. And "none of his abortions had resulted in death." To a 10-year-old that sounded like a good thing. At least it wasn't like the case in Philadelphia.

But what was an abortion? My trusty dictionary defined it as "premature expulsion of a fetus." After I looked up the three big words, it didn't sound like such a good thing. And what did the doctor have to do with it? There hadn't been any mention of a doctor in Philadelphia.

"Home by dark"

Those of us who were children in the '50s probably remember playing outside without any fear of being accosted. "Be home by dark" was the only admonition our mothers needed to give us. As Annie Dillard recalled of growing up in Pittsburgh in that era, "My mother had given me the freedom of the streets as soon as I could say our telephone number. I walked and memorized the neighborhood" (*Childhood*, p. 42). But, again, a look at the newspapers and magazines from 1956 suggests the world was scarier than we realized. During that year the newspapers I was reading covered several kidnappings of young children, all of which ended with the recovery of a body.

In one case a mother left her two-year-old son in a playpen in the family's back yard while she went into the house to do something. When she came back a few minutes later, the child was gone. It took two agonizing months for the police to arrest the kidnapper and recover the body. The case demonstrates how far we've advanced forensically. The police had to compare the handwriting in a ransom note with signatures on voting lists, driver's license applications, and other public records – all manually.

In another case a woman left her six-week-old baby in a stroller outside a Sears store while she went in to shop. Imagine a world where someone feels safe enough to leave an infant unattended outside a large department store! Her plan was to check on the child every ten minutes. On the second check she found the stroller empty.

Both of those incidents happened in or around New York City. In Laurens or Greenville – even in Cincinnati – I did not feel that kind of danger.

"Perfection is achieved, not when there is nothing more to add, but when there is nothing left to take away."

Antoine de Saint-Exupery

The Good Life – Automatically

In 1956, even more than today, ads in magazines and newspapers showed the world as we wished it to be, a perfect world. It was an all-white world, of course, and, apparently, a world in which people had time to read several long paragraphs of text espousing the virtues of the product being advertised, sometimes in vocabulary that would be unfamiliar to a college student today. An ad for a sale on children's clothing in the *New York Times* on May 1 described it as "A Liliputian Bazaar."

Articles and stories were wordier, too. An issue of *Time* or *Newsweek* from 1956 looks as dense as the *Oxford English Dictionary* compared to their modern versions, which feature lots of pictures and white space.

The technological advances made under the pressure of WWII were coming into the public domain. That was both promising and troubling. An article in the Greenville *News* on July 26, 1956, forecast that within fifty years humans would be able to lighten the night sky, control where and when rain would fall, train dolphins to herd fish like collies herd sheep, and defuse hurricanes as they formed. But another article on Sept. 10 predicted that "within a few decades" scientists would be able to control the world's climate to such an extent that weather could be used as a weapon against one's enemies.

In baseball terms the scientists came up 0 for 5.

Convenience and ease are two themes that show up repeatedly in the ads, whether someone is selling stoves, vacuums, garden fertilizer, or food. Aluminum foil was introduced in March of '56 in a two-page spread in *Life*. If something could be prepared "automatically" or "instantly," that became its major selling point. And if it wasn't automatic, it could be "Fotomatic" or "Roto-matic" or "hydromatic."

My favorite ad showed a woman – in the standard housewife's uniform of dress, heels, and pearls – watching a Philco TV. The caption reads: "Her dinner for 8 cooks automatically . . . while she watches television that tunes itself." The Philco electric range lets her "completely escape from the kitchen. All surface units are automatically self-regulating. Every dish cooks to perfection right on time. No burning, no boil-over, no pans to watch."

All that's missing is the Jetsons' robot maid, Rosie.

Not that people weren't dreaming of her. A couple in New Jersey, according to the *New York Times* on May 3, were installing automated features around their house, from push-buttons to open the front door to a thermostatically controlled motor that opened and closed windows. The father of the family was "constructing a radio-controlled teddy bear for the [children] – which may be borrowed for use as a 'silent' butler for adult parties." And which probably put the kids in therapy for years.

"Smoke 'em if ya got 'em"

One of the most striking things about ads from 1956 is how aggressively cigarette makers were running claims of the smoothness, mildness, and great taste of their products. Everyone knew "Winston tastes good, like a cigarette should." The makers of Camels argued that pleasure improves one's disposition, so "For more pure pleasure . . . have a Camel." One of Mickey Mantle's early endorsement contracts was for Camels, but he admitted he "couldn't understand how anyone could derive pleasure by inhaling smoke into his lungs." He sent the cartons of free cigarettes he received home to his father, who swapped them at the grocery store for his preferred brand, Lucky Strike (*The Mick*, pp. 12-13). Other athletes did smoke. Mantle mentions Don Larsen "duck[ing] into the runway for a smoke" during the perfect game (*Octobers*, p. 67).

I was disappointed at the time to see my hero advertising cigarettes. My father smoked until I was nine. I never did like to be around it. While he was quitting we went through a couple of difficult months.

Anyone who watches movies from this era knows how often people lit up in them, almost as often as people today answer a cell phone. Emily Post, in response to a reader who didn't like cigarette smoke in her home, decreed that "unless smoke really makes you ill, you cannot ask guests not to smoke" (Greenville *News*, Mar. 26, 1956). In July, when another reader raised the question, "Shouldn't one ask permission before smoking?" Post replied, "It would be very nice if they would, but it is not necessary because smoking has become too universal."

> *"A cigarette is a perfect type of a perfect pleasure. It is exquisite, and it leaves one unsatisfied. What more can one want?"*
>
> Oscar Wilde

The Cincinnati *Enquirer* reported on one study which concluded "smoking apparently increases the risks of death from coronary heart attacks as well as from lung cancer" (Oct. 8, 1956), but with Doris Day returning home for the premiere of her movie "Julie," such bad news didn't get much attention.

And a TV in Every Living Room

The biggest impact on American life in the mid-'50s came from television. In 1950 it was just a toy for the rich in a few big cities. A town the size of Greenville was lucky to have one network station, NBC. For a fuzzy ABC we relied on a station in Asheville, fifty miles away in the mountains of North Carolina. Early in 1956 a CBS station went on the air in Spartanburg, thirty miles away. By 1956, more than 90 percent of Americans lived within range of one TV station, while 75 percent could get at least two stations. As televisions became commonplace, the medium showed its power. As already mentioned, it contributed to the downfall of the red-baiting Sen. Joseph McCarthy and heightened the nation's awareness of the civil rights struggle.

Politicians were learning, though, that television could work *for* them. The political conventions of 1956 were the first to be staged primarily for TV. Richard Nixon was on the Republican ticket as Vice President because of television. After getting the nomination in 1952, Nixon was accused of accepting lavish gifts from people who expected favors from him. On Sept. 23, on national television, he delivered his "Checkers speech," explaining his finances and challenging his Democratic opponents to do the same. The only gift he had accepted, he claimed, was a little black and white dog which his older daughter named Checkers. The public responded favorably to the speech, although some editorial writers criticized Nixon for stooping so low as to use his family to garner sympathy

(Halberstam, *Fifties*, pp. 239-242).

My family acquired our first TV in October of 1954. Before then we sometimes were invited to a neighbor's house to watch shows like "Boston Blackie," "Joe Palooka," and – my personal favorites – "Superman" and "The Lone Ranger." Reading back over those words, I wonder why I was drawn to heroes whose identity was a secret. Did I feel there was some part of my life I couldn't show to those around me? But Everykid feels that way during puberty.

By 1956, even though most towns had only three network stations and they were not on the air around the clock, television was so much a part of daily life that people were already showing signs of becoming obsessed with it. This article appeared in my hometown paper on April 20, with a dateline from Chicago:

> A 22-year-old wife and mother who said she'd rather have her television set than her husband got her wish today.
>
> Judge Walter O'Malley of Superior Court granted a divorce to Mrs. Darlene Carlson. She testified her husband, Richard, 27, a painter, became violently angry when she stayed up late to watch TV shows. She charged him with cruelty.
>
> The court gave her custody of their two sons, Stephen, 3, and Mark, 1, and ordered Carlson to pay $32.50 a week for their support. Mrs. Carlson was asked if her husband didn't mean more to her than the TV set. She replied:
>
> 'Definitely not.'

Getting – and keeping – a watchable picture required frequent adjustment of the antenna, an interior "rabbit ears" antenna for most people. That could get tricky. According to an article in the Greenville *News* on July 8, a couple in Florida were dissatisfied with the quality of their picture. The husband moved the antenna, then the wife adjusted it. "An argument ensued as to who had done the better job." The wife picked up a pair of scissors to underscore her point, and her husband got his revolver: ". . . while he was attempting to disarm his wife, the gun went off and a bullet struck her in the shoulder."

It gets worse. A couple in Indianapolis were watching a TV show when a character on the show knocked on a door. The husband, who had been drinking, told his wife to answer the door. When she refused, he beat her on the head with a hammer and threw a knife at her. "Meanwhile, she said, he turned off the TV set several times and she turned it back on each time." When he rushed at her with a knife, she took it from him and stabbed him to death (Greenville *News*, Aug. 5). Notice that, in the midst of a literal fight to the death, they kept turning the TV off and on. Of course, we have only the wife's version.

Evidence of TV's influence on viewers was mounting. In Clearwater, Florida, two teenaged boys were watching "Kit Carson." One went into another room and returned with a rifle. He told his friend, "I'm going to kill you," and fired the gun, striking and killing the other boy. The boy claimed he had been "influenced by the TV show" (Greenville *News*, July 2).

For me and a lot of other kids, TV meant the opportunity to watch major league baseball. By 1956 the effect of this exposure could be seen in the number of youngsters who actively imitated their heroes' batting or pitching styles (*Sports Illustrated*, Sept. 10, 1956).

Some people saw television as a baneful influence on American society. Pitirim Sorokin, the controversial former chairperson of Harvard's Sociology Department, took the most pessimistic view in a book published in 1956:

So far, almost the only important achievement of this new instrument of communication has consisted in bringing into millions of our homes the erotically charged, alcoholic atmosphere of night clubs, ugly commercials, and endless murder-and-sex plays. If the majority of our movies concerned the upper region of the moral and social sewers, the bulk of television programs and commercials sink us into the filth. No wonder that many of us, after being immersed in this muck, come out of it feeling physically, morally and mentally dirty. Some of us can and do cleanse ourselves promptly. Other less fortunate television viewers often lose even the very desire to reestablish their sanity, and remain contaminated by the poisons.

Revolution, pp. 32-33

Two questions confronted television in 1956. Was it physically harmful to viewers? And, When would we have color TV?

Some health experts did worry that "television emits X-rays which ultimately damage the eyes," but there was no conclusive evidence this was a problem (Greenville *News*, July 25). The color issue was a big one for me. When would I get to see Mickey Mantle play on green, not gray, grass? In April of '56 WNBQ in Chicago became the first station in the country to broadcast in all-color, even though most of its viewers still had black-and-white sets.

There were only 35,000 color sets in the whole country at that time and predictions about increases in their production had proved overly optimistic. One General Electric executive said he didn't expect large sales until the price of the units dropped below $500. At the time it was $800 (Greenville *News*, Mar. 2), almost half the price of a no-frills car. On the bright side, one decorator assured readers of the *News* they would not have to redecorate an entire room if they bought a color set. Just avoid having a bright colored wall opposite the screen (July 8, 1956).

The first practical wireless remote control came on the market in 1956. The first commercial video-tape recorder was also developed in that year. It changed the way television programs were produced. On April 20 the *New York Times* reported, somewhat sardonically, that "TV engineers noted that the tape recording of video images had some interesting possibilities. Tape can be played back seconds after it has recorded a picture. If an umpire blew a close one, a station could play back the critical happening on the diamond and reassure the city's beer drinkers of their superior wisdom."

Yes, they were talking about instant replay. They just hadn't named it yet. And if they'd had it during Don Larsen's perfect game, a couple of plays would have gotten intense scrutiny. I'm not suggesting the calls would have proved to be wrong, just that it would have been interesting to see them in a replay. And what a treat it would have been to watch Mantle's spectacular catch in the fifth inning several times in slow motion from different angles, just to rub my Dodger-loving friend Mitch's nose in it.

As Long as You've Got Your Health

New food and health products abounded in 1956. Budweiser Brewery introduced Busch beer. Jif peanut butter and Certs breath mints appeared in stores. If you didn't have any Certs handy, be sure to use Gleem toothpaste. Their ads claimed brushing with Gleem *before* breakfast would leave one's breath fresh all day. Studies had proved it.

Special 'miracle' ingredients were all the rage. Colgate toothpaste contained Gardol, while Crest touted Fluoristan. A cold remedy called Bromo Quinine boasted "its exclusive medicinal formula now contains an amazing new Citrus BioFlavonoid." What the hell is a Citrus BioFlavonoid? you may ask. According to an ad from an orange-growers' group, the BioFlavonoids are "mysterious yellow substances in the 'meat' of the fruit." They "affect your family's health in a special way all their own."

There you have the 1956 version of a scientific explanation.

Advertisers must have thought people were concerned about the healthfulness of the foods they ate, but their concept of healthfulness differed from ours today. Trix cereal was introduced as "a real, honest-to-goodness body-building breakfast-food," according to an ad in *Life*. And so convenient. You didn't even have to trouble yourself to put sugar on it. The box pictured in the ad carries the slogan: "The sugar cereal with the FRUIT FLAVOR." I was a Kellogg's "Frosted Flakes" kid myself, with the cavities to prove it.

Jell-o was advertised with a cute jingle:

> Old King Cole was a merrie old soul,
>   And the healthiest King in town.
> For his cooks made Jell-o in a great big bowl
>   And the King just gobbled it down.

"The trade of advertising is now so near perfection that it is not easy to propose any improvement."

Samuel Johnson
(1709-1784)

In ads in *Life, Time,* and the *New York Times* the Sugar Institute touted the healthful qualities of their product. Eating sugar before a meal, they claimed, would curb one's appetite and lead to weight loss. Sugar was the "scientific nibble." That's why 7-Up could claim: ". . . in just 2 to 6 minutes after you finish the bottle, you get new pep! That's because, along with its other special ingredients, 7-Up has just enough pure, natural sugar to renew your energy." Coke bragged about "that bright little lift that puts you at your sparkling best."

Can you spell sugar buzz?

Baseball players of the 1950s seem to have had little awareness of nutrition or healthful eating. Unless one of the high-paid stars like DiMaggio treated the team, the only food available in the clubhouse was hot dogs and soft drinks purchased from a stadium vendor. After a game the routine was to eat and drink pretty heavily. *Sports Illustrated* reported that, when Billy Martin went home to Berkeley, his mother "serves no vegetables. Billy hates them" (April 23, 1956).

The early and mid-1950s also saw the birth of the Big Boy restaurant chain, Kentucky Fried Chicken, and McDonald's. And Velcro was patented in 1955.

KFC, McDonald's, Busch, sugar highs, Velcro, remote controls and instant replay – how could Norman Mailer call this "one of the worst decades in the history of man"?

The Dark Side

All of this processed food meant the introduction into the American diet of various dyes and other chemicals. As early as August of 1956 medical authorities expressed concern about the long-term effects of these materials on consumers. Dr. W. C. Hueper of the National Institutes of Health addressed the problem at an international conference. In spite of the headline on the article, "Cancer Expert Says Dyes In Foods Bad," Dr. Hueper said it was "unlikely that many of the presently used additives and residues introduce hazards of cancer-producing agents into the general food supply." His concern was the lack of mandatory testing of the "long-term or delayed effects" (Greenville *News*, Aug. 11).

One of the greatest fears facing us in the 1950s was polio, especially among children. In some ways it was more terrifying than AIDS because you couldn't avoid it by relatively simple precautions. A child could go swimming one afternoon and be unable to get out of bed the next morning. Two kids in my elementary school had to wear leg braces. Jonas Salk developed an effective vaccine, and mass inoculations of school children began in April of 1954. The results were promising at first, but when

200 cases were caused by the vaccine, leading to 11 deaths, all vaccinations were halted until the problem was isolated. It proved to come from one bad batch of vaccine. By April of 1955, 4,000,000 people had been vaccinated. The statistics tell the story. In 1955, 28,985 cases of polio were reported. In 1956 the number dropped to 14,647, and in 1957 to 5,894.

There were, of course, thousands of victims of the disease, like my schoolmates, who had to cope with the after-effects for the rest of their lives. Few Americans knew how badly polio had crippled Franklin Roosevelt. Instead of serving as an inspiration for those afflicted by the disease, he chose to hide his condition because attitudes toward "crippled" people were so negative at that time. By the mid-'50s discussion of the problem was more open. In August of '56 the *Saturday Evening Post* ran a story entitled "I Married a Polio Victim." The woman who was featured overcame many obstacles to go to college, marry, and have a child. Many others, though, were confined to wheel chairs or encased in iron lungs. Baseball player Vic Wertz contracted a non-paralytic form of polio and missed most of the 1955 season but returned the next year.

There were hints the good life had its price. In an article in the *Saturday Evening Post* on January 28, Hannah Lees discussed why "Our Men Are Killing Themselves." She pointed to a near-epidemic of heart attacks and suicides among men (though she didn't mention smoking) and concluded "most of what is killing off American men seems to be linked with what we think of as progress." The American male felt himself duty bound to support his family at a level of material prosperity which induced stress many men were unable to handle. That gray flannel suit (the movie came out in '56) didn't always fit so well.

When I read Lees' article I couldn't help but think of my dad. He always wanted a better job, more authority – plant manager, vice president. He had more education than anyone else in his family at that date, and we lived in a nicer house and drove a newer car than he had ever known as a child. "More and better" seemed our inevitable goal. And yet my father was a painfully shy man. It must have been difficult for him to move up and have to deal more and more with people and not with the materials of his job.

CHAPTER 16

Moving Day

We arrived in Cincinnati on my eleventh birthday, September 23, 1956, a Sunday. By an ironic twist we would leave there exactly a year later, on my twelfth birthday. But do not pity a boy who spent two consecutive birthdays following a moving van. For that twelfth birthday my mother gave me money and let me take two of my friends to the mall near our apartment house. After a year in Cincinnati, I had only one friend – Mitch – and an acquaintance – a boy named Bobby, who had just moved in across the hall from us a few weeks before – so I didn't have to be selective. I bought them ice cream and they went with me to pick out my presents.

The first thing I worried about was learning to spell the name of the city. As journeyman ballplayer Rocky Bridges said, "It's a good thing I stayed in Cincinnati for four years – it took me that long to learn how to spell it." After only one year in Cincinnati, my family would move to Chattanooga, Tennessee. Thank God I wasn't dyslexic.

But I'm getting ahead of myself. The next morning, September 24, nothing was unpacked and my mother didn't even know where the grocery store was yet, so we went out for breakfast, something my family never did. All I remember about that morning is the fog and Big Boy. The Big Boy restaurants began in California and were franchised under various names across the country in the 1950s. In Cincinnati they were, and still are, Frisch's Big Boy. In some places they are Elias Bros. Shoney's has become the more common franchise across the country, but I still want to call it Frisch's, and I still think of it as a Cincinnati original.

Cincinnati sits in a bowl, and it tends to fog up in the mornings, especially in the spring and fall. The fog that morning was thick. I was in this strange city, on the wrong side of the Ohio River, and I couldn't see anything. If I had to live in this damn Yankee place, I wanted to be able to see it. This problem continued throughout the fall. In mid-October the local papers were reporting that the smog, which was equal to levels in Los Angeles, would continue to be a problem for several more days.

I was relieved to see that the Cincinnati *Enquirer* carried some of the same comic strips that the Greenville *News* did. Rereading them, it amazed me to see that Mary Worth looked older in 1956 than she does today. And Judge Parker's son Randy was just finishing high school; today he's only a few years out of law school.

I thought of Cincinnati as a northern city. The historians and sociologists I've read recently describe it as "the northernmost city in the South" or "the most redneck city in the North." Its Southern connections go back a long way. In the pre-Civil War days slave owners went to Cincinnati the way some people today go to Las Vegas. It was "Sin-city." Free blacks in the city were sometimes kidnapped and forced into slavery. A significant portion of Cincinnati's population consisted of poor Southern whites who could not compete with slave labor.

Racial tensions are still high there today, and the city is inextricably bound to Kentucky, as are other cities on the northern bank of the Ohio River, such as my wife's hometown of Evansville, Indiana. This link is so tight because two people can stand next to one another on a bridge, with one in Ohio and the other in Kentucky.

We had only one car – a black 1950 Chevrolet – so after breakfast we dropped my father at the G. E. plant which had lured him to this eerie, fog-bound place, and my mother took my brother and me to Carthage Elementary School. For the second time in barely a month I would be a "new kid," this time coming in after school had started. My name wouldn't be on any of my teachers' charts here either.

"What's in a Name?"

Not only was I a new kid, I had a new identity. I couldn't help being shy and snaggle-toothed and I couldn't change my last name, but I decided the move to Cincinnati was my opportunity to shed that hated nickname. Now, after hiding it for fifty years, it's difficult for me to tell even close friends, let alone put it into print for the forty or fifty people who might eventually buy this book.

Looking at it rationally, I know it's not a horrible nickname, but I got teased about it so much I still loathe and despise it. I was – still am – an introvert, and I got kidded enough about my last name (Hey, Ding-dong!) and my snaggle-tooth. The nickname became too much to bear. My writers' group finally convinced me that, for this book to work, I needed to spill the beans, and they did not laugh me out of the room when I told them. So, here goes.

My grandfather named his two oldest sons after men he served with in World War I. My uncle got Alvin York; my dad got Albert Atwood, and I got "juniored." The most obvious nickname to come from Atwood is Woody. There have been successful men with that name: coach Woody Hayes of Ohio State, actor Woody Harrelson, musician Woody Guthrie, and comedian/film-maker Woody Allen. A Google search reveals there are several successful men named Woody Bell. But I spent my childhood being called Woody Woodpecker and having other kids do that braying jackass laugh of his.

The scars run deep.

Moving to Cincinnati meant nobody except my parents and my brother would know me. So I told them I wanted to be "Al." My parents didn't see anything wrong with my nickname, but they went along with me. The letter my dad wrote me is addressed to "Al, Jr." My brother was the problem, of course.

On the way to Cincinnati, in the back seat of our car, my brother told me he wouldn't call me "Al" unless I called him "Spin." We were both fans of the "Spin and Marty" series on the "Mickey Mouse Club," especially after Annette Funicello "filled out" the cast. My brother's middle name is Spencer, after our maternal grandfather, so he wanted to pick up a "cool" nickname as I was dropping a hated one. I submitted to his blackmail for a few days, until he forgot about it. For several months, though, like someone in the witness protection program, I lived under the threat that he might slip and call me by my nickname in front of somebody in Cincinnati.

The first day under my new identity at Carthage Elementary did not go well. At lunch I ended up standing in line with two boys I had been sitting next to in class. They were picking on a girl in front of us. The principal came by, observed their misbehavior, and made the three of us stand against the wall at the spot where students picked up their trays. We had to stand there until everybody else had gone through the line. Only then did we get to eat. My protestations of innocence fell on deaf ears. Maybe he couldn't understand my Southern accent.

Disneyland opened in 1955. Without fail in my nightly prayers I asked that I might get to visit the Magic Kingdom and meet the Mouseketeers, in particular cute little Sharon Baird. Both prayers remain unanswered.

Inwardly I raged against this injustice. I had never gotten in trouble in school in my life. I wasn't that kind of kid. If I was still in South Carolina, this wouldn't be happening. My brother smirked at me when he came through the line. This was such a reversal of our usual roles. I didn't mention the incident when my mother picked us up and took us "home" to our apartment. My brother promised not to say anything as long as I called him "Spin."

Apartment Living

We lived in an apartment complex called Swifton Village, on Langdon Farm Road, off of Reading Road in what was then the northeast part of Cincinnati. Our apartment had only two bedrooms, so I was still relegated to sharing with my brother.

Swifton Village was two years old at that time, about 1200 apartments in large, box-like red-brick buildings. Rents started at $85 and included all utilities. I've since learned the place was financially troubled from the beginning. In the mid-1960s the owner, a New York developer, went bankrupt and put the complex up for sale. Another New York realtor named Trump bought it for practically nothing and sent his son Donald, a freshly minted MBA, to oversee the renovation.

In an interview Donald Trump recalled that he lived there for several months (in our apartment? I'll have to ask him sometime). "It was a mess," he said. "When we bought it, it was almost fully vacant. It was falling apart. It was a real disaster. We bought it very cheaply. I fixed it, I made it beautiful, I sold it and we made a great profit on it." He regards this as the beginning of his career as a real estate magnate, but people who actually worked on the project say Trump exaggerates his role in converting Swifton Village into Huntington Meadows.

Something about its location seemed to make the place unmanageable, no matter what it was called or who owned it. The complex fell on hard times again in the 1980s and by 2002 it was crime-ridden, vacant and bankrupt. It was razed and replaced by a more upscale housing development.

Even in September of 1956 Swifton Village seemed scary to me. As I look at family pictures from that time (some of them a bit crooked because I took them) the place appears to have had all the charm of the huge apartment complexes the Russians and East Germans were building for their workers' paradise. I hated the cold and the lack of trees, but I don't suppose there was any real reason to fear anything. The crime and drugs that would eventually overwhelm the place were nowhere to be seen then, at least not by a naive 11-year-old. It was just such a jarring change from our pretty little house on a quiet street in a Southern suburb.

The one thing Swifton Village had over Edgewood Avenue was lots of kids, many of them around my age. Most of them liked to play baseball and none of them knew I had been cut when I tried out for a team.

The buildings that made up Swifton Village were arranged in block U shapes. The building we lived in sat parallel to Langdon Farm Road, with buildings on each side perpendicular to it and running down to the road. Each set of buildings thus had a large rectangular court, enclosed on three sides, where the kids played. It would have been perfect for football and okay for baseball except it was terraced. Mr. Spock made chess a three-dimensional game on "Star Trek," but baseball doesn't work in that form. Dollar-ball did, and I introduced the game to Swifton Village.

I had two other options for satisfying my baseball habit. In the evenings and on weekends my dad would throw with me. Sometimes he would stand on the highest terrace, just outside our door, and throw fly balls so I could pretend to be Mickey Mantle. With him standing on the highest terrace and me two levels below him, I got some amazingly high flies to chase. The only problem was that other kids wanted to join in. Toward the end of his life my dad said he thought throwing those high flies had contributed to the severe arthritis in his right shoulder.

Thanks for that one last guilt trip, Dad.

My other option was to throw an old tennis ball against the wall of an apartment building. One short end of the rectangular buildings had only a single row of windows, from top to bottom. The portion of the wall without windows, which can be seen over my mother's left shoulder, was where the stairs were. I used that part of the brick wall to throw grounders, flies, anything I liked. I could use a piece of chalk to mark a strike zone and even practice pitching.

He Ain't Heavy?

On most of the family-oriented TV shows of the 1950s the family consisted of at least two children, e. g., the three Anderson kids on "Father Knows Best," David and Ricky Nelson on "Ozzie and Harriet," and, of course, Wally and the Beaver. But I envied the kid on "Lassie" – even if he did keep falling down old wells – because he was an only child.

Why my brother and I never got along is a mystery to me, and a source of real regret, one of the greatest imperfections in my life. I wanted to be David to his Ricky, or Wally to his Beaver. My hair was blond while his was dark and the age difference – three years – was about the same, so the analogy would work. We played together when we were younger, but by the time I entered junior high in 1957 we had little to do with one another. I won't try to place blame. We just didn't

The show we think of as "Lassie" premiered in 1954 as "Jeff's Collie." After various cast changes, Jon Provost appeared in 1957 as the orphan Timmy, adopted by Lassie's family, or maybe by Lassie.

get along and, unfortunately, still don't. Settling our father's estate a few years ago proved to be a painful experience.

The year we lived in Cincinnati turned into a Continental Divide in our relationship. After our mother started work in late October, my brother and I came home to an empty apartment. We some-

times went out to play. When the cold weather kept us inside, we often argued.

During one of those arguments he picked up a pair of scissors and started chasing me. I finally had no choice but to hit him. I caught him in the solar plexus and he fell to the floor, gasping for breath. Because I had never seen anyone have the breath knocked out of him before, I was sure he was going to die. But I couldn't kneel over him to see about him because he still had the scissors clutched in his hand.

Moving into Swifton Village was a step backwards for my family, from suburban home-owners to urban apartment rent-ers. But my parents promised that, as soon as they could sell the house in Greenville, they would be able to make a down payment on an even nicer house in Cincin-nati. I just hoped it had three bedrooms and I would live long enough to enjoy one of them.

Oddly enough, the subject of death and Cincinnati recently came up in a "Zippy-the-Pinhead" comic strip. Zippy asked the Shoney/Frisch's Big Boy, who appears often in the comic strip, "What happens when we die, Big Boy?" He is told, "We go to Cincinnati & await further instructions." Zippy wonders, "Do we have jobs? And if so, do they still deduct withholding? Also, when we take public transportation, do we still pay full fare?" Big Boy assures him, "Hey, it's Cincinnati - not purgatory." At the time I couldn't see much difference between the two.

It's All in the Cards

When we weren't playing ball in Swifton Village, we collected baseball cards. I got to Cincinnati late in the season, where I was able to get a few cards that hadn't shown up in the packs I bought in South Carolina. The next summer I went into collecting full-steam. I still have a lot of 1955 Topps cards. My '56 set is missing only #5 – Ted Williams, a pricey card – and my '57 set is complete. By 1958 I was seriously into girls, so my collection dwindled, although I do have Roger Maris' rookie card from that year. A few years ago I sold the odd cards I picked up in the late '50s and early '60s.

"You didn't have to play baseball to collect baseball cards. You didn't even have to be a fan, it often seemed . . . . The only constant of my boyhood was the Red Sox – and the uninspired mediocrity of their play. That and the reassuring presence of my baseball cards: flipping back and forth through the slow summer days"

(Great American . . . Book, *p. 12*).

Baseball cards go back to the beginning of the twentieth century. In the 1950s intense competition – of which kids were blissfully unaware – broke out between the long-established Bowman company and the upstart Topps line. Bowman's 1951 Mantle rookie card is the collector's holy grail. In near-mint condition it goes for about $250,000 today. Mantle attributed much of his post-retirement popularity to the craze for baseball cards, especially autographed cards, and didn't understand why his rookie card should be more valuable than any other player's (Castro, p. 246). He is still the biggest draw in card collecting, no matter how long it has been since he retired or since he died. In early 2006 Topps announced the unveiling of a whole new line of Mantle cards, featuring pictures acquired from his family and other material never before available to the public.

Topps and Bowman signed contracts with individual players to use their pictures on the cards. In the early '50s each company tried to make their contracts exclusive, so some sets are missing players. Sal Maglie does not appear in the Topps set in either 1955 or 1956. Sometimes numbers are missing because the company failed to sign a contract with a player but had already assigned his card a number. The '55 Topps set, which is short to begin with, does not include #'s 186, 203, or 209. The 1956 Topps set contained 340 cards. Sixteen were team cards and two were the presidents of each league, so there were 322 of the major league's 400 players depicted.

In 1956 Topps bought out Bowman and held a monopoly on the card business until 1981. Its 1955 and 1956 sets are regarded as works of art. The black-and-white images in this book do them no justice. An easy way to appreciate the beauty of these cards in color is to visit these web sites: www.vintagecardtraders.com/virtual/55topps/55topps.html and www.vintagecardtraders.com/virtual/56topps/56topps.html

Both sets use a horizontal format, instead of the more traditional vertical. The '55 set shows a head shot of the player, an isolated "action figure" and a team logo against a solid color background.

The '56 set used the same head shot of each player as the '55 set but with a full-color action shot as the background. Even sluggers like Mantle are shown making defensive plays or running the bases. Ted Williams is one of the few players shown swinging a bat.

I still remember the day I got my '56 Mantle card (#135). My mother, brother, and I were in Laurens on a Saturday in July. My cousin Buster and his family were also there. Buster is two years older than I am and we looked and sounded enough alike that we were mistaken for brothers. Our parents gave us a dollar apiece (plus an extra quarter for Buster since he was twelve) and we walked downtown to see a movie. That got us into the movie (twenty-five cents for me, fifty cents for Buster), bought us something to eat and drink (fifty cents – theaters always have made their profit on over-priced concessions), and left enough for a stop at the dime store to buy two packs of baseball cards (ten cents each).

Our route home was South Harper Street, which sloped down to a railroad track and then back up to the neighborhood where our grandparents lived. Today it's the historic district. Back then we just thought of it as a place with a bunch of big, old houses. On the downward slope of the trip we opened our first packs, compared and traded a couple. Everykid knew which ones he had and which ones he needed. We had crossed the railroad track and were on the upward slope when Buster opened his second pack. Mantle was the first card. I was so envious I forgot to open my other pack.

"Oh, shoot!" Buster said, slipping the card to the back of the stack.

"What do you mean? I've been trying to get that card all summer." I grabbed at his hand.

"You really want it?"

"Yeah. Who wouldn't?"

"I don't. You're the one that likes the Yankees. I hate 'em." He held it up, as if examining it, but he was just taunting me.

We had argued before about liking or disliking a team that won so much of the time. We didn't know it, but we were talking across a divide that split the nation. Some people hated the Yankees so much in those days that the players received death threats.

"What are you going to do with that card?" I asked.

"I don't know. Maybe I'll use it for target practice with my BB gun. I bet I could put one right between his eyes."

I knew he wasn't kidding. "Come on, Buster . . . ."

"What'll you give me?"

I didn't hesitate. "I'll give you this whole pack." I held up my unopened second pack. "And a nickel."

James Michener said, "Bennett Cerf, my deceased publisher, always sensed that there was something about him I didn't like, something that kept us from being good friends. He finally asked me what it was, and I told him I could never be comfortable with anyone who was a Yankee fan, which he was. I told him I thought there was something fundamentally sick about being affiliated with the Yankees."

in Los Angeles Times Book Review July 25, 1975

"Ten cards and a nickel for one? You're crazy." He grabbed the pack and allowed me to pull the precious Mantle card out of his hand.

It was – still is – magnificent! Mickey's head-shot is on the right side, his name and "*outfield* NEW YORK YANKEES" in a rectangular box in the upper left corner. In the background he's shown leaping at the wall to rob somebody of a home run. The cards showed a facsimile of the player's signature. Mantle's was still simple at that time. Later it came to have ornate loops on the two M's.

The '56 set was the first to include checklists, which nobody kept, and team cards. The cards were an eighth of an inch larger on each side than modern cards. Topps released their cards in series during the summer. But the later, higher numbered series did not sell as well because kids were going back to school by the time they came out. In 1952 the company was left with a huge surplus of those late summer cards, which it dumped into the Atlantic Ocean. That last series began with #311, Mickey Mantle's card, which is today the most valuable card Topps ever produced. After 1952 they either

printed smaller runs of the higher numbered cards or destroyed leftovers at the end of the season, in less dramatic fashion, so those cards are harder to find and more expensive.

Today baseball cards are divided into "commons" and "stars" and are graded on strict standards. The picture has to be well-centered and the corners sharp. Unfortunately, when the cards were being printed, the machines that cut them just hacked away. Some cards don't even have a white border all the way around. That's a major flaw. Creases or worn edges also knock the value down dramatically.

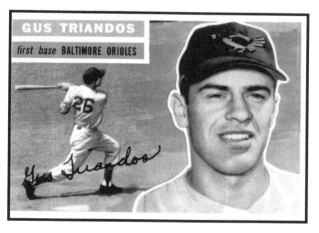

There aren't many cards surviving from this period in "excellent" or "near mint" condition. In 1956 we didn't plan to finance our kids' college education with the things. We just wanted to get as many as we could. But every pack we bought inevitably contained a card or two we already had, usually of some journeyman player on a second-division team ("Oh, man! Not Gus Triandos again!"). Some of those we put on the spokes of our bicycles to make them sound like motorcycles. Or we put a rubber band around them and stuck them in the pockets of our jeans to trade. We usually kept them in numerical order, so the lowest and highest numbers suffered the most damage.

One way of quickly increasing – or decreasing – your holdings was to participate in a "flipping" game. Any number could play. The first kid tossed or dropped a card from shoulder height to the ground or the sidewalk. The next one would do the same. If his card covered any part of the first card, he won both of them. If not, the next player dropped a card until somebody managed to cover part of a card. The player who accomplished that won all the cards on the sidewalk. You could also flip the cards at a wall or toward a line drawn in the dirt. Whoever got his card closest to the wall or the line won all the cards that had been thrown. Many of the cards landed on their corners, of course.

I traded cards, but until I moved to Cincinnati I had participated in a flipping game only once because I didn't like cards with damaged edges. That and I couldn't stand to lose. The only time I flipped in South Carolina, I felt sick watching some kid scoop up five of my cards.

But kids at Carthage Elementary were more into flipping than trading. I wanted to be accepted, so on my second day there I stuck my doubles in the back pocket of my jeans and hung out during lunch at the spot where the action took place. That was where I met Mitch.

Mitch and I were in the same classes, but he sat on the other side of the room from me. I had noticed him because he talked loud and funny. You couldn't help but notice him.

A boy named Jack was running the flipping game. He had greasy black hair and wore the sleeves of his t-shirt rolled up. Away from school he probably kept a pack of cigarettes there. I wasn't sure how to get into the action, but he took care of that.

"You got any cards?" he asked.

"Yeah." I pulled out the fifteen cards I had stuffed in my pocket.

"You wanna play?"

Keeping my head down so the others couldn't see my snaggle-tooth, I shrugged. "Sure."

"What's your name?"

I caught myself before I said Woody. "Al . . . Al Bell." Somehow that didn't sound much better. Maybe I should have given more thought to this name change.

"Well, Ding-dong, let's see what you've got."

At least he didn't call me Woody Woodpecker and nobody did that braying, jackass laugh.

I lost two cards in the first round, but I won the second round – twenty cards.

The bell rang and we started back to class. Mitch caught up with me. "Hey, Bell, you sure got a bunch of cards there. Wanta trade some?" His accent was so different I had to listen closely to be sure I knew what he was saying.

"Which ones do you want?" I wasn't sure which cards I had picked up. Some of them had been face down. I didn't want to trade one and later realize I needed it.

"Didn't I see Carl Furillo in there?"

I shuffled through the stack. "Yeah, here he is."

"I want him. I'm from Brooklyn. Just moved here this summer."

"What'll you give me?"

Mitch fanned the half dozen cards he had left so I could see them. My eye caught the

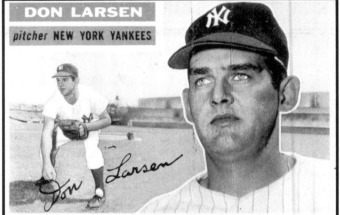

words "Don Larsen, *pitcher* NEW YORK YANKEES." I knew I didn't have him. He was one of those high numbers (#332) that had just been out for a few weeks. The card wasn't in great shape, but I didn't have it, and that was what mattered.

"I'll trade you Furillo for Larsen," I said.

Mitch grabbed the Furillo card so quickly I almost dropped the others. Then he stuck out his cards with Larsen pushed out, like a clumsy magician trying to make me pick the card he wanted me to take.

"Is that all you want?" he asked.

"Yeah. One for one."

He patted me awkwardly on the shoulder. "Thanks. You're a nice guy. I'm a big Dodger fan. Most of these kids make me trade two or three to get one Dodger."

"Well, I like the Yankees. And I already have Furillo."

Some of My Best Friends . . . .

As we walked back to class I studied Mitch. I had expected everybody in Cincinnati to be very different from people I knew in South Carolina. But they weren't. The kids here looked like the kids back home. Carthage Elementary School was all-white. These kids didn't even talk all that different.

But Mitch was different. His short hair was black and curly, his face long and slim, with a hooked nose. As I looked at him closely for the first time, I realized that, except for the beard, he resembled the Pharisees who were always after Jesus in the pictures in my Sunday School lesson books. And he talked so different. His voice had a nasal quality I had never heard before. That was part of what made him difficult to understand. The real problem for me, though, was how fast he talked.

"Whehyafum?" he asked. It took me a second to slow that down and decipher it as "Where are you from?"

"South Carolina."

"Where's that?"

"Right below North Carolina."

"Oh, a wise guy. What other cards did you win? Got any other Dodgers?" He stuck his own cards in his pocket and grabbed the ones I had won.

I think we knew each of us had just found his first friend in Cincinnati.

CHAPTER 18

Latchkey Kids

Mitch, it turned out, lived in Swifton Village, in the rectangular court next to mine. I don't believe the term "latchkey kids" had been coined in 1956, but that's what he was and what my brother and I became when our mother got a job at Rollman's Department Store in the Swifton Center, behind our apartment complex. One of the first indoor malls in the country, Swifton Center was billed as the "largest multi-million dollar retail trade center within the city limits of any metropolitan area" (Cincinnati *Enquirer*, Sept. 30, 1956). It opened one month after we arrived.

> *"Among the other excellencies of man, this is one, that he can form the image of perfection much beyond what he has experience of in himself."*
>
> David Hume

> *While cleaning out my parents' house after my father's death, I found an old flatware knife with the initials MHC on the handle. Since my mother's maiden name was Crisp, I assumed it was a family keepsake, but no one could identify an M. H. Crisp. Then one cousin suggested, "What if it stands for Mars Hill College?" He showed me a knife he still had from his student days, with his university's initials on the handle. I had to conclude that my mother had taken the knife as a souvenir of the place where she and my father met.*

My mother worked after she finished high school and didn't start college until four years later, in the fall of 1941. She met my dad while they were working in the dining hall of Mars Hill College, in western North Carolina. When my dad was at Georgia Tech in 1949-51 she had a paper route and two small children. I wanted to go with her on her route, so one morning she took me along. All I remember is being miserable, but probably not as miserable as I made her. Once she took this job at Rollman's in Cincinnati, she would be a working woman for the rest of her life, almost always doing office work in department stores.

Because we had only one car, my brother and I were already riding the bus to and from school. Dad took the car, and my mother walked to work. What would change when Mom started working, though, was that she would not be home when we got there.

Here was one more measure of the upheaval 1956 thrust upon me. Until that year I had enjoyed an idyllic life in the South. A key element in the formula for that life was my mother's presence. She drove me to school in the morning and picked me up after school every day. She worked hard around the house, and she cooked. She squeezed fresh orange juice and made pies from scratch. My favorite was her cherry pie with the lattice crust. Some mornings we had pancakes. Mickey Mantle endorsed "Batter Up" pancake mix (earning $15,000). I persuaded my mother to buy a box, but they were no match for hers, made from scratch. She didn't do housework in pearls and heels – and my dad didn't say, "Honey, I'm home" – but we weren't too far from the Reed/Cleaver/Anderson paradigm.

Cincinnati and 1956 changed all that forever.

As I grew up, I came to realize my mother wasn't happy playing domestic diva. She enjoyed working outside the home, and bringing in extra money was important to her. A child of the Depression, she could remember when her father's business failed and supper was a piece of bread with butter on it. She was never convinced she and my dad had enough money. My dad lost his last job when he was 59. He started a small sewing company, but my mother supported the two of them for the next ten years until she became too sick to work. After her first bout with cancer she dragged herself back to work long enough to get herself and my dad fully vested in Wal-Mart's medical plan. Within a year after her death Wal-Mart sold the expensive insurance

plan for surviving spouses to another company, leaving my dad with little besides Medicare. But, if your motto is "always low prices," you've got to keep those costs down.

My wife says she's grateful for the survival skills I learned because my mother went to work in Cincinnati. The day she started her job, she saw my brother and me off to the bus and told me, "Wash the dishes when you get home." That worried me all day. The dishes were always washed when I got home. I didn't know how to wash dishes. I used a bar of hand soap and cold water. It's a miracle we weren't all sick. One morning I told my mother I needed a shirt pressed. Her response was, "You know where the iron is."

By going to work my mother joined a social movement (Boyer, pp. 126-127). Women had worked outside the home during WWII, but returning servicemen reclaimed many of those jobs. The economic prosperity of the mid-1950s encouraged women to seek full-time employment. So many women had jobs that the Cincinnati *Enquirer* ran an article on October 10 discussing how stores were having trouble hiring people for the approaching holiday season. The head of the Retail Merchants' Association said, "Never before in peacetime have the stores faced such a problem in getting part-time help."

With both parents working, I had to learn to get around on my own. I became a more urban kid than I had ever been in Greenville. I rode the bus to and from school. I could walk over to the Swif-

ton Center if I had a little allowance money saved up. I took the bus downtown to the orthodontist, and I also rode it to my accordion lessons.

Since I've already revealed my odious nickname, I suppose I can't be embarrassed any further and can admit I took accordion lessons for almost a year. I liked music, but our apartment had no room for our piano or for an old pump organ my dad had taken apart and restored. I chose the accordion as a substitute. In my defense I can say I never tried to play "Lady of Spain."

Between the time my brother and I got home from school and the time my mother got home from work we had about an hour and a half to fill up. On most days that meant getting a snack and watching a little TV. When cold weather set in, shortly after my mother started working, I didn't have much interest in going outside. We may have been just across the river from the South, but we had Northern weather, including snow. As noted earlier, the weather was unusually cold that year. Probably a result of testing nuclear bombs, many people thought.

My mother's instructions were explicit. No other kids were allowed in our apartment, and we weren't allowed in anyone else's apartment if there was no parent at home. That wasn't hard to comply with during the school year. During the summer (of 1957) it meant a lot of time spent outside.

Being outdoors that summer suited me fine. Mom came home for lunch to check on us, but otherwise my brother and I were on our own. And there were kids to play ball with and baseball cards to collect.

The 1957 Topps set differed dramatically from the 1956. It went back to the traditional vertical arrangement and had just one picture of the player, instead of a head shot and a background shot. Most of the pictures were posed exclusively for Topps, and the infielders, who are supposed

to look like they're fielding or throwing, just look like they're posing. A lot of the pitchers appear to be showing how well their anti-perspirant is working.

But it is considered a highly desirable set, the hobby's equivalent of the '57 Chevy. It was larger than the '56 set (407 cards to 340) and included a few cards showing two or more players, such as the "Yankees' Power Hitters" with Mantle and Berra, the last card in the set. Mitch was quick to point out that the card with the "Dodgers' Sluggers" had to be printed horizontally, like the team cards, because it had four guys on it – Hodges, Snider, Furillo, and Campanella. I just reminded him who won the 1956 World Series and who lost.

The '57 Topps set features one of the most famous errors in baseball cards. Hank Aaron's picture was printed backwards, so that he was batting left-handed. The position of his arms covered up "Braves" and the number on the front of his jersey, and the 'M' for Milwaukee on his cap looked right, so no one noticed the mistake in time.

That summer I got all but twelve of the set. I have since acquired those and replaced some that were in poorer condition. The first card I ordered cost me $12.00, more than I spent on all the ones I collected during the summer of '57.

Looking back, I wonder if someone should have called Child Protective Services and reported all the children who were being left alone during the day in Swifton Village. I was not competent to look after my brother. We knew our mother was only a couple of minutes away, but in a real emergency – like when he came after me with the scissors – that distance could have been critical. With so little supervision, it would have been easy for us to become "juvenile delinquents," or JD's, as the breed was known in the '50s.

1,000,000 Delinquents

Since antiquity it has been standard procedure for adults to bemoan the low morals of the younger generation. But statistics support the notion of a problem in youth lawlessness in the 1950s. Nationwide, between 1945 and 1951, the number of youths ages 10-17 who were arrested remained steady at almost 50,000 per year. Starting in 1951, however, the number rose every year, reaching just under 250,000 in 1956. Between 1948 and 1955 the number of youths 10-17 who appeared in court on some charge increased ten times faster than the population of children that age. People living through that era knew something was "going wrong." A lot of soul-searching went on in the mid-'50s. What was the cause of this alarming trend? Could it be stopped?

The Cincinnati *Enquirer* wasn't optimistic: "No one seems to have a definite preventive program that would curb the increase in delinquency" (Sept. 27, 1956). Benjamin Fine of the *New York Times*, in a book published in 1954, predicted the nation would soon be confronted with 1,000,000 JD's. The topic of juvenile delinquency "loomed disproportionately large in the decade's mind" (Miller and Nowak, p. 280). Movies like "Blackboard Jungle" and "Teenage Crime Wave" sensationalized it in 1955.

The number of such films is legion. Many of them were set in reformatories or mental institutions, or they portrayed high schools as enemy territory, controlled by gangs of hoodlums. The open way – for that time – they dealt with subjects such as sex and drugs alarmed many people. Some featured established actors. Ginger Rogers and Michael Rennie starred in "Teenage Rebel" (1956). Sal Mineo, James Whitmore, and J. Carrol Naish appeared in "The Young Don't Cry" (1957). Others introduced actors who went on to significant careers. Jack Nicholson's first featured role was in "The Cry Baby Killer" (1958). "Crime in the Streets" (1956) was John Cassavetes' first film, while Sally Kellerman made her debut in "Reform School Girl" (1957). These films tended to be shown at drive-ins, or "passion pits." Jerry Lewis spoofed the genre in "The Delicate Delinquent" (1957).

Conservatives usually blamed delinquency on individual young people who just refused to measure up to social norms in an era when conformity was all-important. The answer to the problem was for caring adults to instill some discipline and purpose into the lives of the young. That was the message of "The Delicate Delinquent." A concerned policeman (Darrin McGavin) takes an interest in Lewis' character and "saves" him. The moral is undercut to some degree by the plot line: Lewis stumbled into trouble by unwittingly being on the scene when a gang committed a crime. He is no hardcore JD, the sort of character so often played by Sal Mineo.

Government was thought to be vital. The governor of Florida outlined his state's plan to keep teenagers in school in the summer and not give them enough time to get into trouble (*Life*, May 12, 1956).

Liberals, on the other hand, emphasized the problems of urban life which led young people to join gangs. Psychological terminology, coming into vogue in the '50s, was used to explain that JD's were "sick." Such diagnoses were applied especially to girls who were promiscuous, or just behaved flirtatiously ("Girls in the Night," 1953; "JD Girl," 1957). The number of films from the '50s with titles like "Teenage Bad Girl," "Hot Rod Girl," or "Teenage Doll" boggles the imagination when one sees them in a list, such as can be found at www.thevideobeat.com. Click on the page "JD, Bad Girl & Hot Rod Movies."

Juvenile delinquency rated attention in both of the newspapers I read in 1956. The Greenville police department sent an officer to a three-month Delinquency Control Institute at the University of Southern California (*News*, Feb. 28, 1956). The officer later reported on his work to the Greenville Council of Church Women, which helped to fund his trip. Echoing a common theme of those who worked with JD's, he said "There is so much more temptation for children today." He displayed weapons taken from juvenile offenders, including a switchblade knife and a zip-gun, a spring-action, single-shot weapon which could be made from a small piece of pipe, a ball-point pen, or a car's radio antenna.

The zip-gun was so closely identified with JD's that the lyrics to a popular song had to be changed. "I Fought the Law," written by Sonny Curtis of the Crickets in 1959, originally contained the line "Robbin' people with a zip gun." Record producers changed it to "six gun" in the more popular version released by The Bobby Fuller Four in 1965.

The most common attempt at a solution to the problem of delinquency was a curfew law. Cities across the country enacted them, with mixed results. As one police officer said, "Youngsters who are prone to get into trouble will ignore the law, and the others are going home anyway" (Cincinnati *Enquirer*, Oct. 7, 1956). The mayor of Cincinnati appointed a commission to review a report from the Citizens' Committee on Juvenile Delinquency and study how best to implement the committee's recommendation for a mayor's committee on youth (*Enquirer*, Oct. 18, 1956). Perhaps they should have taken Henry Wadsworth Longfellow's advice and had them play baseball:

    [Ball playing] communicated such an impulse to our limbs and joints, that there is nothing now heard of, in our leisure hours, but ball, ball. I cannot prophesy with any degree of accuracy concerning the continuance of this rage for play, but the effect is good, since there has been a thoroughgoing reformation from inactivity and torpitude.

Apparently there was a need for some work on this problem in Ohio in particular. An article in the *Enquirer* on Sept. 27 pointed out that the state's juvenile delinquency rate was rising faster than the national rate. Oddly enough, it was rising faster in rural areas than in the cities.

"When You're a Jet . . . ."

In June of '57 Mitch spent a couple of weeks with family in Brooklyn. For most of May that trip was all he talked about. Since the Dodgers would be playing home games for part of his time there, he would get to see them in his beloved Ebbets Field.

With no one to throw to, I resorted to throwing an old tennis ball against the wall of one of the apartment buildings. The wall did have one advantage – it could catch better than Mitch and return the ball more accurately.

After shagging a few flies, I chalked a strike zone on the wall to work on my pitching. Mantle was still my idol, but the memory of Don Larsen on the mound in that perfect game just would not go away. Like a lot of youngsters, I imitated the no-windup delivery Larsen used so successfully in the game. Bob Turley also used it in Game 6 of the '56 Series and pitched his best game of the year, a 4-hitter, only to lose 1-0 in the tenth inning. Some baseball pundits were afraid young pitchers would ruin themselves by trying to mimic the style (Cincinnati *Enquirer*, Oct. 14, 1956).

Larsen was off to a decent start in '57 and would finish with a 10-4 record. If the no-windup worked for him, I thought, why not try it?

But I was throwing an old tennis ball, not a baseball. The movement, or break, a pitcher is able to achieve with a baseball is due to the ball's raised seams and the air resistance they create. No matter how I gripped the smooth tennis ball or how hard I threw, I couldn't get it to "move." It just went straight to the spot I was aiming at.

I was trying to figure out what grip to use for a curve ball when someone came around the corner of the building and said, "What the hell do you think you're doing?"

That wasn't how Casey Stengel approached his pitchers on the mound.

This guy was a teenager, several years older than me but about three inches shorter. His hair was swept back in ducktails and his tight t-shirt showed off his well-developed arms and chest.

"Hey! I said, What the hell do you think you're doing?"

"I'm just playing ball."

"No, you're makin' this THUD, THUD noise. I can't hear nothin' inside except that THUD, THUD."

"Sorry. Nobody ever complained before."

"I guess 'cause I ain't never been here before, talkin' to my girl."

Then, over his shoulder, I noticed Debbie, a 15-year-old bombshell who lived in that building. She had spoken to me once.

"Sorry," I said again. "I'll . . . come back when you're gone."

He stepped closer to me. "No, you won't, 'cause it's none of your business when I come or go. You gotta stop doin' this shit."

"You don't live here. You can't tell me what to do." The words got past my braces before I had a chance to think them through.

He reached behind his back and whipped out something that looked like a handle. When he pushed a button, a long blade popped out. "I don't think you understand me, kid. I want you to stop throwin' that damn ball against the wall." He laughed. "Hey, I'm a poet." He grabbed the tennis ball out of my glove and jabbed the point of the knife into it. Then he sliced it in half and dropped the halves back into my glove.

"If you bother us again, that's what I'll do to any other balls you've got."

CHAPTER 19

The Good (?) Ol' Days

Today when people lament the moral state of America, they usually hark back to the 1950s as a time when everybody was as virtuous as the families on "Donna Reed" or "Ozzie and Harriet." According to those shows, the biggest problem we had to face was how to conceal a broken vase from Mom and Dad. But why bother? They always found out, and they always forgave the kids.

People who lived through that era, though, saw it differently. On April 14, 1956, Msgr. Harold S. Engel, director of the Youth Activities Department of the New York Catholic Charities, worried in the *New York Times* that "the appreciable increase in youth problems last year reflected a continued decline in moral and spiritual values."

I would argue that the country as a whole was not going through a decline but was hitting puberty in the mid-1950s. We still could be as innocent as a Doris Day movie (she was from Cincinnati), but we were also exploring, and we were rebels, with or without a cause. At times we seemed eager to rush into exciting, unknown territory; at other times we wanted to hang back where we knew we were safe. Movies of the 1950s were wholesome or titillating, depending on whether they starred Doris Day and Rock Hudson or Marilyn Monroe and Robert Mitchum.

Monroe and Mitchum co-starred in "River of No Return" in 1954. I didn't see it until it came to Greenville's Skyland Drive-in in June of 1956. My parents seldom went to movies, and when they did they preferred drive-ins because they didn't believe in babysitters and because drive-ins played three features. Since South Carolina didn't observe Daylight Saving Time, the first show started reasonably early. My brother and I could enjoy the playground and stay awake for most of the first feature. Then my parents could watch another show or two in peace and quiet.

Monroe and Mitchum did their own stunts for the movie. Production was delayed when Marilyn broke her leg.

My dad must have picked this particular triple feature. After Marilyn, the second movie starred Jane Russell and the third showcased Betty Grable and Sheree North. If we'd had "Hooters" in those days, we probably would have gone there a lot.

"River" was largely forgettable. The scene that remained burned in my memory was when Marilyn got thoroughly soaked going down a river on a raft. Mitchum took her ashore and into a cave, where she undressed and wrapped herself in a blanket. She was cold and shivering, so Mitchum had her lie down and gave her a vigorous rub-down – back, shoulders, legs. I'm sure I

> *"It is best to overlook most things, and not be too solicitous about perfection."*
>
> Rutherford B. Hayes

wasn't the only male wondering, What did she feel like under that blanket? (When I see it on TV today, I wonder, How many takes did they have to do?)

The mid-'50s saw a number of serious, now-classic, films produced. Hollywood seemed to be emerging from the terror of the Red-hunting and the Blacklist inspired by McCarthy. Many of the films, like "The Day the Earth Stood Still," dealt with the fear of nuclear war. Others, like "The Wild Bunch" and "The Blackboard Jungle," tried to understand the rise in juvenile delinquency. My family, if we went at all, tended toward less controversial movies. My first date was with a girl who lived three houses down from my grandparents. We walked downtown in May of 1956 to see "The Lone Ranger."

Under the mattress

As further evidence for America's rush into puberty I would point to the debut of *Playboy* in1954, with its women airbrushed to perfection. Follow that with the publication in 1955 of *Lolita* and in 1956 of Grace Metalious' *Peyton Place*, a potboiler novel that wouldn't rate more than a PG-13 today but which created a scandal when it came out. At a time when married couples on TV and in movies slept in twin beds, Metalious' book admitted they actually had sex, and not just with their spouses. And their kids were doing it, too! Called "probably the most controversial novel ever written," it quickly outsold *Gone with the Wind*.

By 1959 psychologists Eberhard and Phyllis Kronhausen were trying to distinguish pornography from eroticism in their book *Pornography and the Law*, while admitting that "the question of what is or is not 'obscene' is of small importance in a world which is faced with the problem of physical survival" (p. ix). Even though they were writing in a sober, scholarly manner, the Drs. Kronhausen felt they could not repeat the language used in the books they were studying but had to resort to "bracketing the more acceptable synonyms for the expressions used" (p. 108).

Even the serious literature of this period struck many readers as scandalous. Controversial sociologist Pitirim Sorokin lambasted American literature as "largely centered on sex, especially its pathological forms" (*Revolution*, p. 19). Sorokin felt Hemingway, Faulkner, Steinbeck and other major American writers had "paid their tribute to sex, either by making it the main topic of many of their works, or, what is perhaps more symptomatic, by devoting to it much attention in works supposedly dealing with problems quite different" (*Revolution*, p. 23).

The greatest outcry of social critics in the 1950s was leveled against comic books and pulp fiction novels. Fredric Wertham, in his *Seduction of the Innocent* (1954), claimed comic books corrupted children's morals. Wertham was a reputable psychologist who directed a mental health clinic in Harlem. His scholarly article on "Psychological Effects of School Segregation" was part of the evidence submitted to the Supreme Court during its deliberations in the *Brown* v. *Board* case.

Much of Wertham's work was with juvenile delinquents in the New York court system. As he interviewed them, he became aware, he said, of how many of them read crime comics. Even defenders of the genre today admit that, in the early '50s, many comics deserved Wertham's criticism. The goriest and most violent were those published by William Gaines' EC Comics. Wertham also asserted that Superman was a Nietzschean incitement to fascism, that Batman and Robin were homosexual lovers, and that Wonder Woman was a lesbian devotee of bondage. (Wonder Woman's creator did eventually admit to a fondness for handcuffs and ballgags.)

Wertham's book, though shoddily written and poorly documented, was excerpted in popular magazines. The furor led to Senate hearings on the comic book industry in 1955. Rather than wait for government regulation, the producers of the comics set up the Comics Code Authority to police themselves. The worst offenders simply shut down. Comic book aficionados still revile Wertham as the man who castrated the industry. William Gaines was left with only *Mad* magazine, which one of my older cousins introduced me to in 1957 while we were in Laurens.

My introduction to pulp novels was of my own doing. Shortly after we arrived in Cincinnati my parents got me an appointment with an orthodontist to get braces to correct my snaggle-tooth. His office was in Carew Tower, the tallest building in downtown Cincinnati (49 floors). With both parents working, I had to ride the bus downtown twice a month to have the braces tightened. I made sure my brother got on the school bus and then I caught a bus straight downtown.

One afternoon the session took longer than usual and I missed the bus I rode home. It would be twenty minutes before the next one. It was February and cold, so while I was waiting for the bus I stepped into the newsstand on the corner to check out the latest comic books. I wouldn't have believed it at the time, but my affection for comics was a trait shared by several major league ballplayers, including Don Larsen (*Perfect Yankee*, p. 47).

I went to the comic books, now nicely sanitized thanks to Dr. Wertham, and found the latest "Superman." What really drew me to the character, I think, was his X-ray vision. What would it be like, I wondered, to see through things – things like Lois Lane's clothes? Would you be able to stop your X-ray vision when you got to her underwear? To her skin? Or would it go on into her insides? Would you see a naked woman or a skeleton?

Those were important questions to an 11-year-old with super-charged hormones.

The newsstand had a lot of magazines and paperback books, most selling for 25 cents each. I had recently read my first Perry Mason mystery, so I spotted other Erle Stanley Gardner titles on the racks. Then I noticed another rack behind that one, where you couldn't see it until you were right up on it. The book covers on that rack showed either two muscular, shirtless men or two voluptuous women. One, titled *Bitter Love*, had a blurb describing it as "the story of a queer marriage."

"Son, you don't need to be back there," the store owner said from behind the counter.

Because of the growth spurt I was experiencing I was often mistaken for someone in his mid-teens, but I obviously needed to be even older to read these books. What I was observing unwittingly was a cultural explosion, the crest of a wave of gay/lesbian pulp novels that ran from right after WWII until the early 1960s. People like Gore Vidal and Truman Capote wrote some of those books under pen names.

Being homosexual in the 1950s was, in many ways, more difficult than being black or Communist. Accusations of homosexuality had to be couched in the vaguest terms, and the response had to be equally cautious. When Liberace visited England in September of 1956 he objected to press descriptions of him as an "unmanly man." The charges upset his mother – who was accompanying him – so much she had to be hospitalized. In a masterly piece of obfuscation Liberace told a news conference, "Just look at the number of woman fans I have. I'm just like God made me and I don't intend to change . . . . Censorship should not hide the truth, but if the truth is of degeneracy, I think that censorship should take place. I guess everyone has to expect a certain number of nonbelievers and I suppose that's why they shot Abraham Lincoln" (Greenville *News*, Sept. 30, 1956).

Given the meaning of certain terms today, one can't help but chuckle at some things published half a century ago. In its March 20, 1956, issue *Look* ran an article titled "Spring Girdles Go Gay." Elvis Presley recorded a song that year, "Paralyzed," in which he sang about his reaction to being in love: "I'm gay every morning/At night I'm still the same." In a "Gasoline Alley" strip on Feb. 29 Skeezix asks his son "How about girls, Chipper? Do they interest you?" Chipper says, "Not like boys." Skeezix seems to want some reassurance. "They're all right at parties, aren't they?" "Yeah," Chipper concedes. "They look smooth an' smell nice. But they're always thinkin' about gettin' their clothes mussed. Give me boys every time."

At a conference of juvenile judges in North Carolina concern was expressed about the dramatic increase in the amount of pornographic material in circulation. A Pittsburgh police officer speaking to the conference said "the number of illustrations and photos of nude men found in circulation indicated in his opinion the tremendous increase in homosexuality" (Greenville *News*, Aug. 16, 1956).

When I turned back to the rack of more acceptable paperbacks, my eye fell on one called *The Baby Doll Murders*, by James O. Causey. (It had nothing to do with the movie "Baby Doll," starring Carol Baker, which caused a sensation when it came out in June of '56.) The covers of the Perry Mason novels were about as provocative as this one. For that matter, some of the illustrations accompanying the stories in the *Saturday Evening Post* aroused my interest as much as this cover.

So I bought the book.

I tucked it, along with my "Superman" comic, into the backpack I carried (one my dad had used in the Marine Corps) and headed for the bus stop. I figured I would have to keep it in the backpack. Some kids I knew hid stuff under their mattresses, but I didn't feel anything I put there would be safe from my brother. I wasn't sure when I would get a chance to read it, or even why I had bought it.

The outspoken Professor Sorokin made no secret of what he thought about the type of book I had just purchased:

> . . . in this pulp writing, sexualization has gone much farther, and has assumed much uglier forms than in the serious literature. The sham literature of our age is designed for the commercial cultivation, propagation, and exploitation of the most degraded forms of behavior . . . . this pornographically illustrated pulp-literature demoralizes and dehumanizes millions of readers. Its audience, as well as its quantity, is incomparably larger than that of serious literature . . . . In addition, some of this material is turned into popular movies, is brought into millions of homes by radio and television, and is even dramatized on the legitimate stage. All in all, this stuff has become omnipresent in our lives, and everyone of us is incessantly and increasingly exposed to its deadly radiations.
>
> (*Revolution*, pp. 24-25)

Sorokin may have been an alarmist, but he was right in one regard: *Peyton Place* was made into a movie and, eventually, a TV series.

CHAPTER 20

"During adolescence imagination is boundless. The urge toward self-perfection is at its peak."

Louise J. Kaplan

Those Oldies but Goodies

While in Cincinnati I began taking music seriously. My accordion book contained some arrangements of classical theme, which I liked. For Christmas of '56 I got a radio and began listening to WLW, which played a mix of music. Gradually I began to tune to stations which played more rock and roll. Obviously a guy who plays the accordion isn't going to back up Elvis, but some of the music appealed to me, especially the slower songs.

A history of rock and roll's origins is far beyond the scope of this book. A couple of items included in the bibliography can lead the curious reader to fuller information. What I hope to do in this chapter is to give a snapshot of the impact the music was beginning to have in 1956-57 and show some ways it affected my own life at that time.

Suffice it to say that the roots of rock and roll can be traced to Cleveland radio personality Alan Freed. In 1952 Freed became aware that white teenagers were listening to, and buying, rhythm and blues (R&B) records by black artists. He persuaded his station manager to let him start a program he called "Moondog's Rock and Roll Party." Freed chose the term "rock and roll" to distance the music from the racial connotations of R&B. "Rock and roll" was black slang for dancing but also for sexual intercourse. Freed's show proved enormously popular. He went on to stage concerts and produce movies featuring black performers. Chuck Berry was practically the co-star with Freed of "Go, Johnny, Go" in 1956 (Miller and Nowak, pp. 295-299). Freed's career ended when he was caught up in the Payola scandal at the end of the decade.

Go, Cat, Go!

Much of the hand-wringing over the moral decline of youth in the mid-1950s was directed at popular music, which by that time was in a state of transition. The Big Band era was over, but some people hadn't figured that out. In July of '56 NBC started a new radio program, "NBC Bandstand," five days a week, from 10:30 until noon. It would reunite "some of the greatest names in the business . . . . [F]eeling that band music is being revived, and equal to the 'crush' years in the '30's, NBC has brought them all together" (Greenville *News*, July 25). Who could pass up a chance to hear the Dorsey Brothers, Guy Lombardo, Johnny Mercer, and all the rest?

Even defining a performer's genre in the mid-'50s could be difficult. Patsy Cline was popular with general audiences as well as on the country charts. Some of the earliest rock stars, such as Bill Haley and the Comets, performed what is known as "rockabilly," using rhythms borrowed from country music. Teresa Brewer, whose voice was more strident than a typical big-band singer but definitely not rock and roll, was voted outstanding female vocalist in 1955 and 1956. In the summer of 1956, she co-wrote "I Love Mickey," about my hero. Mantle says a few words near the end of the song, making it the most collectible of Brewer's recordings. In mid-September *Sports Illustrated* reported the record was "doing well."

The tension in popular music was probably best summed up by Kay Starr's song, "The Rock-and-Roll Waltz." It described how a teenager saw her parents trying to waltz while playing a hit song on her "record machine." ("Rock- two-three, roll-two-three.") Some lack of focus can also be seen in the Cincinnati *Enquirer*'s list of the top ten songs in town as of October 13, 1956, a list "based on reports from high school correspondents":

1. Love Me Tender – Elvis Presley
2. Green Door – Jim Lowe
3. Walkin' in the Rain – Johnnie Ray
4. Out of Sight, Out of Mind – Five Keyes
5. Every Day of My Life – McGuire Sisters
6. Blueberry Hill – Fats Domino
7. Don't Be Cruel – Elvis Presley
8. Friendly Persuasion – Pat Boone
9. Tonight You Belong to Me – Lawrence Welk
10. Miracle of Love – Eileen Rogers

Elvis, Fats Domino, Pat Boone, the McGuire Sisters, and Lawrence Welk, all on one list? Can you spell 'eclectic'? Even more amazing is the fact that on Sept. 18 Welk's song was number one, with Bing Crosby's "True Love" at number two. "Don't Be Cruel" ranked number 6 that week. Mitch Miller and Doris Day also had songs in that list.

My dad liked a duo, the Bell Sisters, who recorded throughout the 1950s, appearing with Bob Hope, Dinah Shore, Bing Crosby, and others. At the time we wondered if they were related to us. I've since learned they were from California and took their name from one of their grandmothers. I saw them on the "Mickey Mouse Club" in 1955. One can now watch that performance, and others, on their web site. Their style was definitely big band. Their biggest hit, "Bermuda," was used in the 1996 film "Grace of My Heart," and they were the pop culture reference *du jour* of a "Zippy the Pinhead" comic strip in 2005.

Radio and records were where one heard Elvis and Fats. TV was still the domain of the big-band sound. Each week my family watched the "Lawrence Welk Show." The "lovely little Lennon Sisters" were the attraction for a shy 11-year-old boy who was hitting puberty with a vengeance. Man, that Peggy was *so* hot. But my adoration may have had a subconscious baseball aspect as well. Unless they were in one of the show's inane production numbers, the girls stood in a diamond formation, with Janet at home plate, my beloved Peggy at first, Diane at second, and Kathy at third.

On May 6 the *New York Times* reported that Welk and his sponsor, Dodge, would present a second show designed "strictly for teenagers." That show, "Lawrence Welk's Top Tunes and New Talent," ran from 1956-59. Welk was so afraid of the double meanings in the lyrics of some popular songs he had a member of his staff assigned to ferreting out any potentially offensive words. I never met a teenager who watched the show.

Ford Motors had its own plans in the works for a show featuring Tennessee Ernie Ford which would "also be aimed at youth." One wonders how they defined "youth," with guest stars such as Greer Garson, Zsa-Zsa Gabor, and Adolphe Menjou. Ernie sang mostly old standards and hymns, but he did occasionally do pop tunes like "Love Me Tender" or "Way Down Yonder in New Orleans." My father had an excellent bass voice, so we usually had to listen to him singing along with Ernie.

On "Your Hit Parade" Gisele MacKenzie, Dorothy Collins, Snooky Lanson and others sang ballads and show tunes. "Hit Parade" was a carry-over from radio and never had particularly high ratings. Its format of presenting the top seven songs of the week plus an old favorite (the "Lucky Strike Extra") put it in a bind when one song remained at the top of the charts week after week. How many different ways can you stage "How Much is that Doggie in the Window"? But, except for a hiatus in 1958, the show stayed on the air until 1959.

By 1956 the "mainstream" music industry had its finger stuck in the dike, trying to hold back the flood waters of rock and roll. *Life* magazine said the craze began "last summer as demurely as the first fuzz on the chin of a growing boy," but by early 1956 "a rage for teen-age lyrics has reached a full, luxuriant growth" (Mar. 5). Some of the more traditional singers tried to appeal to teens with songs like Eddie Fisher's "Dungaree Doll" and Gale Storm's "A Teenage Prayer." Perry Como got on the bandwagon with "Jukebox Baby." The songs were just as vapid as one might imagine, and yet, when I mentioned them to my wife, she said, "Oh, yes, I remember 'A Teenage Prayer'."

Rockin' Around the Clock!

Alan Freed's movie "Rock Around the Clock" played in Greenville in May of 1956. It often evoked strong reactions from teenagers viewing it. By September it was showing in England and police had to use dogs "to help break up a riot . . . . One policeman was knocked into the seats by dancing teenagers who went wild in the theater aisles. The incident . . . was similar to others in theaters elsewhere in the London area" (Greenville *News*, Sept. 12, 1956). A week later the BBC reported its weekly call-in show "Any Questions?" drew "twice as many inquiries on rock 'n' roll as it did on Suez" (*News*, Sept. 21, 1956)

The performers who starred in the movie also staged live shows, with unpredictable results. Bill Haley and other performers were scheduled to play in Greenville in May, but a bomb threat caused a cancellation (Greenville *News*, May 24, 1956). A concert in Raleigh, North Carolina, went off as scheduled but with seventeen arrests. The audience was "separated but included both Whites and Negroes at the same performances. Police said most of those arrested were Negroes" (*News*, May 25, 1956). A concert in Miami drew 10,000 in a "non-segregated" audience, where "except for one arrest of a youth who refused to obey a policeman, the two-show concert went on without incident" (*News*, May 29, 1956).

In San Jose, California, though, a riot broke out among 2,500 teenagers attending a show and dance where Fats Domino was performing. The incident was provoked by someone throwing a beer bottle at the dancers. In the resulting melee hundreds of bottles were smashed, "chairs and tables broken and the railing on the bandstand torn down." It took police an hour to get the situation under control. Ten people were arrested (*News*, July 9, 1956).

Domino and his band were also playing at an enlisted men's club in Newport, Rhode Island, when another riot erupted, complete with flying beer bottles and chairs. As the music "reached a frenzied tempo," someone shut off the lights and pandemonium ensued. The admiral who investigated the incident concluded there were no racial overtones, even though the crowd was integrated, and "the only cause of the melee . . . was the excitement accompanying the fever-pitched 'rock-n-roll'." Therefore, he banned the music (Cincinnati *Enquirer*, Sept. 19, 1956).

In light of such incidents, adult reactions to the music were predictable. Regina McLinden, head of the Miami Board of Review, "put aside her anti-comic book crusade temporarily to wage war on the 'worm wiggle' . . . . 'I'm not against jazz,' Mrs. McLinden said. 'That's here to stay and it has some merit. But this worm wiggle, with its suggestive movements, is dangerous for children'." She feared that young people became addicted to the music and it created a "form of mood . . . which could lead to something more. I don't approve of it" (Greenville *News*, May 29, 1956).

That fear of "something more" stoked many adults' objections to the music. Judge John J. Connolly of Boston's juvenile court, saw a connection between the music and "the climb in immorality among youngsters . . . . Innocent girls get into trouble when they go unsupervised to record hops. Older boys, excited wise guys, sell them a bill of goods, and what happens is shameful" (Greenville *News*, June 21, 1956).

People on the streets of Greenville, when asked if rock and roll was "a bad influence on teenagers," were divided in their views. Those who, to judge from the pictures, were older voiced opinions such as "Very definitely. It gets them into a sexy mood. I understand several cities have outlawed it," or "It is not good Christian music. The teenagers should have more interest in finer types of music." Those who appeared to be younger, including two unmarried women, seemed more tolerant: "I don't think it is a bad influence. I like it. Rock and' Roll is not high class music, but it is good listening music" (*News*, June 17, 1956).

Established musicians like Mitch Miller denounced the form. "The reason kids like rock and roll," he said, "is that their parents *don't*." As Artist and Repertoire director of Columbia Records, Miller kept the label from signing any rock artists throughout the 1950s. Frank Sinatra thought rock was created and performed by "cretinous goons" and was "the most brutal, ugly, desperate, vicious form of expression it has been my misfortune to hear." He had so much influence at his label, Reprise Records, that they would not record any rock music until Sinatra's daughter, Nancy, wanted to make a record in 1966. Composer Billy Rose dismissed rock as "obscene junk, pretty much on a level with dirty comic magazines." He also called the music's performers "a set of untalented twitchers and twisters" (Cincinnati *Enquirer*, Sept. 24, 1956).

It should be no surprise that sociologist Sokorin (*Revolution*, p. 31) was as critical of popular music as he was of popular books. He thought the sexuality of modern music had become

> naked, seductive and abductive, lusty and perverse in popular jazz and song hits and in the bulk of night club, television and radio music. References to kissing, embracing, and going to bed are essential to their lyrics. The songs are monotonously chanted by voiceless crooners innocent of the art of bel-canto. Their bleating is underscored by their gyrations, contortions, and bodily rhythms all too clear in sexual innuendo and undisguised meaning. Records of this sort of 'music' are sold by the millions and their nauseous repetition occupies the lion's share of radio and television programs. The composers and crooners of these 'hits' are idolized by millions, and are financially remunerated many times more amply than are the composers of the serious music of today.

Burl Ives was more open-minded: "I understand some people are worried that rock 'n' roll is immoral and promotes juvenile delinquency. Horsefeathers! I'd say if a young person is going to get into trouble it doesn't matter which he listened to: rock 'n' roll or Rachmaninoff" (Greenville *News*, June 10, 1956). Dinah Shore said, "I like anything with a beat, and for too many years there hasn't been much of a beat in music . . . . I think the music is exciting and fun" (Cincinnati *Enquirer*, Sept. 20, 1956).

The great hope of adults was that rock and roll would be short-lived. The editors of the Greenville *News* (June 8, 1956) were confident it was

> a temporary fad. Others have come and gone before it. It may or may not be as good as the addicts think or as bad as the critics claim. As for us, we question whether it really is music, unless there is music in the primitive emotional outbursts of celebrating savages. We do know for certain, however, that the lyrics of many of the numbers are, to say the least, in extremely bad taste and we are surprised that radio stations would play some of them for broadcast.

By the summer of 1956 America was embroiled in what *Look* called "The Great Rock 'n' Roll Controversy" (June 26). The "craze" had "frightened parents, turned the music-publishing business upside down and sent psychiatrists to their textbooks for new ways to say 'adolescent rebellion'." The editors did conclude with a concession: "in the name of fairness, it must be added that the music is vital, exuberant and affirmative." It had the misfortune, though, of becoming popular "at a time when juvenile delinquency was getting more publicity than ever before, perhaps more than it deserved. The musical craze provides a convenient scapegoat for adult failures."

As the recording industry woke up to the income potential of this new style of music, they felt it could not continue to rely on black artists. White singers began to "cover" original songs by black singers and groups. The cover versions were usually sanitized. LaVern Baker's "Roll with Me, Henry" became Georgia Gibbs' million-seller "Dance with Me, Henry." Where Joe Turner had sung "You wear low dresses/The sun comes shinin' through" in "Shake, Rattle, and Roll," Bill Haley changed the line to "You wear those dresses/Your hair done up so nice" in his cover. The Crew Cuts, a group so white they were Canadian, enjoyed great success in the mid-1950s by covering such tunes as "Earth Angel" and "Sh-Boom." One source noted, "The only original recording the Crew Cuts ever made was a 1956 Budweiser commercial" (Miller and Nowak, p. 298). The put-down isn't literally accurate. A number of their own songs made the charts in Canada but never succeeded in the U. S.

For two reasons 1956 proved to be a watershed year for rock and roll. First, Little Richard's "Long, Tall Sally" became the first record by a black artist to outsell the white cover (by Pat Boone). And, second, Elvis Presley blazed onto the national scene with three #1 songs in one year, two of them on one record.

The King – but not yet

Elvis had already been on some local TV shows in the South. From January to March of 1956 he went national, appearing six times on the Dorsey Brothers show, then twice with Milton Berle, and in July on Steve Allen's show, where he had to sing "Hound Dog" to a basset in a tuxedo. Allen's show aired opposite Ed Sullivan's juggernaut and signing Elvis was a pure ratings ploy that worked. It was the first time Allen's show topped Sullivan's in the ratings.

Sullivan had not wanted Elvis on his show, but he couldn't ignore the numbers, so he signed Presley to three appearances, the first on September 9, 1956. After that there was no turning back. As Danny and the Juniors would proclaim, "Rock and Roll is Here to Stay." In that first appearance Elvis was introduced by actor Charles Laughton, who was substituting because Sullivan had been seriously injured in an auto accident several weeks before. Laughton was in New York and Elvis in California, where he was filming "Love Me Tender." Elvis appeared again on October 28, when Sullivan proclaimed him a "real decent, fine boy." It was not until his third appearance, on January 6, 1957, that Sullivan decided to show him only from the waist up.

The controversy surrounding Elvis in his early days is old news, but it is worth sampling a few of the comments made about him. Jack Gould had this to say in the *New York Times*, June 7, 1956:

> Mr. Presley has no discernible singing ability. His speciality is rhythm songs which he renders in an undistinguished whine; his phrasing, if it can be called that, consists of the stereotyped variations that go with a beginner's aria in a bath-tub. For the ear he is an unutterable bore. He is a rock-and-roll variation of one of the most standard acts in show business . . . the virtuoso of the hootchy-kootchy.

A critic in the *New York Journal American* concluded that "he can't sing a lick" and his gyrations on stage resembled "an aborigine's mating dance." Elvis' ability as an actor was also called into question. In a review of "Love Me Tender" *Time* magazine asked, "Is it a sausage? It is certainly smooth and damp-looking, but whoever heard of a 172-lb. sausage six feet tall?"

In a feature article on August 27, 1956, *Life* called him "a different kind of idol" and expressed concern that his movements on stage created "shock waves of hysteria" in his heavily female audiences, who went "into frenzies of screeching and wailing, winding up in tears." A judge in Jacksonville, Florida, threatened to have him arrested on a charge of "impairing the morals of minors," while teenagers in a Baptist church in the city prayed for his salvation. Reactions to him were seldom neutral. One 14-year-old girl in East Meadow, New York, ran away from home because her parents

objected so strongly to her playing Elvis' records. Her mother said, "We quarreled all the time about Presley . . . . She played Presley records all day and all night. It's like a frenzy" (Greenville *News*, July 22, 1956).

I missed Elvis' first appearance because that was when my mother, brother, and I were staying at my grandparents' house, just before the move to Cincinnati. If you were at their house when the church doors were open, you went to church, Sunday morning, Sunday evening, and Wednesday evening. In addition, South Carolina was not on Daylight Saving Time, as New York was, so Sullivan's show was starting as we were going into church, at 7 p. m.

Being only ten at the time, I wasn't quite ready for rock and roll. The couple of times I had heard Elvis – and I did see him singing to the basset hound on Steve Allen's show – he had the same effect on me that he did on a lot of people: he scared me. Music so powerful, so raucous, I just could not comprehend. By the next summer, though, with all sorts of new hormones surging through me, I found a connection with it, particularly with the slow-dancing, broken-hearted songs.

Who wears short shorts?

The first girl I danced with was Ruth Ann. She moved into a building in our U-shaped court in Swifton Village during the winter. By the time she and I emerged from hibernation I stood 5'6" and my voice had changed. When we went to Laurens for Easter, I was taller than all of my older cousins except one. Mitch, who was maturing more slowly, said I was definitely ready for my Bar Mitzvah.

Ruth Ann was 12, one of the other kids told me, about 5'3", and sported the figure of a 16-year-old. She had red hair. Mitch wondered one day if her "other hair" was red, too.

"What do you mean?" I asked.

"You know. Down there." I really didn't know what he was talking about.

Ruth Ann also wore braces. I had hated mine since the day they were put on, but at least on the infrequent occasions when I smiled now, people didn't think, 'Oh, he's got a snaggle-tooth.' They thought, 'Oh, he's wearing braces.' Unlike a snaggle-tooth, braces are a normal part of growing up. That realization did a lot for my self-esteem, and the braces themselves were my point of contact with Ruth Ann. The first thing she ever said to me was, "I see you've got to wear braces, too. Don't you hate them?"

Ruth Ann's mother worked in one of the stores in Swifton Center and her stepfather worked in a gas station, so she was also a latchkey kid, originally from

somewhere in the mountains of Kentucky. She called the man her stepfather, but one day, while we were sitting on the steps in front of her building, she told me that he and her mother weren't actually married.

"I'm not supposed to tell anybody," she said, lowering her voice and putting her hand on my thigh. "I'm telling you because I trust you so much."

My mother met Ruth Ann's mother while walking to work. I overheard her describe Ruth Ann's mother to my dad as "white trash." She resisted the woman's overtures of friendship. I didn't like her much either. She had a shrill voice and smoked. And she snapped at Ruth Ann even more harshly than my mother sometimes talked to my brother.

Ruth Ann rarely played ball with us. When she ran, parts of her moved like I had never noticed a girl moving before. We were both chasing a fly ball once and bumped together. I had called for it, but she didn't get out of the way. She grabbed hold of me and we ended up on the ground. I missed the ball and, with her on top of me, I couldn't chase it. When I pushed her away she laughed and gave me a look I had seen only in ads for certain kinds of movies in the paper.

Most of the time Ruth Ann just sat on the steps in front of her building and watched us play. Whenever I looked her way, she was watching me. And I looked in her direction a lot because she always wore shorts and tied her blouses in a knot so her bellybutton showed.

How much skin women should show in public was a hotly debated topic in the mid-1950s. John Marquand could even write a humorous article about it in *Sports Illustrated*: "Are Shorts too Short at Happy Knoll?" The town of East Hampton, New York, approved an ordinance requiring women to "cover that portion of the body from midway between the knees and hips to and including the shoulders." Offenders could be fined $5 to $100 (Greenville *News*, May 11).

In White Plains, New York, two women were cited "for wearing shorts that bared more leg than the law allowed." One, a visitor from Kansas, received a suspended sentence because she was unaware of the law "that a lady's leg must be covered at least halfway from thigh to knee." The other, the 17-year-old daughter of a New Rochelle doctor, was arrested "for wearing 'real short' shorts" (Greenville *News*, June 28, 1956).

A letter writer to the *News* on May 27 endorsed a stand the paper had taken:

> I found myself heartily in agreement with what you said editorially in one of last week's issues on the impropriety of people going shopping clad, or scantily clad, in shorts. I would go a step further and say that such a practice ought to be regarded as an insult to the public conscience.
>
> It is strange to note that women are the chief offenders along this line. Since the women are supposed to be the symbols of modesty among us, it is rather disappointing to note this trend.

One of the age-old arguments for women covering themselves is that the sight of a scantily clad female body is a distraction to men. That was certainly the case in Ionia, Michigan, where two policemen emptying parking meters dropped the bag and had to reroute traffic while they scrambled after the coins. "The red-faced pair admitted they'd gotten absorbed watching a pretty girl in shorts walk by" (Greenville *News*, June 8, 1956).

In early August a woman wrote to Emily Post to complain about women who came into stores wearing shorts. "They also walk through the town in shorts and do all their marketing dressed in this fashion. To me this is in shockingly bad taste." Mrs. Post could only agree and "find the custom very unpleasant." I doubt she was amused by the song "Short Shorts," by the Royal Teens, which came out in 1958 and reached #3 on the charts.

Obviously I had seen girls in shorts before, but there was something special about the way Ruth Ann looked in them. And the way she would rub her hands on her legs. She reminded me of some of the voluptuous women in Al Capp's "Li'l Abner" and in his spin-off strip, "Long Sam," which ran in the Cincinnati *Enquirer*.

Happy Birthday, Baby

One hot Monday afternoon in June there weren't any other kids around. I had just gotten back from a week in Laurens and Mitch was visiting his family back in Brooklyn for a couple of weeks. My brother had taken off to the next court to play with some of his school buddies. Ruth Ann and I were sitting in front of her building, just talking. Well, I was also looking at her as much as I could. She had on the shortest pair of shorts I had seen her in yet.

"You missed my birthday," she said.

"When was it?"

"Yesterday. I was thirteen. Are you thirteen yet?"

"No. I'm . . . twelve." Well, I would be twelve in September. But nobody believed me when I told them I was eleven. In Laurens a group of us had gone to a movie. Under twelve, you got in for a quarter. Twelve and over, it was fifty cents. My cousin Buster, who was thirteen, paid his fifty cents. Then I stepped up and tried to get in for a quarter. Since I was taller than Buster, the ticket lady wouldn't believe me. She wouldn't even believe the four cousins who were with us. On the way back to Cincinnati I decided that, if people thought I was twelve, I might as well *be* twelve a few months early.

"Would you like a piece of my birthday cake?" Ruth Ann purred.

"Sure. Thanks."

She stood up and opened the door to the building. "Come on, then."

I had assumed she would bring the cake out to the porch. I didn't want to tell her that my mother wouldn't let me go into anyone else's apartment if there were no parents home . . . . Shoot, I would just stay long enough to eat a piece of cake. Who would know?

I followed Ruth Ann up the stairs to her apartment on the third floor. Hell, with her shapely bottom and legs just inches above me, I would have followed her up the stairs all the way to the 49th floor of Carew Tower.

The living room of her apartment was as messy as my brother's half of our room. Socks, t-shirts, and a couple of pieces of women's underwear were lying on the sofa and the big chair that was pointed at the TV set. On the coffee table were some magazines. One of them, *Playboy*, Mitch had told me about, but I had never seen a copy before.

"Let's eat in the kitchen," Ruth Ann said.

Not that the kitchen was much of an improvement. What looked like a couple of days worth of dishes were piled in the sink. By now I had learned to wash dishes in hot water and detergent. Apparently Ruth Ann's mother hadn't assigned that task to her. I watched to make sure she got clean plates out of a cupboard.

"When is your birthday?" Ruth Ann asked as she cut two pieces of yellow cake with chocolate frosting and opened a couple of Cokes. The cake was made from a mix and didn't have any decoration – like mine and my brother's always did – just holes where the candles had been.

"In September," I said. Upon reflection I guess she took that to mean I would be thirteen in September.

"I can't wait till I'm sixteen," she said. "Then I'm going to leave here. Get away from my mother and her damn boyfriends. I may not even wait that long. My mother got married when she was fourteen."

I didn't know what to say to that.

"Let's listen to some music," Ruth Ann said. "I got money to buy records for my birthday." She went to the portable record player in the living room and stacked several 45s on the spindle. Elvis' "Love Me Tender" was the first one, an oldie from 1956.

When Ruth Ann sat back down at the table her leg touched mine. I moved my leg, and she moved hers so it was touching mine again.

"I love that song," she said. "And I really love Elvis. Do you like him?"

"Yeah, he's good." What could I say? I wasn't going to run home and get my accordion. "I like Ricky Nelson, too." Ricky's first two songs had come out that spring. He was more familiar, safer. I had watched him grow up on TV.

She brushed my hair with her hand. "You know, if you'd let your hair grow a little and comb it back, you'd look kind of like Elvis. You've got nice lips, like his."

The next record was Pat Boone's "Love Letters in the Sand."

"You want to dance with me?" Ruth Ann asked. She sounded almost like she was begging.

"I don't really know how to dance."

"It's easy. I'll show you. Come on."

She took my hand and led me into the living room. As Pat Boone finished and Elvis started "Love Me," a hit from earlier in the year. Ruth Ann took my left hand and guided my right hand to the small of her back. Then she pressed herself against me, her left hand on my shoulder and her head on my chest.

"I can feel your heart beating," she said, "just like in the song. 'So close to mine'."

I could feel something else, and I was afraid Ruth Ann could feel it, too.

One day earlier that spring I had been on my way out to play, but my mother told me I couldn't "because of that." The "that" she was pointing to was the noticeable bulge in the crotch of my jeans, which were tight because that's how we wore them and because I grew six inches during the year we were in Cincinnati. She told me to go back to my room for a while.

Ruth Ann and I swayed back and forth for a couple of minutes. I wasn't really leading her, just trying to get away from her.

When the song's last "Oh, yeah" had faded away, I peeled Ruth Ann off of me and said, "Thanks for the cake. I need to go. I'm not supposed . . . I mean, I'm supposed to keep an eye on what my brother's doing. I'd better go find him."

"I'll see you later," she called after me as I trotted down the stairs.

That night Ruth Ann did call me, the first phone call I'd ever gotten from a girl. I had to take it in the living room while my parents and my brother were watching TV. She did most of the talking. "It was fun dancing with you," she said. "I know what you really wanted, though, and it's all right with me, any time."

"To be thirsty and to drink water is the perfection of sensuality rarely achieved. Sometimes you drink water; other times you are thirsty."

Jose Bergamin

Behind Closed Doors

Years later I realized Ruth Ann was probably a victim of sexual abuse. Her situation was a classic scenario: divorced parents, stream of mother's boyfriends, daughter who matures physically at an early age.

We don't think of that sort of thing happening in the 1950s, but it did. We just didn't hear about it as much as we do today. Marilyn Van Derbur, Miss America of 1958, didn't reveal for years that her father sexually molested her from the time she was five until she left home at eighteen (*Miss America*). Even in that supposedly puritanical age, the Greenville *News* reported incidents of fathers molesting or raping their daughters, one 13, the other 11 (March 8, April 1).

CHAPTER 21

> *"The essence
> of being human is that
> one does not seek
> perfection."*
>
> George Orwell

Ah, Sweet Mystery!

When Mitch returned from Brooklyn he was as excited as Moses must have been when he climbed down from Mt. Sinai. And he had something we considered as valuable as those stone tablets. The day he got back he took me aside and showed me a deck of playing cards featuring nude people, mostly women but also some couples. They weren't doing much, but they were naked and they were showing everything. For my raging hormones, that was enough.

"Where did you get these?" I asked when I got my breath back.

"My cousin, the one I stayed with, showed them to me. When I was packing, I took them."

"Won't he be mad?"

"What can he do? He can't come out here to get me. And what's he going to tell his parents? 'Mitch stole my deck of cards with the naked people on them'?"

I had started puberty earlier in 1956, at age ten. When I took swimming lessons that summer in Greenville I was already sporting what felt to me like a lot of body hair. It must have looked that way to others, too. A kid standing near me said to someone else, "Who's the gorilla?" I now know I'm no hairier than average, but I have not worn a pair of shorts outdoors since that day. (I've never learned to swim either and was amused to learn my idol, Mickey Mantle, never took to the water.) My mother, after noticing the results of a wet dream in my pajamas, I think, sat me down in the front bedroom of my grandparents' house while my dad was in Cincinnati and gave me "the talk" in five minutes.

The confusion she created took several years to clear up.

As an adult I came to wonder at her ineptitude in explaining such things. She let me see a couple of letters, out of two dozen, which she had written to her family from California. She and my father were married there while he was in the Marines in 1944. The letters displayed her sharp wit and hinted that she enjoyed the physical aspects of marriage. She told me I could have them when she died, as long as I promised not to publish them. On my first visit home several weeks after her death, I went to the trunk where she had kept them for fifty years, only to find they weren't there. I asked my dad where they were.

"I burned them the day after her funeral."

"Why did you do that? Mother said I could have them."

"They were private," he said.

By some miracle one of my mother's letters did survive. It was one she wrote my father when I was three months old. I cried when I read it and also saw where I might have gotten some of whatever writing talent I possess, if such a thing can be inherited.

In the mid-1950s if a pubescent boy didn't get the instruction he needed at home, there wasn't a lot of reliable information "on the street" to help him. Some schools may have taught the basics, but not the ones I attended. When Skeezix, in the comic strip "Gasoline Alley," undertook to have a "man-to-man talk" with his son, he started by saying, "There are questions which come up, and it is well to have the right answers." Chipper assured him, "I understand, Pop. I'll tell you anything you want to know."

Margaret Truman reported her father found his wife Bess burning letters he had written to her. "You oughtn't to do that," the former President protested. "Why not? I've read them several times." "But think of history," Truman urged. "I have," Mrs. Truman replied.

I think I was more typical in having no easily accessible source of information. I found things in newspapers and magazines that raised all sorts of questions, questions which some instinct told me not to ask my parents, especially not after "the talk" with my mother.

Several stories that appeared in the spring left me wondering. On March 8 the *News* ran this article on the front page, right under the headline:

A West Berlin high school teacher was sentenced to 18 months in prison today for taking nearly 6,000 nude pictures of girls between 12 and 18 years of age in his apartment.

Dr. Gustav Roessler, 41, told the court he had taken the photographs only to illustrate a scientific work on sex problems in large cities.

The court, however, held a considerable part of the work was obscene. It said it could see no scientific purpose in pictures of girls wearing nothing but top hats, neckties and walking sticks.

I spent a long time trying to imagine those girls in their top hats and neckties, but certain areas remained out of focus.

So, when Mitch whipped out that deck of cards with the naked people on them, it was like the veil of the temple had been rent in twain, the mystery revealed. I thought he must know . . . something. But, even though he had the deck, he didn't understand any more about what it all meant than I did. He just thought it was fun to look at them. He was giggling; I was aroused.

As was my habit, I decided we should look up some things.

We looked up all the body part words we knew in the dictionary. Not much help. For example, "penis" was "the male organ of copulation." Look up "copulation" and you find "act of coupling or joining; union; conjunction; sexual union; coition." Look up "coition" and you find "sexual intercourse." 'Round and 'round you go. I had never copulated with my penis, as far as I knew. I did pee with it and the dictionary made no mention of that function, unless that was what one of those other words meant.

"Breast" was defined as "the fore or ventral part of the body, between the neck and the abdomen; hence, a part, as of clothing, covering the breast; a mammary gland; a teat." That last one broke Mitch and me up, as it sends every pubescent boy into paroxysms of laughter.

As part of our misinformation exchange Mitch showed me the Song of Solomon. I knew it was in the Old Testament because Pa-Pa expected all his grandchildren to memorize the books of the Bible, but I had never read it. Chapter 7 was Mitch's favorite: "Your rounded thighs are like jewels . . . . Your two breasts are like two fawns."

Some of the ads I saw left me plain mystified. One product always showed a beautiful woman in a lovely gown, usually off-the-shoulder with some cleavage, and the words "Modess . . . because." Because what? I wanted to know. All I could learn from the ads was that Modess, whatever it was, didn't chafe. That's a far cry from commercials now, like the one where a woman takes a tampon out of her purse and plugs a hole in a leaky boat.

Some magazine ads of that day showed women in their undergarments. Those intrigued me, even though a woman wearing such things looks fully clothed compared to the models in today's ads. One ad that appeared on the comics page of the Greenville *News* (Feb. 14, 1956), right between "Pogo" and "Li'l Abner," really left me wondering. For sixty-five cents, it said, someone could buy "the first self-deodorant, self-antiseptic, and mildew-resistant rayon panty. Retains its hygeinic [*sic*] effect indefinitely. Hand washable."

Self-deodorant? Antiseptic? Mildew? What the hell was going on down there? Maybe those were questions Mickey Mantle was trying to answer with the "bizarre collection of provocative women's underwear that [he] kept as trophies" of his sexual conquests (Castro, p. 244).

Those Modess ads are now collectible. The pages, torn from magazines, go for $15 to $20. The value is less if the text, which usually ran across the bottom of the page, has been cut off.

Women's unmentionables were mentioned a lot in the spring of 1956 as panty raids became the rage on college campuses. The Greenville *News* dutifully reported that boys at Mars Hill College left "only with a few towels from a laundry room." At East Carolina and Western Carolina colleges damage was done to the women's dorms which were raided and both administrations "refused to consider it a prank." The men at Western Carolina "carried away a number of lacy trophies." At the University of California "coeds were carried out of their [sorority] houses in pajamas or in the nude." The University of Kansas expelled over 50 men for their part in a panty raid at nearby Baker University.

The virtue of being virtuous

The personal behavior of politicians and media celebrities is not the best gauge for judging the moral standards of an era, but such people do have an enormous impact on how the mass of people behave. When Clark Gable, in "It Happened One Night," took off his dress shirt and revealed he wasn't wearing an undershirt, sales of the garments plummeted. John F. Kennedy practically killed the American hat industry overnight by appearing hatless at his inauguration.

Did people have a higher standard of sexual morality in the 1950s than they do today? Was that what made that era different? Better?

Rock and roll music glorified kissing and holding hands and making someone "thrill with delight," but characters on TV and in movies never went any further than innocent flirtation. Married people slept in twin beds, and Wally Cleaver or Bud Anderson never had to worry if a girl they knew was late with her period. Doris Day was "the professional virgin." No man could have her until he placed a wedding ring on her finger. Even sexpots like Marilyn Monroe and Jayne Mansfield were, ultimately, "good girls." The characters they played ended up married, and they married off-screen as well.

But there were those, like sociologist Pitirim Sorokin, who thought America was a modern Sodom and Gomorrah, even in 1956:

> Sexual infamy is almost a necessary condition for becoming a star of stage, movie, or television; sometimes, it is found to be the only talent possessed by these performers, who are otherwise perfectly innocent of the art of artful acting. Among our public officials, there is a vast legion of profligates, both heterosexual and homosexual.

Sex Revolution, p. 44

A public figure, especially a woman, who did not adhere to the standards could find herself shunned, even vilified. Ingrid Bergman shocked the world when she openly began an affair with director Roberto Rossellini in 1950. Both were married to others, but Bergman became pregnant before they divorced and remarried. She did not make any movies in the U. S. during the early and mid-1950s. Colorado Senator Edwin C. Johnson condemned her as "a powerful influence for evil."

The blatant sexuality (and homosexuality) of the modern media would have caused widespread heart palpitations in the 1950s. Young people heard from parents, teachers, ministers, and every other authority figure in their lives the virtues of being virtuous. The personal lives of celebrities and political and sports figures were not fodder for magazines at the check-out counter of every supermarket or gossip shows on TV masquerading as "entertainment news."

And yet Everykid knew who the "bad girls" were and which ones had "gotten in trouble." One of the most discussed questions in newspaper advice columns was the difference between necking and petting and "how far" it was appropriate to go at certain stages of a relationship. The Gilbert Youth Research Company surveyed 15,000 teenagers and found that those in cities with populations under 50,000 tended to start dating earlier, to go steady at a younger age, and to think marriage at 17 or 18 was a good idea (Cincinnati *Enquirer*, Sept. 9, 1956). The third date was considered optimal for the first kiss.

But teenagers did engage in premarital sex. Advice columnist Dorothy Ricker responded to a letter from a girl who had done so and offered this counsel (Cincinnati *Enquirer*, Sept. 25, 1956):

> Yours was a serious mistake and one which should not be shrugged off lightly. But you are more fortunate than some of the girls who write to me about similar problems. You have been given a second chance – without having to pay the tragic price of bearing an illegitimate child, of knowing public censure or of breaking your parents' hearts – to say nothing of experiencing the trapped feelings of desperation which these girls describe.
>
> While I certainly cannot condone what you did, you should not let it ruin your life. You should be very thankful for your 'escape' and show your gratitude by being the right kind of girl from now on.

Norman Vincent Peale didn't exactly display "positive thinking" in his response to a girl's letter in his column in *Look*:

> My heart goes out to you, for you have made such a bad mistake. And it is more than a mistake; you have sinned against God and your own girlhood. Boys only "use" girls who conduct themselves as you have done. That is why you have lost their respect. You can be a good girl and find happiness again. Stop what you are doing at once. Go to your minister and tell him all about it. He will help you find God's forgiveness and build your life anew.

"Under God"

For better or for worse, the 1950s was a time when standards of conduct were clearly defined, even if they weren't always observed in the intimacy of a car parked on a Lovers' Lane or at a drive-in movie. And those standards were religiously based. People weren't afraid to talk about religion, and church attendance was at an all-time high. In most schools the day began with a devotional reading, prayer, and the Pledge of Allegiance. Dr. Peale, Billy Graham, Oral Roberts, and Bishop Fulton J. Sheen appeared regularly on television and in popular magazines. *Life*'s first issue of 1956 featured an article by Dwight Eisenhower, "The Testimony of a Devout President." The editors saw evidence of "an unprecedented revival in religious belief and practice everywhere in the U. S."

One reason for this "revival" may have been the desire to get God on our side in the struggle against atheistic Communism. Supreme Court Justice William O. Douglas reported on his trip to the Soviet Union in "Religion in the Godless State" (*Look*, Jan. 10, 1956). On Feb. 21 a letter to the editor suggested it would be "wonderful if we had 500 Justice Douglases to go behind the Iron Curtain and preach Christ to those people."

That growing religious impulse came into conflict with forces in American society which seemed to threaten what most Americans regarded as core values. The '50s may have been the last decade in American history when we were convinced that we were right and that it was our obligation to uphold what was right. There was no multi-culturalism, no sense that everyone was entitled to hold a divergent opinion, or to be different from the norm which we saw every day in the media.

Looking back, that is one of the most amazing things about my friendship with Mitch.

Autograph Hounds

Mitch and I were the quintessential odd couple – the soft-spoken, naive, blond Baptist from South Carolina and the loud-mouthed, dark-haired Jew from Brooklyn who was always working on some kind of deal. Our friendship was as unlikely as that between Whitey Ford and Mickey Mantle. As Ford saw it, "No two people could have been more different: me from the streets of New York, a know-it-all city kid, him a hick from Oklahoma" (*Slick*, p. 99).

As with Ford and Mantle, what drew Mitch and me together was baseball.

Even though he couldn't hit, catch, or throw, and could not have beaten my mother running from home to first, Mitch followed the Dodgers avidly. But his interest could expand if money was involved.

One Saturday morning in April of 1957 he met me on the steps of one of the apartment buildings where we usually hung out, away from the buildings where we each lived. From an envelope he took out a sheet of paper and unfolded it.

"Take a look at this," he said, sticking it under my nose.

I studied the paper for a moment. Then I realized it was a list of a dozen players on the Cincinnati Redlegs, each name with an address beside it. "These addresses are all here in Swifton Village, aren't they?" I said.

"That's right. My dad made the arrangements with the team for the players to rent apartments here during the season. I found this on his desk." He was wiggling with excitement.

"But why would these guys need apartments? Don't they have their own houses?"

He slapped me on the back of the head, something he did whenever he thought I was being obtuse. It bugged me; I didn't like people messing with my hair. "Just because they play for the Redlegs, that doesn't mean they're from Cincinnati. Your guy Mantle plays for the Yankees, but when the season's over he goes back to whatever cowboy place he's from."

"He's from Oklahoma."

"Yeah, fine. But during the season he lives in a hotel or an apartment in New York. That's what ballplayers do."

"Gus Bell lives in Cincinnati. I read that in *Sports Illustrated*. And Johnny Temple bought a house here. I saw that in the paper." Temple was the Redlegs' second baseman.

"Okay, a few of them live where they play. Most don't."

"So what are you going to do with this list?" I asked.

"We are going to get some autographs."

"Why do we want these guys' autographs? You don't like the Redlegs any more than I do."

"But other kids around here do. How much do you think they'll pay for an autograph? Maybe fifty cents?"

"But if you've only got one autograph from each player, you aren't going to make much."

"I said *we* are going to get some autographs."

I had an uneasy feeling about this, but it was hard to say no to Mitch. "Okay, so we'll have two of each player."

"If we take your brother along, that's three. And if I ask them to sign one for my brother, who's home sick . . . ."

"You don't have a brother." Mitch was an only child. That was one of the few things for which I envied him. That and the ease with which he could tell lies.

"Does Johnny Klippstein know I don't? Does Herschel Freeman?" Mitch jabbed a finger at the list, almost knocking it out of my hand. "Are you going to tell them?"

"What if my brother wants to keep the autographs?"

"I thought he wasn't interested in baseball. He never plays with us."

"He's not, but he might keep them just out of meanness."

"We'll give him a dollar. Or I'll beat him up."

Imagining that made me chuckle. I was afraid of my brother, even if he was three years younger than me and several inches shorter. The one time I'd seen Mitch in a fight, he'd looked like a girl, flailing his arms in front of him, slapping the other boy with his open hands. He said it was judo.

"When do you want to do this?" I asked.

"I checked the schedule. They don't play on Monday, so let's go right after school."

"Won't the players get annoyed at us for bothering them at home?"

"Nah. We're fans. Players love to have fans. In New York some of the players ride the subway to and from the game. You can sit next to them and ask them why they dropped a ball or took a third strike. They don't mind."

The next Monday we didn't even go home when we got off the bus. My brother threatened to tell our mother when she got home from work because we were supposed to go straight home. Mitch and I each gave him fifty cents and he trailed along as we knocked on apartment doors and asked for autographs. Mitch had a pack of note cards. The players seemed surprised somebody knew where they lived, but none of them refused to sign. A couple of them invited us in. I hate to admit it, but my brother, being small and – arguably – cute, may have been responsible for that.

I especially remember going into the apartment of a pitcher named Raul Sanchez. I had an odd sense of being transported to another world, standing there in Cincinnati beside my Jewish friend from Brooklyn in the home of a man from Cuba who barely spoke English. There seemed to be a

Sanchez' episodic major league career (1952, 1957, and 1960) totaled 89.2 innings pitched and a 5-3 record. He had a reputation as a "head-hunter" and was involved in several fights as a result, notably in 1957 (Zim, p. 22) and 1960.

dozen people in Sanchez's apartment, none of whom spoke my language. Several women of different ages stood in the kitchen door. One looked like a grandmother, fat and gray-haired. Two little kids clung to her apron. Spanish music blared from a record player. The cooking smells almost knocked me down. The most exotic spices in my mother's and grandmother's recipes were salt and pepper.

We did pretty well on the deal, netting three dollars apiece. That bought a lot of baseball cards. But there was no way we could replenish our stock. How many times could the same kids show up at a player's door?

Mitch, ever the entrepreneur, started selling the addresses to other kids for fifty cents each. And he didn't cut me in on the profits. But that turned out okay. When some of the players complained and Mitch's dad found out what he had done, I could honestly say I had nothing to do with selling the addresses.

Years later I found out we weren't the only kids working this angle. Mickey Mantle used to sign batches of publicity photos for his speaking engagements, only to be unable to find them later. One of his sons, he discovered, was "taking them around from house to house, selling them" (*The Mick*, p. 211).

CHAPTER 23

"I fear I am not in my perfect mind."

William Shakespeare

Our Story Thus Far

The Dodgers won the first game of the 1956 World Series 6-3, behind Sal Maglie's ten strike-outs. I heard about it on the news Wednesday night and didn't want to read about it the next morning, but the Cincinnati *Enquirer* lay on the kitchen table where my dad had left it, with the sports page on top. We both read that first. So, like someone driving past a bad wreck . . . .

Mantle hit a two-run homer in the first inning, but he also hit into a double play to end the game and didn't do much in between. He was slow getting to a couple of balls that fell in for hits, but he denied he was having injury problems. Whitey Ford was the losing pitcher. Going against his usual strategy, Casey Stengel started Ford in Ebbets Field, so friendly to right-handed hitters, because he felt Ford was "the best I got." Ford beat the Dodgers twice in the '55 Series, but in Yankee Stadium both times. In the 1953 Series he had failed to last through the first inning in a start in Ebbets Field. This time he was taken out in the fourth inning, after giving up five runs, the victim once again of what he himself called "the Ebbets Field curse" (*Slick*, p. 112). The headline on one of the *Enquirer* articles added insult to my injury: "Favored Yankees Far Outclassed."

The second game, on Thursday, was rained out. With no travel days scheduled for the Series, that day off was actually welcomed by both teams, except for Dodger pitcher Don Newcombe, who feared the extra day of rest might affect his control (*Enquirer*, Oct. 5, 1956). On Friday Newcombe and Don Larsen faced off in Game 2. From a kid at school who had a radio I learned, just before we went in from lunch, that the Yanks had gone ahead 6-0 in the second inning on Yogi Berra's grand slam. I faced the afternoon with confidence. Given that kind of lead, they were a cinch to win.

I didn't learn until I got home that, in the bottom of the second inning, Joe Collins misplayed a grounder to first which should have been a double play. His error opened the flood gates for the Dodgers to score six runs of their own and to ultimately win, 13-8. The *Enquirer*'s sports editor called it "from an artistic standpoint . . . probably the worst game ever played in the long history of World Series competition." There are no style points in baseball, but it was indisputably the longest game in Series history to that date, three hours and twenty-six minutes. For Mickey Mantle, "the second inning seemed to take up most of it" (*Octobers*, p. 65). Larsen was taken out in the second inning. Newcombe didn't get past the third.

The Dodgers tried not to sound too confident after Game 2. Manager Walter Alston reminded their fans the Dodgers had lost the first two games of the 1955 Series, only to come back and win. The Yankees might well do the same thing. I certainly hoped he was right. The *Enquirer* didn't think the Yankees had much chance.

I watched the third and fourth games of the Series over the weekend with my dad. Safely back in Yankee Stadium, Whitey Ford pitched a complete game victory on Saturday and Tom Sturdivant did the same on Sunday. My dad didn't pull for either team; he just enjoyed the game. As a former catcher he appreciated the performance of two of the greatest ever to play that position: Roy Campanella and Yogi Berra. Both had been MVP in their respective leagues in 1955, as they also had been in 1951.

During Sunday's game my dad surprised me by saying, "We'll have to be sure to see some games at Crosley Field next summer. Maybe when the Dodgers come here."

"That would be great," I said, but I didn't really expect it to happen. He had promised to take me to see Greenville's minor league team, but never found the time. He tended to take me – or the family – to places and events *he* enjoyed. On the rare occasions when we went out to eat it was always to a steak house, even though my mother and I preferred seafood. Once he took my brother and me fishing at a commercially stocked lake. We hadn't asked to go. I trace my antipathy to the whole fishing experience to that interminable afternoon. It wouldn't have made any difference if we had caught anything. While we were in Cincinnati he took my brother and me to a hockey game. Pro, college – I couldn't tell you. I just know I was bored to tears.

I don't mean to sound ungrateful. I know he was trying to be a good father, and he didn't have much of a model from his own childhood. But all I wanted was for him to take me to a baseball game.

I did get to see two games in the summer of 1957. Mitch's dad took us when the Dodgers came to town and again to see the Giants. I got to see Roy Campanella, Willie Mays, Duke Snider, Gil Hodges and some other great players. The much-despised (by me) Johnny Podres pitched one of the games I attended. The Reds' – excuse me, Redlegs' – pitcher was being very careful in pitching to Podres. A fan yelled, "Pitch to him! He ain't Willie Mays." Podres ripped a double. As he pulled into second base standing up, Mitch shouted, "Hold up, Willie!"

After the victory in Game 4 Casey Stengel told reporters, "This Series is more even now than it was."

I guess you had to be there . . . and be eleven.

But on that Sunday, October 7, after the Yankees won, 6-2, and evened the Series at two games each, I went outside, hoping to see Mitch and, I have to admit it, looking forward to gloating a little. I felt it was my turn after all his talk about a sweep when the Dodgers took the first two games.

How I Got "World Series Fever"

Mitch and I agreed Monday's Game 5 would be crucial. If the Dodgers won, they would go back to cozy Ebbets Field needing to win just one game to repeat as World Champs. If the Yankees won, they would be in sight of another championship and, even Mitch conceded, the Dodgers' chances wouldn't be very good. Once the Yankees got a lead on you, they were almost impossible to stop.

"Man, I would *love* to see that game," Mitch said.

"Too bad they don't play the games at night," I said. Night baseball wasn't unusual in 1956. *Sports*

Illustrated could even say "the night game is now unques-tionably the backbone, the blood, the meat and potatoes of the national pastime" (Sept. 10, 1956). But the World Series was considered too important to stage under the lights.

The game started at 1:00 New York time, but in the 1950s there was no nationally established rule for Daylight Saving Time. Individual states, even cities, could decide when, or if, they went on it and off of it. In October, 1956, New York was still observing DST, while Ohio wasn't.

"You know," Mitch said slowly, "we could see it."

"How? It starts at noon. We don't get out of school until three."

"What if we . . . skipped school?"

I'm pretty sure the look in his eye was the same one the serpent gave Eve when he suggested she take a little nibble in the produce department. But, like Mopsy, Flopsy, and Cottontail, I was a good little bunny, if I may mix literary allusions. Years later my mother told me, "I never had *any* trouble with you. You just seemed to know what needed to be done and you did it." Now, though, I was being invited to step into Mr. McGregor's garden, tempted to pull that alluring piece of fruit right off the tree.

If I'd still been in South Carolina, I'm sure I wouldn't have done it. But this wasn't South Carolina. I was in this strange new place called Cincinnati. Everything about my life felt different, as though I was watching someone else's life. I was a new kid with a new name. My body was changing so fast I didn't know what I would see when I showered each morning. (Sadly, now that I'm sixty, I'm having the same experience.) My new best friend was someone I couldn't have imagined even knowing a month ago. I'd already gotten in trouble on my first day in a new school and made a D on the first test I took, so why not do something else I'd never done before?

And, besides, Mitch's family had a color TV.

The perfect plan

Next morning, on the way to school, we put the plan into operation. We told my brother that Mitch and I were going to ride the "Z bus" home. The "Z bus" was a public bus that school kids could ride for free in the morning and the afternoon instead of the school bus. It came earlier than the school bus, and it ran straight from Swifton Village past Carthage Elementary School and reversed the route in the afternoons. I liked riding it because most of the other passengers weren't kids and it had real seats, not those school bus torture racks. My brother was in the third grade and the school bus stopped right in front of our apartment building. By now he knew which bus to get on, so he could get home without my help.

With my brother taken care of, Mitch and I would skip lunch, go directly out to play and work our way toward the edge of the schoolyard. Neither of us had made any other friends, and we usually sat and talked, unnoticed on the margin of things. We went to lunch at 11:45, so we could slip around the corner of the building and run up the street to the next stop on the "Z bus" route. We couldn't ride free at that time of day, but we would have our lunch money for the fare. Our destination would be Mitch's apartment. My mother hadn't started working yet, and both of Mitch's parents did work.

My resolve faltered on the way to school, but two of the teachers in our morning classes were absent. Several other kids were also missing. Mitch convinced me they had stayed home to watch the Series. "If they can do it, why can't we?"

"But, if my mom finds out, I won't get out of my room until Christmas."

"Oh, come on! This is *the* game. You saw what the paper said this morning, didn't you?"

I had read the *Enquirer*'s account of Sunday's game and their speculation about today's: "As we see it Monday's game is MUST for Stengel's Bombers, as it winds up the firing on their home range for the Series, and the records show they've lost their last five outings at Ebbets Field, including the first two this year."

I wasn't optimistic because the paper mentioned Don Larsen would be pitching for the Yankees. After his poor outing in Game 2, I didn't want to sit there and have Mitch cackling in my face when the Dodgers pounded him again. And Maglie, who beat the Yanks in Game 1, would be pitching for the Dodgers again.

By lunch, though, the vision of that color TV had overcome my reluctance to participate.

If I were writing a story about this little adventure, I would have to turn it into a *mis*adventure. Conflict and problems make for good stories. Somebody would spot us leaving school, or there would be somebody we knew on the bus, or my brother would get on the wrong bus and end up in Kentucky, or Mitch's dad would decide at the last minute to take the afternoon off to see the game. But – fiction and life being two different things and life being much less interesting – nothing went wrong. The bus driver did smile at us, but he didn't say anything. He had a transistor radio propped up beside him, tuned to WLW, the station broadcasting the Series.

At 12:05 we were in Mitch's apartment and the Yankees were taking the field.

Imperfect Lives in the Perfect Game

The team taking the field behind Don Larsen consisted of a mix of veterans and young players. All of them reached the pinnacle of baseball success, playing on some of the best teams of all times. As mentioned earlier, there were twelve Yankees who played on all five of the record-setting World Series champs between 1949 and 1953. Three of that twelve – Hank Bauer, Yogi Berra, and Joe Collins – were on the field on October 8, 1956. Along with their six teammates that day, they are the only men who can say they took part in a unique experience, a perfect game in the World Series.

"Imperfection is in some sort essential to all that we know of life. Nothing that lives is, or can be, rigidly perfect."

John Ruskin

And yet imperfection – even tragedy – overshadowed many of them. By 1960 only Berra and Mantle were still with the Yankees. Three of the perfect gamers – Bauer, Larsen, and Andy Carey – were traded to Kansas City in 1960 in the deal that brought Roger Maris to New York.

The two biggest surprises in the line-up might have been Enos Slaughter in left field and Joe Collins at first. The Yankees had younger, stronger players at both positions – Elston Howard in left and Bill "Moose" Skowron at first. But Howard and Skowron both batted right-handed and Casey Stengel wanted left-handed hitters Slaughter and Collins to face right-hander Sal Maglie.

One intriguing bit of trivia about the starters is that three of them were not playing under the names their parents gave them at birth. While name changes are common in the music and movie businesses, they occur more often in baseball than one might suspect. Roger Maras/Maris' was mentioned earlier. Sometimes the names were changed to Americanize a European ethnic name. Cornelius McGillicuddy was one of the greatest managers of all time – under the name Connie Mack. For years Johnny Pesky starred in the infield for the Boston Red Sox, but few would have recognized the name on his birth certificate: John Paveskovich. Other players took the name of a step-parent or adoptive parent. How many Dodger fans in the early '60s knew their star left-hander was born with the aristocratic sounding name Sanford Braun and picked up the name Koufax from his stepfather?

"What is life, after all, but a challenge? And what better challenge can there be than the one between the pitcher and the hitter?"

Warren Spahn

The Battery

Gooney Bird

If you had asked knowledgeable baseball people in 1956 which pitcher might be the most likely to throw a perfect game in a World Series, you would have heard names like Whitey Ford, Don Newcombe, or Robin Roberts. Ford was at the top of his form, recording 19 victories in '56. Roberts was past his peak but still a strong pitcher. Newcombe finished the '56 season with a 27-7 record. Even **DON LARSEN'S** opponent in Game 5, Sal Maglie, seemed a better candidate. He had pitched a no-hitter against Philadelphia on Sept. 25. Another Dodger pitcher, Carl Erskine, had pitched a no-hitter against the Giants on May 12 and another in 1952. If it even occurred to anyone to mention Larsen's name among such company, it would have drawn snickers. Maybe even some three musketeers and a Mars bar. Mickey Mantle called him "an odd candidate for immortality" (*Octobers*, p. 66). As Yankee public address announcer Bob Sheppard said, "If Sandy Koufax had done it, if Don Drysdale had done it, I would have nodded and said, 'Well, it could happen.' But Don Larsen?"

Larsen, born in 1929, had a career record of 30 wins and 40 losses at the end of the 1956 season. More than half of his losses were piled up in 1954, when he joined the infamous circle of pitchers who have lost 20 or more games in a season. But losing 20 games doesn't mean a pitcher is bad. As one baseball pundit observed, "If you lose 20 games, you must be pretty good or the manager wouldn't keep putting you out there."

Larsen finished the '54 season at 3-21 with the struggling Baltimore Orioles, the team formerly known as the struggling St. Louis Browns. (He would become the last active Browns player in the majors.) Two

of his wins were over the Yankees. Several of his losses were low-scoring, one-run games. Against the Yankees he took a no-hitter into the eighth inning, only to have it broken up by Andy Carey, who was taking the field as the third baseman in Game 5.

In 1955 Larsen came to the Yankees in a trade involving eighteen players, the largest trade in baseball history. He was 9-2 that year and gained a reputation for what the *New York Times* discreetly called his "volatile, eccentric and unpredictable . . . off-the-diamond activities." Mickey Mantle was more blunt: "He liked to drink and he was a champion in that league" (*Favorite Summer*, p. 201). Larsen says his mantra was "Man . . . oh Manochevitz . . . Let the good times roll" (*Perfect Yankee*, p. 41). Whitey Ford admitted Larsen was a party animal, but "he was one of the most decent and nicest men I knew . . . . a damn good pitcher and a great competitor" (*Slick*, p. 114). On a tour of Japan Larsen's teammates nicknamed him Gooney Bird after a long-legged, crane-like bird native to that area.

A tall, lanky right-hander (6'4", 215 lbs), Larsen was generally recognized as a gifted athlete who never developed the discipline to become one of the top pitchers of his day. Casey Stengel often said, "He can be one of baseball's great pitchers any time he puts his mind to it." In spite of some personal problems, such as his first marriage breaking up, the 1956 season had been his best, with an 11-5 record.

For years afterwards there was some controversy over just how well-prepared Larsen was to pitch Game 5. Third-base coach Frank Crosetti had a tradition of letting a pitcher know he was going to the mound that day by putting a warm-up ball in his shoe in his locker. Larsen says he did not know until he walked into the clubhouse and found the ball in his shoe that he was going to pitch this pivotal game (*Perfect Yankee*, pp. 30, 33; Doyle). He must not have looked at the papers. I knew he was going to start when I read the Cincinnati *Enquirer* that morning.

Rumors abounded that Larsen had been out partying until all hours the night before. Friends and teammates came to his defense. Mickey Mantle claimed to have seen Larsen enjoying a sedate meal the evening before the game and returning to his hotel across the street at a reasonable hour (*Favorite Summer*, p. 202). The only problem with the story, Larsen says, is that he didn't live in that particular hotel. But he staunchly denied any misbehavior: ". . . we were in the middle of the greatest competition in the history of sport, the World Series. I would never have gotten myself out of top physical or mental condition on the eve of such an important game" (*Perfect Yankee*, p. 30).

Larsen never lived up to the potential which the perfect game suggested. As he himself said, "I'm not sure what people expected from me" (*Perfect Yankee*, p. 216). He was 10-4 in 1957 but ineffective after that. Traded to Kansas City, he bounced around the majors, compiling a record of "unbroken mediocrity punctuated with flashes of competence" (Acocella). He did have the satisfaction of returning to Yankee Stadium in 1962 with the San Francisco Giants and got credit for a win over the Yankees in a World Series game. He finished his career in 1967 with an 81-91 overall record. As of this writing he lives in Idaho with his second wife.

Catcher

Someone has described a catcher's equipment as "the tools of ignorance." Baseball is a non-contact sport, but catchers get foul tips ricocheting off their masks and hands and have base-runners sliding into them, intent on knocking them over or jarring the ball loose. Even if they avoid such damage, catchers have to squat down 120 or more times during a typical game. It is one of the most demanding positions in any sport. I caught one game for my softball team when I was still relatively young and swore I would stop playing rather than go through that again.

> "A catcher and his body are like the outlaw and his horse. He's got to ride that nag till it drops."
>
> Johnny Bench

Great teams usually have great catchers. As Miller Huggins, Yankee manager in the 1930s said, "A good catcher is the quarterback, the carburetor, the lead dog, the pulse taker, the traffic cop and sometimes a lot of unprintable things, but no team gets very far without one."

The man who would catch Game 5 of the 1956 Series for the Yankees already owned six World Series championship rings. **YOGI BERRA,** born in 1925, joined the Yankees at the end of the 1946 season. He would go on to win ten World Series rings and set records for Series games played (75) and at-bats (259). He was also the first player to hit a home run as a pinch-hitter in a World Series (1951).

But few were impressed with him when he arrived in the majors. He was described as having "a homely face, no neck, and the build of a sawed-off weight lifter" (*Ten Rings*, p. 12). Some of his teammates dubbed him "the Ape." His fingers were so stubby one of the Yankees' pitchers told him to "grow some hands."

> Berra quit school after the eighth grade. And yet he has become famous for his wit and wisdom. He even received an honorary doctorate. When asked how he liked school, he replied, "Closed."

During his first couple of years in the majors Berra split time between the outfield and catching, as he would again toward the end of his career. Whatever his limitations in the field, he was simply too good a hitter to keep on the bench. When Casey Stengel became the Yankees' manager in 1949, he decided to make Berra his full-time catcher. Retired great Bill Dickey was brought in to instruct the struggling Berra, who credits Dickey with making him the complete player he became.

Berra grew up in a poor Italian family in St. Louis. His father did not want his sons wasting time on frivolous things like baseball. The older brothers, all talented athletes, finally prevailed on their father to let Yogi have the chance they had been denied. Berra followed a path trod by many ballplayers of the 1940s: signing a contract in his late teens, doing military service during WWII, and spending time in the minors afterwards to polish his rusty skills.

Larsen could not have asked for a more experienced catcher if he was going to pitch a no-hitter. In 1951 Berra caught both of Allie Reynolds' no-hitters. Berra was also behind the plate in Game 4 of the 1947 World Series when Floyd "Bill" Bevens took a no-hitter (but with 8 walks) into the ninth inning. Bevens got two outs, but then a walk, an intentional walk, and a double ruined the no-hitter and meant a loss for the Yankees. Berra blamed himself. When the first base-runner tried to steal second, Berra's throw to Phil Rizzuto was high and the runner was safe. That set the stage for the intentional walk – to set up a force play – and the game-winning double (*Ten Rings*, p. 35).

Berra stayed with the Yankees through their glory years. He managed the team to a pennant in 1964 but lost the World Series and was fired. In 1965 he joined Casey Stengel with the New York Mets and stayed on when former Dodger Gil Hodges became manager. The "Miracle Mets" won the 1969 World Series. When Hodges died during the 1972 season, Berra took over as manager, to the dismay of Mets fans, many of them former Dodger and Giant fans and Yankee-haters, who, in the words of Rube Walker, "had a few years without baseball to get even nuttier." Berra led the team to the World Series in 1973 but lost to Oakland and was fired.

Berra rejoined the Yankees as a coach and managed the team in 1984. In April of 1985 he was fired unceremoniously. The news was delivered to him by one of his coaches. "I took it real bad . . . . [Owner George Steinbrenner] apologized after fourteen years of me staying away from the Stadium, and it's over" (*Ten Rings*, pp. 211-212).

Like several of the perfect gamers, Berra has known disappointment in his family life. His son Dale played shortstop for the Pittsburgh Pirates, Houston Astros, and briefly for the Yankees during Yogi's last year as manager. Yogi says his three sons "always did right by listening to their mom" (*Ten Rings*, p. 210), but in 1986 Dale Berra was fined heavily by baseball Commissioner Peter Ueberroth for using amphetamines.

Yogi now lives in New Jersey. He and his children have created LTD Enterprises to manage Yogi's appearances and sell merchandise linked to him.

The Infield
First Base

Anchoring the Yankees' defense at first base was **JOE COLLINS**, born in 1922. His father, Collins says, "changed his original name, Kollonige . . . . I had to use it in the service. But I changed it right after the war. It was tough for the kids going to school. No one could pronounce it" (in *Men of Autumn*, p. 167).

"I worked real hard to learn to play first. In the beginning, I used to make one terrible play a game. Then, I got so I'd make one a week, and finally, I'd pull a real bad one maybe once a month. At the end, I was trying to keep it down to one a season."

Lou Gehrig

A steady and occasionally brilliant player, Collins joined the Yankees in 1948, after spending ten years in the minor leagues and military service. He was one of those Yankee minor leaguers who found himself in a log jam behind several very good players at his position, making his advancement to the majors take longer than it should have. While in the minors he severely injured his left shoulder in a collision with a telephone pole. Although he would recover, in the long run the injury affected his ability to throw and shortened his major league career.

In the 1951 World Series Collins hit a home run to win Game Two. Another home run gave the Yanks the lead in the first game of the 1953 Series, and two more homers contributed to their win in Game One of the 1955 Series. He seemed to have a knack for driving in a crucial run or advancing a runner into scoring position. Over his career Collins compiled a .256 average, with 86 home runs and 329 rbi's.

Billy Martin complained about Collins' lackadaisical play in the 1956 Series, accusing him of having "the shortest arms" of any first baseman he'd ever seen. Statistics don't bear out Martin's gripe. With Moose Skowron taking over regular duties at first in 1956, Collins played 43 games there and 51 in the outfield. He committed only one error, and that was in the outfield. As mentioned earlier, in Game 2 of the '56 Series, Collins did make a costly error in the second inning that allowed the Dodgers to tie the game. It was his first error in 24 World Series games.

In 1957 the Yankees sold him to Philadelphia, but Collins decided to retire and go into the trucking business. He died in 1989.

"Second base
is anything but magic.
If it's anything at all, it's speed,
sureness with your hands,
and lots of hard work."

Nellie Fox

Second Base

During the 1956 season Casey Stengel seemed to be playing fruit-basket turnover with his infield. **BILLY MARTIN** played second, short, or third. His 1956 Topps card describes his position as "2b-shortstop," but second was his natural position. Martin, born in 1928, may have been the most hot-headed major leaguer of his generation. His later explosive confrontations with his bosses and his players as a manager are beyond the scope of this book, but they did not surprise anyone who had followed his career. They wouldn't have surprised anyone who read a 1956 article about him in the *Saturday Evening Post*: "He's Never Out of Trouble." I first read it as a 10-year-old. Knowing what happened to the man later gave it a new poignancy when I reread it in my research for this book. The article is practically a prophecy of Martin's subsequent career.

From his earliest days with the Yankees, Martin displayed a legendary temper. Some said that, with an Italian mother and a Portugese father, he came by it naturally. Anyone reading his first book gets a vivid picture of what a temper his mother had.

What is less clear is how Martin came by his name. Various sources, including baseball cards from the '50s, say his birth name was Alfred Manuel Martin, but a few sources report it as Alfred Manuel Pesano (Cincinnati *Enquirer*, Oct. 7, 1956). According to Martin himself, his mother was married

BILLY MARTIN
2b-shortstop N. Y. YANKEES

briefly to a man named Pesano, but his father was named Martin (*Number 1*, pp. 31-33). One source gives the man's name as Pisani (*Last Yankee*, p.16). According to different sources his grandmother called him "bello" or "bellitz" (a corruption of "bellisimo" or "very handsome" in Italian), from which came Billy.

Unraveling the story of Martin's early life is nearly impossible, even when relatives are interviewed. It's possible Martin's parents never married and his mother worked as a prostitute in her sister's "house." Martin's mother threw his father out when she caught him in an infidelity, or he left because of her infidelities (*Last Yankee*, pp. 20-23). Martin, only a toddler at the time, harbored enormous resentment toward his father (*Number 1*, p. 34) and became almost a foster son to Casey Stengel. Stengel coached Martin in the minor leagues in Oakland in 1948 and urged the Yankees to sign him when Stengel became manager in 1949.

With a .257 average and 64 home runs for his career, Martin was not an exceptional hitter, but he burned with a desire to win and would not let his teammates get by with anything less than all-out effort. He was a player who stepped up with big hits in big games. He hit .500 in the 1953 World Series and .320 in 1955. He began his career in grand style in 1950, getting two hits in one inning in his first major league game – the first player ever to accomplish that feat.

Martin's most famous defensive play occurred in Game 6 of the 1952 World Series. First baseman Joe Collins lost a high pop-up in the sun and pitcher Bob Kuzava couldn't locate it. With the bases loaded and two out and a 3-2 count, the runners had taken off with the pitch. If the ball hit the ground, two – probably three – runs would score. Martin himself said, "Nobody was moving, so I just took off and the wind kept blowing it back toward the stands and I kept running after it. It seemed the harder I ran, the more the wind took it" (*BillyBall*, pp. 83-84). News photos show the rest of the infield – and base-runner Jackie Robinson – watching as Martin caught the ball at his knees to preserve a 4-2 Yankee win. General Manager George Weiss, who never liked Martin, said he "made an easy play look hard."

In 1950 Martin married. He and his wife had a daughter, but his wife filed for divorce in 1952, saying, "I never saw him, even when I was pregnant. You can't stay in love with a newspaper clipping." The divorce wasn't finalized until 1955. Between 1951 and 1956 Martin was treated for insomnia, hypertension and "acute melancholia." During those years, he admitted, he was addicted to sleeping pills and pain pills. Some who knew him from his youth wondered if he could stand up to the pressures of playing in the major leagues. Poverty, the lack of a father, his small size – all contributed to making him a young man who thought he had to be a fighter to prove himself. In many ways he was the "tough guy" James Dean and Marlon Brando were portraying on the screen, or the "juvenile delinquent" who seemed to be in the newspapers every day.

Some critics felt Casey Stengel did not restrain Martin. In fact, he seemed to use the fiery second baseman as a "hit man." If Casey wanted someone to make a hard slide to pay back an opposing infielder or start a fight to spark the Yankees, he designated Martin to do it. When Phil Rizzuto received a death threat, Stengel had Martin wear Rizzuto's number in a game. Martin seemed to relish such assignments. He was drafted into the Army after the 1953 season and did not return to the Yankees until late in the 1955 season.

Martin and Mickey Mantle became great friends. To escape his domestic problems, Martin spent time in the off-season with Mantle in Oklahoma. Although the brash, big-city Martin was a surprise to small-town Sooners, Mantle says "they got to love him and he loved everybody in Commerce. Even one of my best friend's wife" (*The Mick*, p. 114).

At the beginning of spring training in 1956 Martin still had not signed a contract. An article in my hometown paper called him "pugilistic" – I had to look that one up – and "the most stubborn of a handful of major league baseball holdouts" (Greenville *News*, Mar. 2). Casey Stengel intervened and persuaded management and Martin to come to terms – $20,000 for the year, according to my paper. I asked my dad how much he made and was told $5,200 a year.

Martin came into the 1956 World Series with a grudge against the Dodgers. Like all the Yankees, he wanted to avenge the loss in the '55 Series. But for Martin it was personal. Whenever the New York papers did comparisons of the Dodgers and Yankees, position by position, they always gave the Dodgers the edge at second base because they had Jackie Robinson or Junior Gilliam. Mickey Mantle could see "that drove Billy to play harder and to want to win even more" (*Favorite Summer*, p. 148). Martin himself took pride in pointing out that, in every World Series he played against the Dodgers, he outhit their second baseman (*BillyBall*, p. 83).

Martin's first book shows what tricks memory can play even on participants in a momentous event, and how inattentive editors can sometimes be. He says the Yankees went into the perfect game trailing in the Series: "The Dodgers had us down two games to one, and I was more concerned with winning the game than with his perfect game" (*Number 1*, p. 143). Uh, Billy, it was Game **5** of the Series. You can't be down 2-1 in Game 5.

George Weiss finally found an excuse to trade Martin in 1957, after he and several other Yankees were accused of fighting at a New York nightclub where they had gone to celebrate Martin's birthday.

Martin's second marriage also ended in divorce. His daughter by his first marriage was arrested for drug smuggling in Colombia. Securing her release took him two years and cost him $30,000 (*Number 1*, p. 58) or $40,000 (*Last Yankee*, pp. 216-218). Martin died in an automobile accident on Christmas Day, 1989.

Third Base

Joe DiMaggio wasn't the only Yankee to marry a gorgeous actress in the 1950s. In 1955 **ANDY CAREY** married Lucy McAleer, who, under the name Lucy Marlow, played supporting roles in half a dozen movies between 1954-56. Carey was another of those Yankees playing under a name he wasn't born with. How Andrew Arthur Hexem became Andy Carey, I haven't been able to determine. His birth name is also sometimes given as Nordstrom (Cincinnati *Enquirer*, Oct. 7, 1956). Carey had three children. A son, James, was killed in an automobile accident. Carey's daughter, Jennifer, who became a blues/rock singer, took the last name James to honor her brother.

> "Next to the catcher, the third baseman has to be the dumbest guy out there. You can't have any brains to take those shots all day."
>
> Dave Edler

Born in 1931, Carey joined the Yankees in May of 1952, playing in only 16 games that year and 51 the next season. From 1954-1956 he played in at least 122 games each season, but his batting average plummeted from .302 to .257 to .237. Although not noted for off-the-field antics, Carey was a prodigious eater. Don Larsen stood in envy of the third baseman's appetite: "He was the only guy I can recall who I couldn't keep up with" (*Perfect Yankee*, p. 133). Because of Carey's huge tabs, penny-pinching General Manager George Weiss canceled the players' privilege of signing for their meals. In future that perk was extended only to superstars like Mantle and Ford (*The Yankees*, p. 109).

Casey Stengel wanted Carey to learn to play several infield positions, as Gil McDougald and

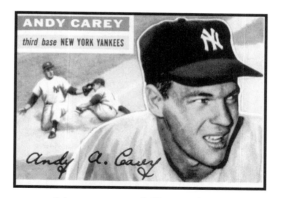

others had done. But Carey insisted he was a third base-man. In spring training of 1956 he drew a line between third and shortstop to make it clear third base was his position. He did try to adapt to the Yankees' suggestion that he become a pull hitter instead of spraying the ball around the field. That may have been one reason for the decline in his batting average.

It was ironic that Carey should back up Don Larsen in the perfect game and make a couple of sterling plays to preserve it. He seems to have had a penchant for breaking up no-hitters, especially against pitchers named Don. As mentioned earlier, he had ruined Larsen's no-hitter in 1954. But, even before that, Larsen was pitching a no-hitter for the St. Louis Browns in 1953 until Carey got a hit in the seventh inning. On May 12, 1956, Don Ferrarese of the Orioles completed eight innings of a no-hitter against the Yankees, but Carey led off the ninth with a single.

"I'll play first, third, left. I'll play anywhere – except Philadelphia."

Dick "Richie" Allen

Carey struggled offensively in the late '50s. He offered his own reason for the slump: "Maybe it was because I was married" (in *Sweet Seasons*, p. 47). After the 1958 season he came down with mononucleosis. He had not fully recovered when the next season began and played in only 41 games. In 1960 he was traded to Kansas City and in 1961 to the Chicago White Sox. Due to a back injury he saw limited playing time and was traded to Philadelphia. Like Joe Collins, he retired rather than play for the Phillies. Former Yankees didn't want to go slumming in the City of Brotherly Love, it seems. Maybe because the pinstripes are the wrong color. Carey did return to play one more year with the Dodgers in 1962.

"The thing that makes a good shortstop is the footwork involved. If you have good footwork, if you can get to the ball, you can set up and get your body out of the way so you can make the throw."

Larry Bowa

Shortstop

The 1956 season was **GIL MCDOUGALD**'s first as the Yankees' starting shortstop. Since joining the team in 1951, when he was Rookie of the Year, he had played behind Phil Rizzuto or at second or third. The years finally caught up with Rizzuto in 1956. He saw only limited action and was released in late August.

McDougald admitted his batting stance was peculiar. "I probably ruined more players who tried to emulate my batting stance than any other player" (in *Men of Autumn*, p. 155). But in 1956 he had his best year, hitting .311 and finishing second in the MVP voting behind Mickey Mantle. McDougald holds some "only" distinctions. He was the only rookie to hit a grand slam in a World Series and the only player to play three different positions on three different World Series championship teams.

In 1956 some Yankee fans still blamed McDougald for a "bone-head" play in Game 7 of the 1955 Series. I was one of them. I didn't see that game, but I had seen film of it and read a lot about it. Sandy Amoros' spectacular catch of Yogi Berra's slicing line drive to left field saved the game and the Series

for the Dodgers. But what happened after the catch was just as important.

The Yankees had runners on second and first at the time. Like everyone else in the park, McDougald, on first, thought Amoros had no chance of catching the ball, so he was already around second base and on his way to scoring the tying run. When Amoros made the catch, McDougald had to return to first. Since he had already touched second, he had to touch it again on the way back. The relay from Amoros to Pee Wee Reese to Gil Hodges beat McDougald easily. The Yankees went from two men on and no outs, to one man on and two outs.

McDougald seemed well on his way to stardom until he hit Cleveland pitcher Herb Score in the face with a line drive in 1957. The incident shook McDougald profoundly. To compound his despair, a few days later he hit Detroit pitcher Frank Lary on the knee. Lary had to be carried off the field. Then, in a game in Baltimore, he hit a line drive so close to the head of pitcher Skinny Brown that "his cap flew off, and the ball went right between his cap and his head" (in *Men of Autumn*, p. 162). Newspaper headlines dubbed the Yankee shortstop "Killer McDougald."

What are the odds? Gil McDougald was the second cousin of umpire Babe Pinelli's wife

(Great No-Hitters, p. 16).

Score came back to pitch, although never as effectively as before the accident. As a result of these incidents, McDougald altered his batting stance and tried to pull all of his hits to the left side of the field. His average plummeted.

In an eerily prophetic incident in Game 4 of the 1956 Series McDougald hit first base umpire Babe Pinelli with a line drive foul, but Pinelli recovered and was behind the plate that Monday afternoon as Game 5 got underway.

In a case of what some might call karmic justice – or maybe just irony – McDougald was hit in the ear by a line drive during batting practice before a game in 1958. His hearing rapidly deteriorated after that. He retired in 1960. After his children were grown, he and his wife adopted three more. McDougald reported that he had seen only two games after his retirement: "I don't miss the game . . . . I'm not much of a baseball fan" (in *Men of Autumn*, p. 164).

The Outfield

Left field

ENOS "COUNTRY" SLAUGHTER, born in 1916, was best known for scoring from first base on a single in the 1946 World Series on the so-called "Mad Dash," when he was playing for the St. Louis Cardinals. As mentioned earlier, Slaughter had been acquired by the Yankees in 1954 and traded to Kansas City in 1955, where he played until August of '56.

Don Larsen felt Slaughter was not popular with his teammates. Some regarded him as still a Cardinal at heart and others resented the way he pushed younger players (*Perfect Yankee*, p. 108). Coming from an era of tough players, Slaughter certainly

"Gee, it's lonesome in the outfield. It's hard to keep awake with nothing to do."

Babe Ruth

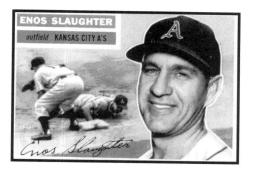

had the credentials to act as a model for younger men. In the fifth game of the 1946 World Series he was hit on the elbow by a pitch. He played the rest of that game and Games 6 and 7 with a broken elbow.

In Game 6 of the '56 series a line drive got over Slaughter's head to score the winning run in the bottom of the 10th inning. Whether Slaughter could or should have made the catch is still debated. Lou Smith, sports editor for the Cincinnati *Enquirer*, who was at the game, concluded Slaughter could have made the play if he had not first broken in on the ball. But he pointed out Slaughter also "lost a ball in the high sky in the third inning" and "quit on Labine's high fly doubt along the left-field line in the eighth."

After that loss Billy Martin stormed into Casey Stengel's office and demanded Slaughter and Joe Collins be replaced for Game 7 by Elston Howard and Moose Skowron, even though the Dodgers would be starting a right-handed pitcher. Whatever influence Martin may have had, Howard and Skowron did start the final game of the series and contributed mightily to the Yankees' 9-0 victory.

Slaughter's personal life was tempestuous. He had married for the fifth time in January of '56 and his wife was expecting a child at the time of the World Series. Although he first became eligible for the Hall of Fame in 1964, Slaughter was not elected to the Hall until the Veterans' Committee voted him in in 1985. His attitude toward black players in the major leagues, mentioned earlier, probably contributed to the delay (Mantle, *Octobers*, p. 72). He died in 2002.

Center field

MICKEY MANTLE. One hardly needs to say more than those two words. The raging debate during the 1950s was whether Mantle, Duke Snider, or Willie Mays was the greatest center-fielder of all time. As David Halberstam said, loving baseball in the 1950s meant "you have to accept the lore of the bubble gum card, and believe that if the answer to the Mays-Snider-Mantle question is found, then the universe will be a simpler and more ordered place."

My friend Mitch, the avid Dodger fan, tried to argue for Duke Snider, but he couldn't make the case against Mantle and

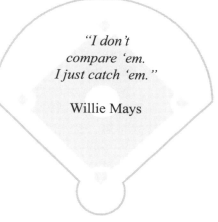

"I don't compare 'em. I just catch 'em."

Willie Mays

Mays. Both could run, and both could hit for power, but, as Billy Martin said, "I don't think baseball has ever known a player who had Mantle's combination of power and speed" (*BillyBall*, p. 75).

What finally gave Mays an edge in the record books was his freedom from injuries, which nagged Mantle throughout his career. Before each game he had to tape his right leg from thigh to ankle. Cleveland pitcher Early Wynn, after playing with Mantle in an All-Star game, said, "I watched him bandage that knee – that whole leg – and I saw what he had to go through every day to play. And now I'll never be able to praise him enough. Seeing those legs, his power becomes unbelievable" (*Octobers*, p. 62). And yet he was as likely to beat out a bunt as to park the ball in the stands. Nellie Fox of the Chicago White Sox summed up the opinion of Mantle's contemporaries: "On two legs, Mickey Mantle would have been the greatest ball player who ever lived." Don Larsen concurred: "The good Lord never put a better ballplayer on the face of the earth" (*Perfect Yankee*, p. 68).

Mantle's career got off to a slow start, though. He describes himself as looking like a character out of "Li'l Abner" when he joined the Yankees in 1951, wearing "blue jeans which were rolled up at the bottom . . . white sweat socks and shoes with sponge-rubber soles, a tweed sports coat and a tie that was about twelve inches wide and had a peacock painted on it" (*Favorite Summer*, p. 23). A cardboard suitcase completed his ensemble.

Billy Martin was impressed by Mantle's "forearms like a lumberjack" (*BillyBall*, p. 76), built up by work in the lead mines around his home town. Casey Stengel raised expectations about Mantle with statements like this in the spring of 1951: "He should lead the league in everything. With his combination of speed and power he should win the triple batting crown every year. In fact, he should do anything he wants to do."

The shy youngster found it difficult to live up to that billing. In the middle of the '51 season he was sent back to the minors and almost quit baseball. His father used a little tough love to get his son's career back on track (*Favorite Summer*, p. 157). Mantle grieved deeply when his father died in 1952, at the age of 39: "I stood before my father's grave, remembering a thousand things from the past . . . So many chances then to let him know how much I loved him – and I never said it, not once" (*The Mick*, p. 88).

"Tough love" is putting it mildly. Mantle says his father told him, "I thought I raised a man, not a coward." Just what a stressed-out 19-year-old needs to hear.

Some of Mantle's injury problems went back to the osteomyelitis which afflicted him when he was in high school. This condition is a chronic infection that settles in the bones after an injury, usually the long bones of young people. Mantle had been kicked in the lower leg while playing football in high school. In 1946 he was hospitalized and treated with a new drug, penicillin, which he believed saved his life and prompted a growth spurt (*Favorite Summer*, p. 54). His most infamous injury occurred in the 1951 World Series when he caught his cleats in a drain cover while running for a fly ball. All reports agree he went down like he had been shot, with his right knee severely damaged.

The Yankees' team physician just wrapped the leg and sent Mantle home. The next morning he and his father, who was in town to see his dream fulfilled, realized Mickey needed to get to a hospital. While he was there his father collapsed and was hospitalized in the same room. Doctors discovered he had inoperable cancer.

Although he was the best-known and most widely popular of the perfect gamers, Mantle's life off the field was probably the most imperfect. Or maybe it just seems that way because he was the most

gifted athlete among them, the one with the greatest potential. He overcame a number of physical ailments to achieve great things, but one must always wonder how much more he could have achieved if he had been able to sort out his personal life. As Mantle himself ruefully observed, "Sometimes I think if I had the same body and the same natural ability and someone else's brain, who knows how good a player I might have been."

Only late in his life did Mantle make known some of the emotional problems which tormented him. When he was in elementary school he was sexually molested numerous times by his older half-sister and some of her friends. Probably because of that trauma, he was a bed-wetter until he was sixteen (Castro, pp. 11-12).

In December of 1951 Mantle married Merlyn Johnson, a hometown girl. But he later admitted he married her, as he did so many things, to please his father. To do so he had to break off a serious affair with a New York nightclub entertainer (Castro, p. 112). Life in New York overwhelmed the two young Sooners. Merlyn admitted she was even afraid to use a rotary dial phone (*Hero*, p. 44). Mantle found he enjoyed the night life that went along with being a Yankee star. He, Billy Martin, and Whitey Ford made the rounds of the watering holes. All three developed serious problems with alcohol.

Mantle's wife, left alone with Mickey on the road and aware of his constant womanizing, also became an alcoholic. They had four sons who, as adults, became Mickey's drinking buddies (*Hero*, p. 13). Billy – named after Billy Martin – died in 1994 while in a detox center. The other three sons also had alcohol and/or drug problems. In his autobiography Mantle admitted, "I gave Merlyn everything she wanted except having me around enough. I was no better father than I was a husband" (*The Mick*, p. 211). Mickey and Merlyn separated in 1980, but they never divorced and continued to celebrate birthdays and anniversaries together. Toward the end of his life Mickey could call her "the only woman I loved for a lifetime" (*Hero*, p. 27), although he was living with his agent, Greer Johnson, at the time.

Mantle retired from baseball in 1969. Over the next few years the Yankees invited him back now and then as a celebrity coach, and he tried his hand at being a sportscaster. In 1983 he was suspended from all contact with baseball by Commissioner Bowie Kuhn when he was hired to promote a casino in Atlantic City. Commissioner Peter Ueberroth reinstated him in 1985.

Mantle finally began to try to deal with his alcoholism in the early 1990s. In an article in *Sports Illustrated* he admitted he had mistreated and embarrassed his family, friends, even fans, because of his drinking. He entered the Betty Ford Clinic for rehab, but the damage was already done. In June of 1994 he received a liver transplant. During the surgery doctors discovered inoperable cancer. Mantle died on August 13, 1995.

> *"You start chasing a ball and your brain immediately commands your body to 'Run forward, bend, scoop up the ball, peg it to the infield.' Then your body says, 'Who, me?'"*
>
> Joe DiMaggio

Right field

HANK BAUER was born in 1922. He served in the Marines in World War II, was wounded twice and received two Bronze Stars. His older brother, whom Bauer considered a better ballplayer than himself, was killed in the war. After the interruption to his minor-league career, Bauer debated whether to return to baseball or to go back to being an iron-worker, where he could earn some real money, $3.00 an hour. Don Larsen, who played with him and for him when Bauer became a manager, called him "a pro's pro, a gritty, no-nonsense, in-your-face warrior . . . . Why he isn't in the Hall of Fame, I'll never know" (*Perfect Yankee*, p. 39). Mickey Mantle, who roomed with Bauer, found "if you leveled with him, he was a pussycat; if you struck a nerve, you had a tiger on your hands" (*The Mick*, p. 72).

Even though he wasn't one of my favorite players, I developed some affection for Bauer once I learned from his baseball card that his middle name was Albert, the same as my first name. He thought of himself as a singles hitter, not a slugger. In an article in the Greenville *News* (July 1, 1956) he complained he was hitting too many homers and his average was dropping. "I'd gladly take those 16 homers of mine, break them down into total bases, and take them as singles instead." But a few days later the headline on the sports page read "Bauer Belts Grand-Slam in 6th." A week after that, Bauer was featured on the sports page again, this time with his wife and their new-born daughter.

Bauer, whose face reminded some people of a clenched fist, played in nine World Series with the

Yankees (53 games) and collected the winners' share seven times. Players' salaries were low in those days, and General Manager George Weiss would always remind those who complained that they would get a World Series check. For the lowest-paid players that could be almost 50% of their annual salary. Teammates who weren't putting out a full effort would hear Bauer snarl, "Don't mess with my money!" Under Casey Stengel's platoon system, Bauer did not play every day, but he credited that practice with extending his career (in *Men of Autumn*, p. 68). He hit for power and yet possessed enough speed to bat in the lead-off spot until late in his career. He hit 18 lead-off home runs, a sure way to demoralize an opposing pitcher.

Derek Jeter and Manny Ramirez have hit in 17 consecutive post-season games, but for the purist there is an irreconcilable difference between "post-season" – the league play-offs – and World Series. Reggie Jackson is credited with more "post-season" homers than Mickey Mantle. As Mantle said, "False reporting. What they did was combine his post-season and World Series home runs"

(The Mick, *p. 259*).

Bauer enjoyed his best season in 1956, hitting 26 home runs. He had already had at least one hit in each of the first four games of the '56 Series. He would go on to hit in 17 consecutive World Series games from 1956-1958, a record that stands today.

After he was traded to the A's in 1960, Bauer became a player/manager. For one fan Bauer embodied "the proud Yankee tradition." Seeing him playing right field for the Athletics "was a little like coming home from school and finding my mother dressed up in combat fatigues" (Boyd and Harris, p. 145). Bauer managed the A's for a couple of seasons with little success. In 1966 he managed the Baltimore Orioles, climaxing the season with a four-game sweep of the still hated (by me) Dodgers in the World Series, for which I still bless his name.

CHAPTER 25

*"Perfection
is the child of time."*

Bishop Joseph Hall

The Other Guys

The nine Yankee players weren't the only guys on the field that day, of course. In the interest of completeness and fairness, I'm going to do a quick survey of the Dodger players in the game, about whom I knew very little in 1956, aside from what I had read in articles about them in *Sports Illustrated* and my newspaper that summer, and the umpires, about whom I knew nothing beyond their names.

'Dem Bums'

It is important to acknowledge that the Dodgers were damn good because it underscores the magnitude of Larsen's achievement. Throwing a perfect game against a hapless team is still an accomplishment, but to do it against a team that had dominated their league since 1949 and had beaten the Yankees in the 1955 World Series – after losing the first two games – was nothing short of a spectacular achievement.

The Dodgers led the National League in total runs scored in 1951-53, the first team ever to lead their league in that category for three straight years. Now, with their second consecutive pennant in hand, perhaps they were ready to cast off the role of tragic heroes, perpetual losers, what Roger Kahn called "a national team, with a country in thrall, irresistible and unable to beat the Yankees" (*Boys of Summer*, p. xii). Even though Don Newcombe had compiled a 27-7 record in 1956, Sal Maglie was generally considered the man who put the Dodgers over the top with his 13 wins, some of them in crucial spots. *Sports Illustrated* described him as "heretofore respected but not particularly loved as a cold-blooded, hard-boiled, unsmiling gangster of a pitcher . . . who with the Dodgers became a full-blown white-armored hero . . . an old man turned young, and a villain reformed" (Oct. 8, 1956).

The Dodgers' line-up for Game 5 would intimidate any pitcher: Junior Gilliam, Pee Wee Reese, and Duke Snider, followed by Jackie Robinson, Gil Hodges, Sandy Amoros, Carl Furillo, Roy Campanella, and Maglie, a pitcher who was no slouch with the bat. Four of them – Reese, Snider, Robinson, and Campanella – would make the Hall of Fame. And, even being an inveterate Dodger-hater, I don't understand why Hodges and Furillo haven't joined them. Look at these statistics compared to three Hall of Famers from the same era:

	AVG.	HR.	RBI
Hodges	.273	370	1274
Furillo	.299	192	1058
Luis Aparicio	.262	83	791
Lou Boudreau	.295	68	789
George Kell	.306	78	870

Aparicio made it to one World Series (1959), as did Boudreau (1948), but Kell never played on a pennant-winning team, even though his stellar career spanned from 1943-1957. The three of them together hit only 229 home runs.

If Hodges' statistics didn't earn him a place in the Hall of Fame, his personality probably should have. He had the reputation of being an all-around nice guy. Charlie Dressen, Dodgers' manager in 1951, urged Hodges to argue with the umpires now and then about their calls, but "he's such a nice guy he wouldn't even do that. The umps think he is the nicest guy in the league. But you don't have to be that nice." When I spoke at a conference and mentioned I was working on this book, a woman approached me and said she had grown up in the same block where Hodges lived. "Gilbert Ray was such a nice man," she said. "Not like that awful Duke Snider."

As mentioned earlier, the Dodgers' line-up was filled with veterans nearing the end of their careers. An article in *Sports Illustrated* at the end of the

On Oct. 6, 1956, a Cincinnati woman sued Duke Snider for damages from injuries suffered in 1954 when he "did negligently and wantonly knock a pitched ball with such force and violence as to strike plaintiff with great force and violence." Snider was alleged to be "an expert with a bat and a home run artist" but he "wobbled and swayed his body in such a wanton manner as to cause the ball to take a wild course other than a home run."

(Cincinnati Enquirer)

season admitted "Brooklyn's Money Men" had come through in the clutch, but they seemed tired. In Casey Stengel's view, "That Brooklyn club is smart. Old but smart . . . . but I'm not afraid of 'em" (*Sports Illustrated*, Oct. 1, 1956).

By way of comparison, the oldest Yankees on the field for Game 5 were Slaughter (40), Collins (34), and Bauer (34). Because of Casey Stengel's platoon system, his older players got more rest than the Dodger veterans. The Yankees' line-up for Game 5, however, boasted only three players who would make the Hall of Fame: Berra, Mantle, and Enos Slaughter, and Slaughter was voted in by the Veterans Committee on the basis of his long career with the Cardinals.

Jackie Robinson retired after the 1956 World Series. The other senior citizens on the Dodgers team finished out their careers about the time the team moved to Los Angeles in 1958. Roy Campanella was confined to a wheelchair after an automobile accident that year. PeeWee Reese became Dizzy Dean's "li'l podner" in weekly broadcasts of ball games in the early 1960s.

"The best umpired game is the game in which the fans cannot recall the umpires who worked it. If they don't recognize you, you can enjoy your dinner knowing you did a perfect job."

Bill Klem

The Umps

Someone has said an umpire has the best seat in the house for a baseball game, but he has to stand. During the 1956 season a couple of umpires spoke out about their unappreciated work. Larry Goetz criticized "crybabies" who "try to shift the blame for their own incompetence onto the umpires"(*Saturday Evening Post*, Apr. 14). Gil Stratton, Jr., a Pacific Coast League umpire, admitted umps sometimes called close plays on appearances rather than reality. If a first baseman, for instance, actually kept his foot on the bag until the ball was in his glove, Stratton argued, many of them would be injured by the runners' spikes. Or if the second baseman really had to stay on the bag to turn a double play, many of them would be seriously hurt. So, as long as the play looked reasonably close, Stratton said, umpires called the runners out (*Sports Illustrated*, Aug. 6).

In the World Series two extra umpires are used, along the left and right field lines. That practice would figure decisively in Game 5 of the '56 Series. In the 1950s umpires were still limited to working in one league, so the crews for the World Series were made up of three from the National League and three from the American. Today umpires are simply Major League umpires and can work games in either league.

ED RUNGE, from the American League, was the right field umpire. Runge began umpiring in the minor leagues in 1947 and came to the majors in 1954. His definition of umpiring fits well with the theme of this book: "It's the only occupation where a man has to be perfect his first day on the job and then improve over the years." In the perfect game Runge called two long balls hit by the Dodgers foul. The home plate umpire said he would have called one of them a home run from his vantage point. Runge maintained both were foul by inches. Runge had been Don Larsen's manager in a pick-up league in San Diego in 1955. But he also managed Sal Maglie in his younger days (*Perfect Yankee*, pp. 92, 143), so he shouldn't be accused of favoritism. Carl Yastrezemski once jokingly told Runge, "Ed, you're the second-best umpire in the league. The other 23 are tied for first." Runge, whose son and grandson became major league umpires, died in 2002.

The left field umpire was TOM GORMAN, from the National League. Gorman actually had very little to do that day. He was active from 1951-1976 and is best known for saying, "Any time I got those 'bang-bang' plays at first base, I called 'em out. It made the game shorter." His son also became a major league umpire. Gorman's autobiography is listed in the bibliography of this book.

Third base was the domain of American League umpire LARRY NAPP for Game 5. In a game when one team has no baserunners and the other scores only two runs – one on a home run – there obviously isn't a lot of action at third base. Napp holds the distinction of being the only umpire involved in two perfect games. He was at first base for Catfish Hunter's game in 1968. He was a judo expert and a boxing instructor.

LYNTON "DUSTY" BOGGESS considered his involvement in Larsen's perfect game the greatest thrill of his National League umpiring career, which ran from 1944-1962. Boggess covered second base that day and did have to make a couple of calls on Yankee baserunners. During his career he asked every umpire he worked with to sign a baseball. His will directed that those balls be buried with him. When Boggess died in 1968 the *New York Times* noted "he had no immediate survivors." His book is also listed in the bibliography of this book.

First-base umpire HANK SOAR did have a busy day and had to make a couple of close calls. Soar played football for the New York Giants before becoming an umpire and reaching the American League in 1950. His career lasted until 1975. Highly regarded by players and coaches, he died in 2001.

Calling the balls and strikes for Game 5 was RALPH "BABE" PINELLI, from the National League. Which umpire works in which position is purely a matter of a rotation. The umpires work in crews. After the first game in a series, they move ninety feet. The pattern is for the home plate umpire in one game to move to third, where there is likely to be less action, for the next game. The first base umpire moves to home plate. In the World Series, with two extra umpires, the work load gets spread a little thinner. In Game 4, when Pinelli was the first base umpire, he was hit hard by a line drive off the bat of the Yankees' Gil McDougald.

Pinelli had been an infielder in the major leagues from 1918-1927 and was considered to have a "soft thumb," that is, he was reluctant to eject players or coaches from a game. As luck would have it, Game 5 of the 1956 Series was Pinelli's last game behind home plate and the Series was the last assignment of his 22-year career. He had also been behind the plate for Jackie Robinson's first game.

National League umpires were believed to have a slightly different interpretation of the strike zone than their American League counterparts. The National Leaguers allegedly tended to call low pitches strikes more often than American Leaguers, who allegedly favored higher pitches. When Sal Maglie was traded by the Cleveland Indians to the Dodgers, he said he was happy to be back in the National League because American League umpires "won't give you the low ball" (Greenville *News*, May 20, 1956). Whether the presence of an American League umpire behind the plate would have affected the outcome of Game 5 is one of those topics rife with possibilities for debate.

One might also wonder about the after-effects of an argument which erupted between Babe Pinelli and the Dodgers in a game against Pittsburgh on Sept. 24, a loss that dropped the Dodgers back into second place. Jackie Robinson was especially vocal in his criticism of Pinelli: "He called Gil Hodges out before the ball even left the pitcher's hand . . . . And he missed two on Dale Long in the eighth inning" (Cincinnati *Enquirer*, Sept. 25, 1956).

One story says that after the game a reporter asked Pinelli if he had been aware of the perfect game. Pinelli replied, "Perfect game? I knew it was a no-hitter. You mean I called a perfect game?" The reporter said, "No, Larsen pitched a perfect game."

Babe Pinelli died in 1984.

CHAPTER 26

> *"That soul
> that can be honest is the
> only perfect man."*
>
> John Fletcher

I don't think we're in Laurens any more

Being in Mitch's apartment was another new, strange experience for me, the weirdness of it heightened by my awareness that I shouldn't be there. Growing up as a Southern Baptist, I had been taught to be suspicious – even fearful – of Jews, of anybody who wasn't a Southern Baptist, really, but especially of Jews. All that Christ-killer nonsense was still *au courant* among Southern Baptists in the 1950s. We didn't like Catholics, either, because they worshiped the pope and did it with that Latin mumbo-jumbo. Who could tell what they were plotting? When John Kennedy ran for president in 1960, my grandfather, a life-long Baptist and a life-long Democrat, told me, "I'm going to hold my nose and vote for Nixon."

There was nothing unusual about Mitch's apartment, though. Even with the windows open on a pleasant fall day, it had a stuffy odor I hadn't smelled since my dad quit smoking. The furniture looked old and heavy, but it seemed to fit in an apartment better than my parents' stuff. Mitch said they had lived in an apartment in Brooklyn, so I guess they bought their furniture to fit that sort of space. When we moved from South Carolina my parents had to leave some things behind and my mother was still shifting things around every few days.

At the moment, though, what mattered was that Mitch's TV set was bigger than ours, and it was color. It swiveled on its stand so it could be seen from the kitchen table. Mitch turned it on and there was the World Series – in glorious black and white.

"You said you had a color TV."

"We do, but they're not broadcasting the Series in color."

"Why not?" I was playing hooky and risking a punishment I could barely imagine. I ought to at least get to see the game in color.

"I don't know. They're just not."

Whatever he'd been doing the night before and no matter when he learned he was going to pitch that day, Don Larsen looked sharp from the moment Babe Pinelli cried 'Play ball!' Junior Gilliam, the Dodgers' lead-off man, already had two strikes on him as Mitch got out something for us to eat.

"Come on, Gilliam!" Mitch said. "Base hit! Get it started."

But Gilliam went down on strikes, and so did the next batter, Pee Wee Reese. Larsen ran the count to ball 3 on Reese, the only ball 3 the Dodgers would see all afternoon. Duke Snider then hit a harmless fly to Hank Bauer in right field.

"Good start," I said.

"Yeah, but Larsen got off to a good start on Friday," Mitch reminded me. "Then the Dodgers jumped all over him."

I could have mentioned Joe Collins' crucial error that led to several Dodger runs, but I didn't want to start an argument. Mitch thrived on confrontation, while I did all I could to avoid it. That may have been one reason I got along so well with my mother. So, instead of rising to Larsen's defense, I just concentrated on getting myself some lunch.

I had heard that Jews ate strange food and had peculiar rules about how you had to eat it. There was nothing strange or peculiar about the pimento cheese Mitch pulled out of the refrigerator, though, so I relaxed a little.

Then he asked, "You want whole wheat or rye?"

The two bags he held up looked like bread bags, but I had no idea what the stuff in them was, especially the stuff in his left hand that was so dark it looked burned.

"Whole wheat or rye?" he repeated, raising each bag in turn.

The whole wheat at least looked edible, so I pointed to it.

Mitch pulled out two slices of the rye for himself. "What kind of bread do you guys eat?"

"Just . . . regular bread." Until that moment I had not known bread could be anything but white. At least the potato chips he got out of a cabinet were the same brand my mother bought. Then he offered drinks.

"Dr. Pepper or ginger ale?"

In my family Coke – or as we were more likely to call it, Co-Cola – was the soft drink of choice. We did tolerate a few Pepsi heretics, but there were none of the 'RC Cola and a moon pie' cult among us.

The only thing better than Coke was iced tea, real Southern iced tea, with so much sugar in it one comedian called it "40-W tea." Sunlight cannot penetrate real Southern iced tea. To create the perfect chemical bond, the sugar must be stirred in while the tea is still hot. I've given up ordering iced tea in restaurants outside the South. They bring you a glass of unsweetened hot tea into which they dump a couple of pieces of ice – which have mostly melted by the time the glass gets to your table. Then they expect you to stir in a few packets of sugar. The resulting lukewarm watery concoction, with a layer of sugar sludge at the bottom of the glass, bears no resemblance to *real* iced tea. And it's *iced* tea, not *ice* tea.

Some Southerners cut the sweetness of the tea by adding lemon. My family liked to add pineapple juice. Whenever my grandmother opened a can of pineapple, she poured the juice into a small jar that stayed in her refrigerator. That jar – a one-pint cream jar from a local dairy – came to be considered a family heirloom, which I now have. As an adult I wondered why my wife's tea didn't taste the same when I added the pineapple juice. It was the same brand of pineapple and I was using the very jar we used in Laurens. Then I realized my wife had started buying pineapple packed in its own juice, not in heavily sugared syrup. I haven't really enjoyed a glass of tea since, except at family reunions.

But Dr. Pepper or ginger ale?

I'd heard of both the drinks Mitch offered but had never tasted either one. Why anybody would want to drink something with pepper in it was beyond my comprehension, so I chose the ginger ale and was relieved to find I kind of liked it. I might ask my mom to buy some, I thought. Then I realized she would ask me where I had tasted it. "Oh, what a tangled web we weave . . . ."

During the commercials between the top and bottom of the first inning Mitch hurried to his room and returned with a manila envelope, the contents of which he emptied on the kitchen table: Yankee and Dodger baseball cards in rubber bands and two sheets of paper on which he had lined off columns. One sheet was headed DODGERS, the other DAMN YANKEES.

"What are those?" I asked, blushing at bit at the expletive. That sort of language was entirely foreign to my family and to my life experience to that point.

"They're score cards," Mitch said. "You write the line-ups in the left column and, whatever inning a guy comes to bat, you write down what he did in these boxes." He wrote "Gilliam" in the first column on the Dodgers' sheet, then "Reese" and "Snider" below him. "Gilliam and Reese were called out on strikes, weren't they?"

"Yeah."

"Man, that stinks," Mitch said. Poet Robert Frost put it more eloquently: "One of the hardest things to accept as just is a called third strike" (*Sports Illustrated*, July 23, 1956).

Under the column headed "1" Mitch made a backwards K beside each man's name.

"Why do you use a backwards K if they strike out?"

"One, two, three, and you're out." He drew the three strokes of a K in the air with his finger. "You put it backwards if they take the third strike, frontwards if they swing and miss."

In the first box beside Snider's name he wrote "F-9."

"What's that for?"

"It means he flied out to right field." He looked up at me with a mixture of pity and disbelief. "Don't you know how to keep score?"

The only way I knew to "keep score" was to count how many runs each team got.

"Okay, I'll show you. But first let's arrange the cards in the order of the line-ups. You take your precious Yankees." He shoved a batch of cards over to my side of the table. "I had to use some '55s because I don't have all of them this year."

I took the rubber band off and thumbed through the cards. Between the two years, Mitch had just about the whole team. His cards showed more wear around the edges than mine, and he had drawn mustaches on some. On Mantle's head shot he had drawn a beard and, on the background figure – Mantle making a leaping catch at the fence – he had drawn the ball falling out of his glove and "Oops!" in a cartoon balloon coming out of his mouth. I hope he was one of those guys whose mother threw his collection away while he was in college so he wouldn't have to think about what his '56 Mantle card would be worth today if only he hadn't . . . .

I knew Hank Bauer would bat first, Mantle third, and Berra fourth, so I put those cards in place. McDougald, Martin, and Carey would be toward the bottom of the order. Enos Slaughter, still with Kansas City when the '56 cards were printed, would be in there somewhere, since he batted left and Maglie was a right-handed pitcher. Joe Collins would probably be at first for the same reason, so I pulled his card out.

"Do you have a Larsen card?" I asked.

"I traded him to you, remember? Why don't you run home and get him? Say hi to your mom while you're there."

"Very funny." I felt guilty enough without that sort of a jab.

The Dodgers' line-up hadn't varied much all year, so Mitch had his cards in order quickly. I looked through the others, especially the '55s. I didn't have many of those. One card caught my attention because the face staring out at me looked so much like Mitch. "Who's Sandy Koufax?" I asked, pronouncing it "coo-fax."

"It's 'co-fax'," Mitch said. "He hasn't pitched much yet, but my mother and his stepfather are some kind of cousins. He autographed that card for me. See, on the back."

Maybe I shouldn't hope his mother threw his cards away. The '55 Topps card was Koufax's rookie card. Rookie cards bring top dollar, because, no matter how many years a player stays in the majors, he has only one rookie year. In excellent condition, Koufax's rookie card goes today for about $750.

Autographed, at least $1,000.

I tossed the card back into Mitch's pile.

"We're gonna kill you guys today," he said. "Four home runs, maybe five. I've just got a feeling."

I wanted the Yankees to win, of course, but I hoped the game would be a quick one, not a three-hour slugfest, like Game 2 had been, or an extra-innings affair. Whatever happened, I needed to be home in time to make it look like I had gotten off the bus at the regular time.

"Hey, the Yankees are up," I said.

"SANDY" KOUFAX   *pitcher* BROOKLYN DODGERS

Up, and down almost as fast. Lead-off batter Hank Bauer popped out to Pee Wee Reese. When Joe Collins came to the plate, I slipped his card into the second spot in my stack. He tried to bunt his way on, but Jackie Robinson threw him out. I crossed my fingers as Mantle came to the plate, but he just flied out to Amoros in left field.

As Mitch scribbled on his scorecard I asked, "What does all that mean?"

"Each position has a number," he said. "The pitcher is 1. The catcher is 2. Then the numbers go around the bases: 3 is first base, 4 is second, and 5 is third. Shortstop is 6. In the outfield, the numbers 7 through 9 start in left field and go around to right."

"So Mantle in centerfield is . . . 8?"

"Yeah." Mitch smiled, like our teachers did when we caught on to something.

"Then why does he wear number 7 on his uniform?"

Mitch grimaced. "That doesn't have anything to do with this. Guys just pick numbers they like for their uniforms. Maybe their mother's birthday. Billy Martin thinks he's king of the world, so he wears number 1. But he plays second base and when you're keeping score, second base is position number 4, no matter who's playing it."

"I still don't get it." Math always was my weakest subject.

"Okay, look. When Collins bunted, Robinson fielded it and threw to Hodges, right?"

"Yeah."

"Robinson plays third. That's position number 5. He threw to Hodges, who plays first. That's position number 3. So I write the play down as 5-3."

"What if Hodges had fielded the bunt and Gilliam covered first?"

"Then I would write 3-4."

"But the out was at first base, not second."

Mitch ran a hand over his frizzy hair. "The numbers are for the *player*, not the base! The second baseman is always number 4, whether it's Jackie Robinson, or Junior Gilliam, or whoever. If he ended up covering home on some crazy play and tagged somebody out there, I would write it down as a put-out by 4."

That didn't make any sense to me. If you're out at home, you're out at home, not at second. "How do you show when somebody gets a hit?"

Mitch punched me on the arm. "Maybe the Yankees won't get any. Maglie pitched a no-hitter a couple of weeks ago. He could do it again."

Mitch today probably remembers that he forecast a no-hitter, even if by the wrong pitcher. There are other stories told of premonitions or predictions of something unusual happening that day (*Perfect Yankee*, pp. 30-31).

Good prophet or not, Mitch did teach me the basics of keeping score. He was one of the people

John Culkin had in mind when he said, "I don't think baseball could survive without all the statistical appurtenances involved in calculating pitching, hitting and fielding percentages. Some people could do without the games as long as they got the box scores" (*New York Times*, July 13, 1976). Whole books have been written on the glory of baseball statistics (Albert, Paretchan, Runquist). Dave Kindred kept score as he, also a victim of "World Series flu," was watching the game that day. Years later he lamented: "Man, I wish I still had that scorebook. I've interrogated my mother and I've accused my sister. I'm afraid the truth is, I just threw the scorebook away."

Today there is an entire organization, the Society for American Baseball Research, devoted to the minutia of baseball statistics. I'd be surprised if Mitch wasn't a member. He would have understood William Weiss' sentiments: "I learned at a very young age that I was no athlete. If I wanted to have anything to do with baseball it certainly wouldn't be on the field . . . . Statistics just seemed like a natural for me and it's what I decided I wanted to do in life" (in Bryan, *Baseball Lives*, p. 234).

Roger Angell summed up the baseball fan's love affair with stats in his essay "Box Scores":

The box score, being modestly arcane, is a matter of intense indifference, if not irritation, to the non-fan. To the baseball-bitten, it is not only informative, pictorial, and gossipy but lovely in aesthetic structure. It represents happenstance and physical flight exactly translated into figures and history. Its totals – batters' credit vs. pitchers' debit – balance as exactly as those in an accountant's ledger. And a box score is more than a capsule archive. It is a precisely etched miniature of the sport itself, for baseball, in spite of its grassy spaciousness and apparent unpredictability, is the most intensely and satisfyingly mathematical of all our outdoor sports. Every player in every game is subjected to a cold and ceaseless accounting; no ball is thrown and no base is gained without an instant responding judgment – ball or strike, hit or error, yea or nay – and an ensuing statistic.

"Dodgers are up again!" Mitch said. "Robinson leads off."
Jackie was digging in against Larsen when we heard a key in the front door.

Busted

Mitch and I looked at one another, our eyes widening. There was nothing we could do. The apartment did have a back door, leading out of the kitchen, but the TV was on and our food and baseball cards were all over the table.

"Hello? Mrs. Birnbaum? Esther? Hello?"

"That's Bob Murphy," Mitch said in a loud whisper. "He works for my dad."

Mitch's dad worked for the realty company that ran Swifton Village. To hear Mitch tell it, he ran the whole operation. He looked old enough to be in charge, but Mitch's mother looked a lot younger, maybe a little younger than my mother. And she was pretty.

"Hello?" A man, about the age of my parents, with slicked-back blond hair stepped into the kitchen doorway and gave a surprised jerk of his head. "Well, well."

Mitch gave him a limp wave. "Hey, Mr. Murphy."

"What are you two doing here?" He sounded more annoyed than amused.

"Watching the World Series."

"Don't you mean you're playing hooky?"

"Yeah, that too. What are you doing here?"

"Well, it's . . . kind of embarrassing to admit it, but . . . that's why I'm here, too."

"You're playing hooky?" Mitch said.

"Yeah, sort of. Your dad sent me out to do some things, and I thought I would . . . stop by here and catch a couple of innings of the game . . . before I went back to the office. Be nice to see it in color."

To me he sounded uncomfortable, the way I did when I tried to lie. "They're not showing it in color," I informed him.

"Oh, I didn't know – "

"Why do you have a key to our apartment?" Mitch asked.

"I . . . we have master keys to all the apartments."

Mitch squinted. "I thought my dad had the lock to our apartment changed so – Holy cow! Did he call Robinson out?"

I had been looking past Mr. Murphy and watching the TV. I hadn't realized Mitch was, too. Mr. Murphy whirled around, but the play was over. Robinson had hit a wicked one-hopper to third baseman Andy Carey's left. As Carey lunged for the ball, it caromed off the tip of his glove straight to shortstop Gil McDougald, who caught it and threw in what looked like the same motion, nipping Robinson at first base.

Mitch raised up out of his chair. "Out? Are you blind, ump?"

"The imperfect man pitched a perfect game yesterday."

New York Daily News, *October 9, 1956*

I thought Robinson was safe, too, but I wasn't going to admit it. It was so close a play I was surprised the Dodgers didn't protest. Umpire Hank Soar's reputation for fairness may have helped silence them.

"Man, a couple of years ago they never would have thrown him out," Mitch groused as he flopped back down in his chair.

That is an oft-repeated assessment of the play. Mickey Mantle subscribed to it (*Octobers*, p. 67). But there's no logic to it. The play didn't happen a couple of years earlier. Just as "there's no crying in baseball," there's no time travel either. You might as well say, 'A few years later they would have had instant replay.'

But they didn't, and Robinson wasn't two years younger. What he was, was out.

Gil McDougald described this crucial play from his perspective: "Jackie had bad wheels. I had a rotten arm. But I threw as hard as I could. It was a race between my arm and his legs. We just did get him" (in *Men of Autumn*, p. 163).

Mr. Murphy rubbed his hands together, like he was nervous, or cold. "Real bang-bang play, huh? Look, Mitch, I'd better get going. How about a deal? I won't tell your dad you skipped school if you don't tell him I was here. And . . . you guys get yourselves some baseball cards." He took out his wallet and dropped two dollars on the table.

Mitch nodded and Mr. Murphy left, looking as relieved as if he was escaping from the principal's office without being punished. We could hear him running down the stairs. We each took one of his dollars and put it in our pockets.

Gil Hodges was stepping into the batter's box when we heard a car starting outside the kitchen. The parking places for the apartments were on the backs of the buildings, and Mitch's apartment was on the second floor.

"That sounds like my mom's car," Mitch said.

"How can you tell?"

"It makes that grinding noise when it starts."

Scooting our chairs, we got close enough to the window over the sink that we could see the parking lot without being seen. Mr. Murphy was running toward a car parked farther down in the lot. A '52 Buick was backing really fast out of a space below Mitch's window.

"That's her," Mitch said. "I wonder why she was here."

First Time Through

As Mitch and I returned to the game, the fifth batter, Gil Hodges, struck out swinging. Larsen then got a couple of strikes on Sandy Amoros before he popped one up. I thought for sure it was going to fall for a hit. Hank Bauer, in right field, looked like he couldn't possibly get to it. Then Billy Martin backpedaled from second base and caught the ball as he tumbled to the ground. He bounced to his feet, holding up his glove to show the umpire he had caught it.

"Shit!" Mitch said. "A bad call and some damn Yankee luck. The way this is going, Larsen could pitch a no-hitter." I was so stunned to hear the expletives coming out of my friend's mouth I didn't even think about the rest of what he said.

The Yankees didn't look much better at the plate than the Dodgers did, though. In the bottom of the second Yogi Berra popped up to Reese. Enos Slaughter had gotten three hits off the Barber in Game 1, but this time he flied out to Sandy Amoros. Billy Martin struck out. Campanella dropped the ball and had to throw Martin out at first. After two innings the game was developing into a pitcher's duel. Larsen later recalled that he felt great confidence in his pitches and "couldn't wait to get back on the mound for inning three" (*Perfect Yankee*, p. 47).

Carl Furillo led off the third inning for Brooklyn. Of all the Dodgers I think I liked him least. He was a tough-looking guy and he always seemed to need a shave. Roger Kahn described him as having "a face from Caesar's legions" (*Boys*, p. 49). Larsen felt the same way about him: "His half-shaven beard and steely demeanor gave me the creeps" (*Perfect Yankee*, p. 174). Television made him look even more menacing, a lesson Richard Nixon would soon learn to his regret. But this time Furillo just flied out to Bauer. Then Campanella was called out on strikes.

"That ball was outside!" Mitch yelled. I was impressed with his ability to make that judgment on the basis of the grainy picture we were looking at.

"You better mark down that backwards K," I said. Mitch's glare let me know he took this even more seriously than I did. And rightfully so, I suppose. My adulation of the Yankees was from afar. He had lived in Brooklyn, had seen these guys play, was even distantly connected to one of them.

Sal Maglie then hit a fly to Mantle for the third out.

The bottom of the Yankees' batting order was as strong as the top of the order for many teams. Gil McDougald was the seventh hitter. Though overshadowed by Mantle's splendid season, McDougald had hit .311 and finished second in the MVP voting that year.

As Mitch and I watched, McDougald grounded out to Jackie Robinson. Andy Carey followed with a foul pop-up to Campanella. Larsen did the same. Three innings were complete and no runner for either team had reached first base safely.

The Second Time Around

I doubt there's any documentation to prove it, but it often seems that the second time through the batting order is a pitcher's undoing. The hitters have seen an assortment of pitches, and these guys are in the major leagues because they can figure out what a pitcher is doing and adjust to it. The middle innings of a ball game are often the most interesting because that's when the offense comes to life.

But that's not how the Dodgers started the top of the fourth inning. On the first pitch Gilliam grounded to Billy Martin at second. Pee Wee Reese hit a checked-swing grounder to Martin, also on the first pitch.

"Two pitches and two outs!" Mitch was screaming by now. "Come on, ya bums!"

Duke Snider took the first two pitches and Larsen fell behind two balls and no strikes. He knew, he later said, that his next pitch had to be a strike because the game was so close. But it was a "mediocre fastball" (*Perfect Yankee*, p. 63) and Snider started it on its way down the right field line toward the stands.

Mitch jumped up, clapping his hands, and Snider was in his home run trot when right field umpire Ed Runge called the ball foul. Mitch groaned so loudly I thought he was going to cry. Snider returned to the plate, took a called strike two, fouled off a pitch, then looked at strike three. Mitch scratched an angry backwards 'K' on his scorecard.

When the Yankees came to bat in the bottom of the inning, I didn't say anything but I knew Mantle would be up third. I hoped there would be a runner or two on base in front of him. Bauer grounded out, though, and Joe Collins took a called third strike. That brought my idol to the plate in a situation he wasn't unfamiliar with. Of his 52 homers that season, 29 were solo shots.

In 1956 Mantle had realized the potential people had been talking about for several years. Not that his previous seasons were poor, but in 1956 he seemed to put everything together for the first time and avoided serious injuries. And it didn't hurt to have Yogi Berra batting behind him. Although Mantle was feared by opposing pitchers, Berra could also drive them crazy. The Yankee catcher had won MVP awards, in 1951, 1954, and 1955. *Sports Illustrated* felt "the most impressive thing about the World Series was Yogi Berra: there's no getting away from it . . . . Berra was incomparably the best player in the Series" (Oct. 22, 1956).

But Mantle was the hero in this game. He hit a low line-drive that wasn't as impressive as some of his monster home runs during the season, but the Yankees had a 1-0 lead. While I was celebrating, Mitch threw a bag of chips at the TV set. Yogi followed Mantle's drive with a liner to center field which Duke Snider somehow managed to snag in a diving, rolling catch.

"Damn it!" I said.

"I told you he was the greatest!" Mitch crowed. "Let's see Mantle match that!"

"Mantle would have caught it standing up," I said.

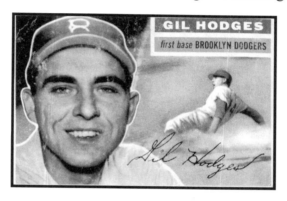

We wouldn't have to wait long to see if Mickey was up to the challenge.

Jackie Robinson started the Dodgers' fifth inning by flying out to Hank Bauer. Then Gil Hodges stepped to the plate. Larsen ran the count to 2-2 before making one of only a few pitches he knew was a "mistake" (*Perfect Yankee*, p. 102). Hodges drove it to deep center field. Mantle took off at the crack of the bat and with his extraordinary speed ran the ball down and caught it backhanded just above his knees. He considered it the best catch he ever made and certainly the most important (*Favorite Summer*, p. 207).

It struck me as curious that, the next day, the Cincinnati *Enquirer* showed Snider's tumbling catch in a sequence of pictures, but not Mantle's, which was much more "artistic," if that's what their sports editor was looking for.

Mitch threw himself back in his chair and clutched his head in his hands. "What do they have to do?" he cried. "What the hell do they have to do? That would have been an easy home run in Ebbets Field."

Hodges' ball clearly would have been a home run in Ebbets Field, where center field was 390 feet. After the game Hodges said, "He'd been climbing if we'd been in Ebbets Field." But the game was being played in Yankee Stadium, where the center field fence stood 461 feet from home plate. As Michael Coffey put it, "deep was something Yankee Stadium had plenty of" (*27 Men Out*, p. 68).

The next batter, Sandy Amoros, gave Larsen and the crowd another cardiac moment. He hit a ball down the right field line and into the stands, but umpire Ed Runge called it foul by inches. When Amoros returned to the plate, he grounded to Billy Martin to end the inning.

Mitch shook his head in disgust as he recorded the outs.

Enos Slaughter led off the Yankees' fifth by drawing a walk. Billy Martin bunted to try to move Slaughter to second, but Sal Maglie threw to second, forcing the 40-year-old Slaughter.

"And they say the Dodgers are too old," Mitch said.

Gil McDougald scorched a line drive that Pee Wee Reese tipped into the air with his glove and caught on the rebound. Martin was running at the crack of the bat, so Reese threw to first and easily completed the double play.

"Damn!" I said, beginning to understand the satisfaction of profanity.

Mitch added to my misery with a cackle. "The number one Billy Martin! Gets himself doubled up on a line drive. Bonehead play, Number One!"

Carl Furillo started the Dodgers' sixth inning with a pop-up to Martin. Campanella did the same, and then Maglie struck out swinging.

Mitch ran his pencil over his scorecard and said, "Hey, the Dodgers haven't gotten *anybody* on base. That's 18 straight outs." He cupped his hands around his mouth. "You're pitching a no-hitter, Larsen! Don't think about it, but you're pitching a no-hitter!"

Oddly enough, Larsen *was* thinking about it. He and several other Yankees report he broke the superstition against mentioning a no-hitter in progress. Mantle said that Larsen quipped to him, ""Well, Mick, do you think I'll make it?" (*Octobers*, p. 67). Other players wouldn't sit near him because they didn't want to be blamed for jinxing him. "They all avoided me like the plague," he later told an interviewer (Doyle). The announcers – Mel Allen and Vin Scully on TV – were coy about what was happening as well. At one point Allen said, "The Yankees have all the hits in the game."

The Yankees' half of the sixth started with a single by Andy Carey. Larsen, with two strikes on him, put down a good sacrifice bunt that moved Carey to second. Hank Bauer came through with a single to score Carey.

I punched Mitch on the arm. "2-0 Yankees!"

Joe Collins followed with a single and Mantle came to the plate in the situation I'd been hoping for during the whole game.

"Come on, Mick!" I shouted. "Two on. Put this one away. One swing. You can do it."

But all my hero did was hit a hard grounder. Gil Hodges fielded it and stepped on first, then threw to home and caught Bauer in a run-down.

"So much for Superman!" Mitch said.

Larsen himself, though, wondered what might have happened if Mantle had hit a home run. "That would have made the score 5-0, and I'm sure I would have relaxed a bit. Maybe too much, like in Game Two, when I blew the big lead" (*Perfect Yankee*, p. 137).

Whitey Ford didn't see Larsen's perfect game. He was in the Yankees' bullpen that day in case he was needed. "So between warming up, and not being able to see the field, I missed the greatest pitching performance in baseball history, and I had to rely on the cheers of the crowd to tell me what was going on."

Slick, p. 117

Third Time's the Charm?

Starting the third time through the order, Junior Gilliam led off the Dodgers' seventh inning. With a 2-2 count he hit a low line drive that Gil McDougald scooped up and threw to Collins at first for the out. Pee Wee Reese followed with a fly to Mantle and Snider flied out to left field.

I hoped the Yankees could add to their lead, but Berra and Slaughter hit easy fly balls for outs. Things looked better when Billy Martin got a hit and Gil McDougald drew a walk. But Andy Carey grounded out to Reese.

A funny thing happens when a pitcher gets through the seventh inning of a no-hitter or perfect game. No matter which team people are rooting for, they want to see the pitcher succeed, just so they can see something that amazing and say they were there. When Don Ferrarese's attempt at a no-hitter against the Yankees was broken up in the ninth inning, *Sports Illustrated* reported "the Yankee Stadium crowd groaned for Don" (May 21, 1956).

I happened to be watching on TV when Randy Johnson threw his perfect game against the Atlanta Braves in 2004. I'm a Braves fan now, but by the seventh inning I was cheering every out Atlanta made, hoping I would see another historic performance. After Larsen's perfect game, Arthur Daley said, "They saw history being made because the odds are at least a million to one that any eyewitness ever will see another perfect game in his lifetime" (*New York Times*, Oct. 9). Mickey Mantle thought even home plate umpire Babe Pinelli wanted to see the perfect game completed (*Octobers*, p. 68).

Jackie Robinson led off the eighth inning. He took a strike; then, as Larsen started his motion for the second pitch, Robinson raised his hand to call time. He may have had something in his eye, as he claimed, or he may have just been trying to disrupt Larsen's rhythm. The ploy didn't work. Robinson grounded to Larsen, who threw him out.

As Gil Hodges came to the plate, Larsen says, he "looked like he stood seven feet tall and weighed at least 300 pounds"(*Perfect Yankee*, p. 162). With two strikes on him, Hodges ripped a low line drive to Andy Carey at third. Carey caught the ball, but he threw to first base to be sure of the out.

"Why did he throw to first?" Mitch said.

"I don't know. Maybe he didn't actually catch it, just trapped it."

Some have questioned Carey making that throw. It was like admitting to the umpires that he hadn't caught the ball on the fly. And if he had made a bad throw, Hodges might have been ruled safe. But if he hadn't thrown and the third-base umpire had ruled he caught the ball after it hit the ground . . . .

Sandy Amoros' fly to Mantle in center field finished the inning.

In the bottom of the eighth the Yankees were reminded that Sal Maglie was also pitching a magnificent game. *Sports Illustrated* called him "a soft-bellied thin-haired 39-year-old gaffer who needed a shave" (Sept. 24, 1956), but he had given up only five hits and two runs. On most days, he would have been the focus of attention. Maglie was due up third in the Dodgers' ninth, so he would be taken out for a pinch-hitter. He finished his day in grand fashion by striking out Larsen, Bauer, and Collins.

"Whiff! Whiff! Whiff!" Mitch shouted as he marked down the K's.

From what I could tell on TV and from all the accounts I've read, the tension in Yankee Stadium as the Dodgers came to bat in the top of the ninth was as thick as an early morning fog in Cincinnati. In that apartment Mitch and I were both sitting on the edge of our chairs. Everyone knew what was going on, but no one quite believed it could happen. Mel Allen couldn't say "no-hitter" or "perfect game." He just kept talking about Larsen's amazing performance. There had never been a no-hitter pitched in the World Series, let alone a perfect game. The Dodgers didn't want to be the victims of the first one.

The Yankees, on the other hand, didn't want to mess up and spoil Larsen's bid for the no-hitter. According to Billy Martin and Joe Collins, "Before we went out for the ninth inning, everyone in the infield talked about getting a glove on any ball that looked like a base hit. The scorer would probably call it an error, not a hit. We weren't thinking about a perfect game. We were thinking about a no-hitter" (in *Men of Autumn*, pp. 142, 171).

Larsen admitted, in a later interview with Harvey Frommer, that "the last three outs were the toughest. I was so weak in the knees that I thought I was going to faint. I was so nervous I almost fell down. My legs were rubbery. My fingers didn't feel like they belonged to me. I said to myself,

'Please help me, somebody'."

The Dodgers obliged. Larsen needed only thirteen pitches to get through the ninth. *Sports Illustrated* described them as his "Thirteen Golden Pitches" (Oct. 15, 1956).

The first batter, Carl Furillo, fouled off four pitches before flying out to right field.

"One down, two to go." I punched Mitch on the arm again, like he was always doing to me. "Can you believe this?"

Roy Campanella fouled off the first pitch he saw, then grounded to Billy Martin at second.

"Two down, one to go!" I stood up.

"Oh, my God!" Mitch gasped.

I looked at him in reproach. "You're not supposed to take the Lord's name in vain. It was one of your commandments to begin with."

Dodger manager Walter Alston sent Dale Mitchell up to pinch-hit. Mitchell had spent his career with the Cleveland Indians until he was traded to the Dodgers during the '56 season, so the Yankees had faced him a number of times. He hit for average rather than power. Gil McDougald believed "he could hit .300 with his eyes closed. I thought sure he'd plunk one in somewhere" (in *Men of Autumn*, p. 161). In right, where the sun created problems for fielders on October afternoons, Hank Bauer felt the anxiety too: "I was saying to myself, 'Dale Mitchell, don't you hit me a low line drive'"

(in *Men of Autumn*, p. 70). Mitchell had pinch-hit three times already in the Series, without a hit. This would be his last bat in the major leagues. Mickey Mantle admitted that Mitchell's ability to spray hits all over the field made him difficult to defend against, so he "just stayed right where I was" (*Favorite Summer*, p. 212).

Larsen's first pitch was called a ball. Mitchell took the second pitch for a strike. Radio announcer Bob Wolff's call of the rest of the at-bat communicates the electricity of the moment: "Count is one and one. And this crowd just straining forward on every pitch. Here it comes . . . a swing and a miss! Two strikes, ball one to Dale Mitchell. Listen to this crowd! I'll guarantee that nobody – but nobody – has left this ball park. And if somebody did manage to leave early, man, he's missing the greatest! Two strikes and a ball . . . Mitchell waiting, stands deep, feet close together. Larsen is ready, gets the sign. Two strikes, ball one. Here comes the pitch. Strike three! A no-hitter! A perfect game for Don Larsen!"

In the words of announcer Vin Scully, "Ladies and gentlemen, it's the greatest game ever pitched in baseball history."

By most accounts that last pitch, Larsen's 97th of the game, came in a bit high but over the plate. Whenever Yogi Berra has been asked about it, he has staunchly maintained it was a strike. And Babe Pinelli was a National League umpire, supposedly tending to call high pitches balls. At the last instant Mitchell started to swing, then stopped. He looked back helplessly as Pinelli's right arm shot up.

Mickey Mantle described that last pitch from a different perspective. In one of his books he said, "I had a clear view from center field and, if I was under oath, I'd have to say the pitch looked like it was outside" (*Octobers*, p. 68). In *The Mick* (p. 128) he was a little more vague about the location of the pitch: ". . . from where I stood in center field it looked like a bad call. Whatever it was, Mitchell took it and Larsen had his perfect game. Yogi caught him in a bear hug, kicked him in the nuts, and then whirled him around. Pandemonium."

POST-GAME

"Oh, hell!" Mitch said as he snapped off the TV. "Do they have to win every time? And a damn no-hitter!" He picked up his score sheets and shredded them.

As I watched him I started to get the same knot in my stomach that I got when my mother lost her temper. Her anger was usually directed at my brother, so I escaped by going to the bathroom, or any other room where I could close a door.

My wife says I still avoid conflict and that her biggest disappointment in me is my unwillingness to argue. She reminds me that she's not my mother, and I know that in my head, but lessons learned early and at an emotional level are hard to unlearn.

I didn't want to stay in Mitch's apartment any longer. "I'll see you tomorrow," I said.

"Where are you going? You can't go home for another hour. Stick around."

"No, that's okay. That Murphy guy walked in. Your mom was here. What if your dad decides to come home early? I don't want anybody to see me here."

He tore Gil McDougald's card in half. "Yeah, okay. I'll see you tomorrow, you damn Yankee-lover."

I don't know how he meant that, but it didn't come across as a term of endearment.

It felt good to close the door of the apartment behind me. It was just after 2:00. I was in the wrong place and I knew it. Something in me wouldn't feel right until I was back where I should be. At this time of day, on a Monday, that was school.

Long story short, I walked/half-ran back to school, where I hid behind a tree on the edge of the playground. A couple of minutes before the bell rang, I got in position at a corner of the building.

When everybody came rushing out, I mixed in with the crowd and got on the bus without incident. My brother got on with a couple of his buddies. We looked at one another but didn't speak.

The hardest thing I had to do was act surprised when I heard about Larsen's perfect game on the news that night.

Mitch and I remained friends for the next year, even though I, as captain of the Safety Patrol in May, got him kicked off the squad for lying down on the job – literally – while his fifth-grade trainee helped kids cross the street. He knew he was guilty and never held it against me.

About the time I learned I was going to be moving to Chattanooga in late September of 1957, Mitch told me his dad had asked to be transferred back to the realty company's New York office. He was ecstatic about seeing his beloved Dodgers again. Then, on October 8, exactly one year after the perfect game, the Dodgers announced they were moving to Los Angeles. When we left Cincinnati I gave Mitch our new address, but I never got a letter from him and I had no new address for him. About a year later I found something I had written when we moved. The new address was on it, but it was wrong, 503 instead of 305. The street we lived on ended in a cul-de-sac. The 300-block was the last block. If Mitch wrote me, he must have gotten the letter back.

I recall Mitch fondly as a friend who helped me get through what would otherwise have been a difficult year. I didn't have a lot of time to miss him, though. In Chattanooga three cute blonde girls near my age lived across the street from us, two brunettes next door, and a red head at the end of our short block. And I was the only boy in sight. My mother kidded me about my harem.

Throughout the 1950s and 1960s I remained a rabid Yankee fan. The only time I got in trouble in high school was when I sneaked a transistor radio into class to listen to the 1960 World Series. And I still can't believe they lost. But when George Steinbrenner bought the team, everything changed.

Maybe the Yankees had always been arrogant and I just never noticed because I loved them so much. Steinbrenner's money translated into free agents who did not seem to understand what kind of class it took to wear those pinstripes – and I am talking about Reggie Jackson. By the late 1970s I had become a rabid Yankee hater. When Bucky f@#*ing Dent hit that home run to win the play-off game over Boston in 1978, I kicked my desk so hard I broke a toe. In 2004, when the Red Sox got up off the mat and came back from a 0-3 deficit to sweep the Yankees in the American League play-offs, I jumped for joy. The Yankees became the first team ever to blow a 3-0 lead in post-season play. It couldn't have happened to a more deserving bunch, I thought.

But in 1956 I adored the Bronx Bombers and wanted them to win every time.

"Perfect, *adj.* finished, complete, from Lat. *perfectus*"

The scene in the Yankees' clubhouse after the game was chaotic. A TV booking agent was rushing around looking for Larsen. Someone heard him say, "Forget Elvis Presley. This guy Larsen is the hottest thing in the country right now" (*Perfect Yankee*, p. 204). A reporter asked Larsen, "Is that the best game you ever pitched?" I've always told my students there's no such thing as a dumb question, but I think that one will force me to re-evaluate my claim. Someone asked Casey Stengel if Larsen had ever pitched better for him. "Not so far," Stengel replied. Dodger players visited the Yankee clubhouse to congratulate Larsen. Manager Walter Alston even asked for his autograph.

Larsen himself was disappointed with the after-effects of the game, especially because the Yankees "did not give me a bonus for pitching the perfect game. During the winter, I tried to get a thousand dollars that I needed for my mother, but George Weiss refused" (*Perfect Yankee*, p. 223). His disappointment is hard to understand when the Cincinnati *Enquirer* reported on Oct. 10 that he was getting $1,000 for each personal appearance or endorsement and his personal manager estimated he would make $50,000 by the next spring. He was voted MVP of the Series, received a Corvette and appeared on a number of TV shows. Someone even wrote a song about the game (*Perfect Yankee*, p, 209).

No one has come close to equaling Larsen's performance, even though there are now many more post-season games in major league baseball. Baseball has expanded (I would say diluted) its play-off system to make more money from television contracts. At least they haven't followed the model of the NBA and NHL and started playing the entire season to eliminate only three or four teams from the play-offs. Before 1969 there could be a maximum of only seven post-season games (barring a tie and a three-game playoff in one of the leagues). Today a team could play a maximum of nineteen post-season games (twenty if a tie necessitated a one-game play-off), and a team which did not even finish first in its division can win (and has won) the World Series.

For the purist, though, there is the World Series, and there is everything else. And there has been only one perfect game pitched in the World Series.

Sources

Acocella, Nick. "Larsen Had One Perfect Day." espn.go.com/classic/biography/s/Larsen_Don.html

Albert, Jim. *Curve Ball: Baseball, Statistics, and the Role of Chance in the Game*, with Jan Bennett. New York: Copernicus Pr., 2001.

Anderson, Dave, et al. *The Yankees: The Four Fabulous Eras of Baseball's Most Famous Team*. New York: Random House, 1979.

Angell, Roger. *The Summer Game*. New York: Penguin, 1990; rprt.

Berra, Yogi. *Ten Rings: My Championship Seasons*. New York: HarperCollins/Perennial Currents, 2003.

Bertschausen, Roger. "Trying to be Perfect in an Imperfect World." www2.fvuuf.org/sermons/perfect.html.

Boggess, Dusty. *Kill the Ump*. San Antonio, TX: Lone Star Brewing Co., 1966.

Boswell, Thomas. *How Life Imitates the World Series*. New York: Viking/Penguin, 1983.

Bouton, Jim, *Ball Four: My Life and Hard Times Throwing the Knuckleball in the Big Leagues*, with Leonard Shecter. New York: World Publ. Co., 1970

Boyd, Brendan C., and Fred C. Harris. *The Great American Baseball Card Flipping, Trading and Bubble Gum Book*. New York: Ticknor and Fields, 1991; 1st ed., 1973.

Boyer, Paul S. *Promises to Keep: The United States Since World War II*. Boston: Houghton Mifflin, 1999.

Bryan, Mike. *Baseball Lives: Men and Women of the Game Talk about Their Jobs, Their Lives, and the National Pastime*. New York: Pantheon Books, 1989.

Bryant, Howard. *Shut Out: A Story of Race and Baseball in Boston*. Boston: Beacon Pr., 2002.

Buckley, James, Jr. *Perfect: The Inside Story of Baseball's Sixteen Perfect Games*. Chicago :Triumph Books, 2002.

Castro, Tony. *Mickey Mantle: America's Prodigal Son*. Washington, DC: Brassey's Inc., 2002.

Coffey, Michael. *27 Men Out: Baseball's Perfect Games*. New York: Simon & Schuster/Atria Books, 2004.

Coontz, Stephanie. *The Way We Never Were: American Families and the Nostalgia Trap*. New York: HarperCollins/Basic Books, 1992.

Creamer, Robert. "The Mantle of the Babe." *Sports Illustrated* June 18, 1956.

Dickey, Glenn. *The Great No-Hitters*. Radnor, PA: Chilton Book Co., 1976.

Dickson, Paul. *Baseball's Greatest Quotations*. New York: HarperCollins/Edward Burlingame Books, 1991.

Dillard, Annie. *An American Childhood*. New York: Harper & Row, 1987.

Dixon, Phil. *The Negro Baseball Leagues, 1867-1955: A Photographic History*, with Patrick J. Hannigan. Mattituck, NY: Amereon House, 1992.

Doyle, Al. "Don Larsen: The Game I'll Never Forget." *Baseball Digest* Oct. 2003.

Dravecky, Dave. *Comeback*, with Tim Stafford. Grand Rapids, MI: Zondervan, 1990.

Falkner, David. *The Last Yankee: The Turbulent Life of Billy Martin*. New York: Simon & Schuster, 1992.

Ford, Whitey. *Slick: My Life in and Around Baseball*, with Phil Pepe. New York: William Morrow and Co., 1987.

Forker, Dom. *The Men of Autumn: An Oral History of the 1949-53 World Champion New York Yankees*. Dallas, TX: Taylor Publishing Co., 1989.

Forker, Dom. *Sweet Seasons: Recollections of the 1955-64 New York Yankees*. Dallas, TX: Taylor Publishing Co., 1990.

Frommer, Harvey. "Don Larsen – The Perfect Game." www.allsports.com/mlb/yankees/frommer.htm

Frommer, Harvey. *New York City Baseball: The Last Golden Age: 1947-1957*. New York: Macmillan, 1980.

Frommer, Harvey, and Frederic J. Frommer. *Growing Up Baseball: An Oral History*. Dallas, TX Taylor Publishing Co., 2001.

Gillon, Steven M. *The American Paradox: A History of the United States Since 1945*. Boston Houghton Mifflin Co., 2003.

Goetz, Larry. "An Umpire Squawks Back." *Saturday Evening Post*, April 14, 1956.

Gorman, Tom. *Three and Two: The Autobiography of Tom Gorman, the Great Major League Umpire*, with Jerome Holtzman. New York: Scribner's, 1979.

Halberstam, David. *The Fifties*. New York: Villard Books, 1993.

Holland, Gerald. "Casey in the Stretch." *Sports Illustrated*, Oct. 1, 1956.

Holtzman, Jerome. "Pitching Perfection is in the Eye of the Beholder." *Baseball Digest*, June, 2003.

Kahn, Roger. *The Boys of Summer*. New York: Harper & Row, 1972.

Kindred, Dave. "The Day Don Larsen Was Perfect." *Sporting News*, February 24, 1999.

Koppett, Leonard. *The Thinking Fan's Guide to Baseball*. New York: Total Sports Illustrated, 2001; rev. ed.

Lally, Richard. *Bombers: An Oral History of the New York Yankees*. New York: Crown Publishers, 2002.

Larsen, Don. *The Perfect Yankee*, with Mark Shaw. Champaign, IL: Sagamore Publishing, 2001.

Leventhal, Josh, ed. *Baseball and the Meaning of Life*. Stillwater, MN: Voyageur Pr., 2005.

Lewis, H. W. *Why Flip a Coin? The Art and Science of Good Decisions*. New York: John Wiley & Sons, 1997.

Mantle, Merlyn, et al. *A Hero All His Life: A Memoir by the Mantle Family*, with Mickey Herskowitz. New York: HarperCollins, 1996.

Mantle, Mickey. *All My Octobers: My Memories of 12 World Series When the Yankees Ruled Baseball*, with Mickey Herskowitz. New York: HarperCollins, 1994.

Mantle, Mickey. *The Mick, an American Hero: The Legend and the Glory*, with Herb Gluck.. New York: Doubleday, 1985.

Mantle, Mickey. *My Favorite Summer 1956*, with Phil Pepe. New York: Doubleday, 1991.

Martin, Billy. *BillyBall*, with Phil Pepe. New York: Doubleday, 1987.

Martin, Billy. *Number 1*, with Peter Golenbock. New York: Delacorte Pr., 1980.

Miller, Douglas T., and Marion Nowak. *The Fifties: The Way We Really Were*. Garden City, NY: Doubleday, 1977.

Miller, Jon. *Confessions of a Baseball Purist: What's Right – and Wrong – with Baseball, as Seen from the Best Seat in the House*, with Mark Hyman. New York: Simon & Schuster, 1998.

Murray, James, "American League? Phooey!" *Sports Illustrated*, June 11, 1956.

O'Neil, Paul. "The Damndest [sic] Yankee of Them All." *Sports Illustrated*, April 23, 1956.

Paretchan, Harold R. *The World Series: The Statistical Record*. South Brunswick, NJ: A. S. Barnes, 1968

Peterson, Richard A. "Why 1955? Explaining the Advent of Rock Music." *Popular Music* 9(1990): 97-116.

Rizzuto, Phil. *The October Twelve: Five Years of Yankee Glory 1949-1953*, with Tom Horton. New York: Forge Books, 1994.

Runquist, Willie. *Baseball by the Numbers: How Statistics are Collected, What They Mean, and How They Reveal the Game*. Jefferson, NC: McFarland, 1995.

Shaw, Arnold. *The Rockin' 50s: The Decade that Transformed the Pop Music Scene*. New York: Hawthorn, 1974.

Sorokin, Pitirim A. *The American Sex Revolution*. Boston: Sargent Publisher, 1956.

Sowell, Mike. *The Pitch That Killed: The Story of Carl Mays, Ray Chapman, and the Pennant Race of 1920*. Chicago: Ivan R. Dee, 1989.

Staten, Vince. *Why is the Foul Pole Fair? Answers to 101 of the Most Perplexing Baseball Questions*. New York: Simon & Schuster, 2003.

Stewart, Wayne. *Fathers, Sons & Baseball: Our National Pastime and the Ties that Bond*. Guilford, CT: Lyons Pr., 2002.

Stone, Isidor F. *The Haunted Fifties*. New York: Random House, 1963.

Stratton, Gil, Jr. "Umpires Ever Wrong? Sure, But With a Purpose." *Sports Illustrated*, August 6, 1956.

Tosches, Nick. *Unsung Heroes of Rock and Roll: The Birth of Rock in the Wild Years Before Elvis*. London: Secker and Warburg, 1991.

Van Derbur, Marilyn. *Miss America by Day: Lessons Learned from Ultimate Betrayals and Unconditional Love*. Denver, CO: Oak Hill Ridge Pr., 2003.

Zimmer, Don. *Zim: A Baseball Life*, with Bill Madden. Kingston, NY: Total Sports Publishing, 2001.

Meet the author:

Albert A. Bell Jr's published works include: historical fiction and mysteries, ***Death Goes Dutch, All Roads Lead to Murder, Kill Her Again*** and ***Daughter of Lazarus***; children's mystery, ***The Secret of the Lonely Grave*** and nonfiction, ***Resources in Ancient Philosophy*** (co-authored with James B. Allis) and ***Exploring the New Testament World***. His articles and stories have appeared in magazines and newspapers from ***Jack and Jill*** and ***True Experience*** to the ***Detroit Free Press*** and ***Christian Century***.

Dr. Bell has taught at Hope College in Holland, Michigan since 1978 and, since 1994, as Professor of History and chair of the department. He holds a PhD from UNC-Chapel Hill. He is married to psychologist Bettye Jo Barnes Bell; they have four children.

Bell discovered his love for writing in high school with his first publication in 1972. Although he considers himself a "shy person," he believes he is a storyteller more than a literary artist. He says, "When I read a book I'm more interested in one with a plot that keeps moving rather than long descriptive passages or philosophical reflection." He writes books he would enjoy reading himself.

Visit the author's website at: www.albertbell.com.

Death Goes Dutch:
A Wooden Shoe Mystery
by Albert A. Bell, Jr.
Claystone Books: Ingalls Pub. Mar. 2006.
ISBN 1932158650, 294p. paperback. $13.95.

Sara DeGraaf reunites adoptees with their biological parents – bittersweet for a Korean-American adoptee unlikely to ever have the same experience. When she finds that her client's mother, a furniture industry heiress, died under mysterious circumstances that were never investigated, her personal commitment takes her farther than agency regulations allow. As long-concealed family secrets unravel, more is at stake than the job Sarah loves and the possibility of fortune for her client. Someone will kill to protect what they've gained.

"The unusual setting and vulnerable but highly appealing female investigator make this initial entry in a new series unique." -- *Library Journal.*

"This new mystery by Albert A. Bell, Jr, ..., is a keeper. ... Bell's plotting is ingenious. "Twists and turns" hardly does justice to the élan with which he leads us down his deceptively well-marked-out primrose path. ... Bell never loses sight of (the characters' feelings.)" – *CML Magazine*

"Sarah is a delightful heroine: witty, sensible, and determined. ... Josh is a little more complicated. ...You want to like him, but you are not sure you can trust him. As you keep reading, you become thoroughly absorbed as the layers to the story unravel. ... DEATH GOES DUTCH is fascinating. It's not heavy, but not too easy to solve either. The balance of dialogue and narrative create a cozy atmosphere that leaves you wanting more!" – *Roundtable Reviews*

Secret of the Lonely Grave
by Albert A. Bell, Jr
Claystone Books: Ingalls Pub
ISBN: 1932158790 trade paperback

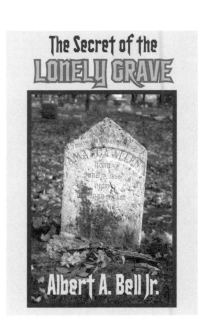

Kids investigate a mysterious grave and solve a 150 year old murder.

One grave in the cemetary stood off by itself. Stever Patterson and Kendra Jordan noticed flowers on the grave for the first time. As they tried to solve the mystery of who left the flowers and why, they discovered a secret leading back to the Civil War and the Underground Railroad. But some people in their small Kentucky town -- even members of their own families -- were not happy with what they found.

ALL ROADS LEAD TO MURDER
by Albert A. Bell, Jr.

ISBN: 097130453X
Illustrations: 30 line drawings by William Martin Johnson from the
first edition of Ben Hur by Lew Wallace, and supplemented with a
glossary of terms.
Hardcover, pp. 248, $21.95
High Country Publishers/ INGALLS PUBLISHING GROUP, INC

"All Roads Lead to Murder is a wonderful historical mystery set in the
Roman Empire during the early Church and St. Luke's timeframes. . .
The author, a classicist, helps the reader experience what it was like to
live during Roman times. The book provides us an education through
the author's superb use of setting and characterizations. Historical figures come alive in his expert hands."
– Bob Spear, *Heartland Reviews*: Rating: ❤ ❤ ❤ ❤ ❤

"All Roads Lead To Murder is a superbly crafted, wonderfully written murder mystery that treats the
reader to a thrilling detective story meticulously backgrounded with accurate historical detail."
– *Midwest Book Review*

"The author brings to the reader the many cultures that were yoked under the politics and power of
ancient Rome. . . The colorful characters, both fictional and historical, are well blended to reveal the
sordid web of money, greed and ruthlessness hidden behind the facade of civilization. One hopes to see
Albert Bell's Pliny again in the future." – Suzanne Crane, *The Historical Novels Review*

"Author Bell does a superlative job of leading the reader into his Roman world, and the element of a
traveling company of near-strangers allows him to develop minor characters to better display the variations of the Roman empire. The plot "worked", and the dialogue seemed just right. A winner all around!"
– Margaret F. Baker, *Past Tense*, publication of the Historical Mystery Appreciation Society

"All roads lead to a masterful blend of history and mystery. Albert Bell has written a wonderful book.
with splendid characters, vivid history and a fair and puzzling mystery. I heartily recommend it."
– Barbara D'Amato, award-winning author of three mystery series, Past President of Mystery Writers
Internationals and Sisters in Crime International
.
"Makes the ancient world a living, breathing entity but never fails to remind us on every page that a
vast chasm separates us from them, 200 years ago. . . . a real historical novel! . . .the best of them – I
do hope that it is the first book in a long series." – Rachel A Hyde, *MyShelf.com*

Visit the author's website for
information about his other books
and ordering at a discount:

www.albertbell.com

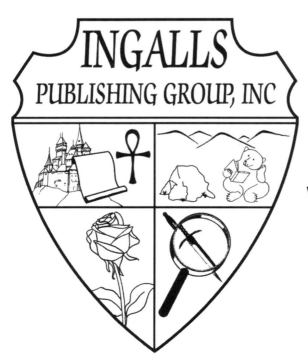

For information about other books
available from
Ingalls Publishing Group, Inc.,
visit the website:

www.ingallspublishinggroup.com